# NEW ZEALAND

## ADVENTURES IN NATURE

W9-DFC-865

Sally McKinney

JOHN MUIR PUBLICATIONS
A DIVISION OF AVALON TRAVEL PUBLISHING

John Muir Publications
A Division of Avalon Travel Publishing
5855 Beaudry Street, Emeryville, CA 94608

Copyright © 2000 by Avalon Travel Publishing
Cover and maps copyright © 2000 by Avalon Travel Publishing

All rights reserved.
Printed in the United States of America.

First Edition. First printing June 2000.

Library of Congress Cataloging-in-Publication Data

McKinney, Sally, 1933–
  New Zealand : adventures in nature / Sally McKinney. —1st ed
    p.  cm.
  ISBN 1-56261-435-5 (alk. paper)
  1. Ecotourism—New Zealand. I. Title.
G155.N5M364        2000
338.4"7919304–dc21                                99-42001
                                                  CIP

Editors: Peg Goldstein, Bonnie Norris
Graphics Editor: Bunny Wong
Production: Marie J. T. Vigil
Design: Janine Lehmann
Cover design: Janine Lehmann
Typesetting: Marcie Pottern
Maps: Kathy Sparkes—White Hart Design
Printer: Publishers Press
Front cover photo: ©Gayle Harper—Dart River
Back cover photo: ©Bill Bachman—Mt. Cook National Park
Title page photo: Destination Northland Limited/Waipoua Forest

Distributed to the book trade by
Publishers Group West
Berkeley, California

*While every effort has been made to provide accurate, up-to-date information, the authors and publisher accept no responsibility for loss, injury, or inconvenience sustained by any person using this book.*

# CONTENTS

# CONTENTS

# ACKNOWLEDGMENTS

Although an author spends long hours in comparative isolation, the writer of a travel guidebook never works alone; in writing this book, I found new teams of helpful people at every turn. I especially want to thank Ron Smith, who subsidized my trip to Los Angeles, and Nigel Speirs, who offered the loan of a laptop computer for 10 days . . . when he didn't even know my name. Without their help, the travel on which the book is based would not have been possible.

Thanks also to Sarah Meikle, international media advisor for the New Zealand Tourism Board, who sent me much-needed e-mail addresses; Stephen Griffiths, an extraordinary researcher for the same organization who answered questions promptly, in great detail, and without ever mentioning how busy he was; Nineke Metz and Fiona Clayton, who were especially helpful in directing me toward the best adventures; Michael O' Neill, who led me toward a greater understanding of ecotourism issues; Tracey and Rem—wherever they are now—who became the wonderful, supportive flatmates I needed when things got really rough; and Petra Eyserth, a herbal practitioner in Epsom, who knew just what I needed to take to begin recovering from the ulcers.

# ABOUT THIS BOOK

*New Zealand: Adventures in Nature* is a guide to New Zealand's most exciting destinations for active travelers who are interested in exploring the country's natural wonders. Along with the best places for hiking and birding and the prime spots for kayaking and sailing, author Sally McKinney recommends outfitters and local guides who can provide gear and lead you to the more remote parts of New Zealand. She also points out places to eat and stay that will help you enjoy local cultures and cuisine. All prices are given in New Zealand dollars.

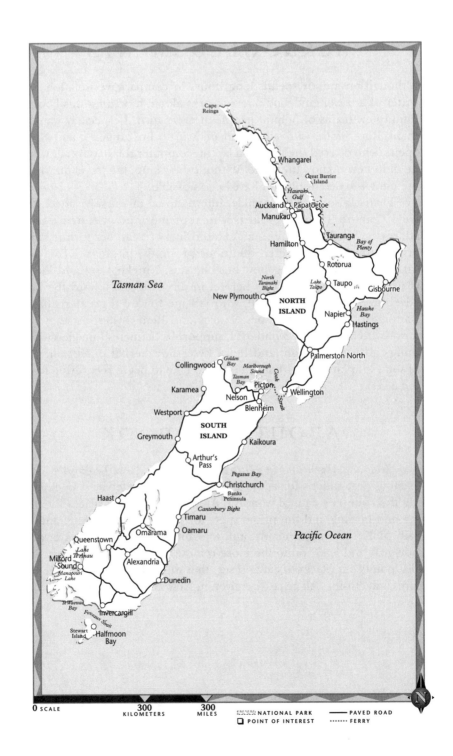

Cape
Reinga

Whangarei

Great Barrier
Island

Hauraki
Gulf

Auckland Papatoetoe
Manukau

Tauranga

Bay of
Plenty

Hamilton

Rotorua

North
Taranaki
Bight

Lake
Taupo

Taupo

Gisbourne

Tasman Sea

New Plymouth

NORTH
ISLAND

Napier

Hawke
Bay

Hastings

Palmerston North

Golden
Bay

Collingwood

Marlborough
Sound

Picton

Cook
Strait

Karamea

Tasman
Bay

Nelson

Blenheim

Wellington

Westport

SOUTH
ISLAND

Greymouth

Kaikoura

Arthur's
Pass

Pegasus Bay

Christchurch

Haast

Banks
Peninsula

Canterbury Bight

Timaru

Queenstown

Omarama

Oamaru

Pacific Ocean

Lake
Te Anau

Milford
Sound

Alexandria

Manapouri
Lake

Dunedin

Te Waewae
Bay

Foveaux Strait

Invercargill

Stewart
Island

Halfmoon
Bay

0 SCALE

300
KILOMETERS

300
MILES

NATIONAL PARK

POINT OF INTEREST

PAVED ROAD

FERRY

N

# CHAPTER 1

# New Zealand Overview

The South Pacific has many lovely island countries, yet New Zealand has become a favorite of outdoor adventurers. People who visit for favorite activities find settings of stunning natural beauty. Skiers from the Northern Hemisphere can swoop down snowy alpine slopes during their summer vacations. Trekkers can follow long challenging trails in regions of awesome scenery. Bird-watchers can observe unusual native species that developed in isolation, separated by water from other land masses.

Your own adventures in nature can take many forms. You can photograph dolphins from the deck of an old wooden schooner. You can study giant kauri trees with evocative Maori names. From the breezy open cockpit of a biplane, you can view the vaporous lakes and volcanic mountains of Rotorua's thermal landscape. From a floating inner tube, you can marvel at glowworms in the wet darkness of a cave. You can camp beside a bay so dark and still that the stars will be reflected in the water—and that's only North Island.

Visit South Island and you can paddle a kayak into tidal estuaries; beyond the wading birds there, you'll see golden beaches, aquamarine bays, and high forested mountains. You can watch herons take flight against a backdrop of lush green rain forest with a snowcapped alpine range behind. Whales, dolphins, and seals swim in the ocean;

if you choose, you can swim with them. You can hike challenging trails through farmland and native forest or help with sheep mustering.

You can also combine nature adventures with historic experiences. At the Buried Village near Rotorua, you'll follow a path through lush stands of bush, where a stream rushes over boulders. You'll walk past remains of Maori and European dwellings, buried by molten lava. Just beyond the stream and across a lake is the powerful volcanic Mount Tarawera, once the source of all that lava.

Along North Island's intricately carved eastern coast, you'll see sheep grazing on green hills, where terraces mark the location of early Maori *pas*, fortifications now draped with grass. Beyond the azure coast, in the deeper blue Pacific Ocean, dolphins break the surface, form an arc, and dive; schools of pink maomaos shimmer in warm currents caught by offshore islands. On a clear night, from a campground on an island, you can spot the Southern Cross in an inky sky.

Indulgences await you as well. In a wilderness lodge with mountain and valley views, you can sip a latte while poring over natural history books. You can waft over a city in a bright balloon, snapping photos of mountains and sea, then celebrate your landing with New Zealand champagne.

New Zealand's seafaring history lives on in the form of adventure cruises. You can board a vintage steamer for a tour of a mountain lake. On a sailing cruise, you can visit nature-sanctuary islands, where populations of once-threatened species are now increasing. You can reach other offshore islands, rich in natural history, by ferry or sea kayak.

The country's well-developed tourist infrastructure (paved roads, island ferries, experienced guides, and well-run soft-adventure tours) enables visitors to easily reach natural settings, even in remote areas. If you want to see brown kiwis feeding in their natural habitat, you can do so on a small nighttime boat cruise to an isolated beach.

Guided tours operate in the most scenic areas, from Cape Reinga in the north to Stewart Island in the south. On a group tour to a deserted island beach, some people might run straight for the surf and dive in. Others might amble off to look at wildflowers, and yet others might stretch out on the sand. Meanwhile, the guide will have boiled the billy for your tea, unwrapped delicious homemade cakes— and probably stretched out for a snooze himself! Another place and time, a different guide will show you how to strap on crampons, hand

## NEW ZEALAND AT A GLANCE

**Climate:** *Temperate maritime*

**Weather:** *Quite changeable. As one New Zealander said, you can experience all four seasons on the same day!*

**Flora:** *Most of New Zealand's plant species (about 84 percent) are endemic to the country; they can be found nowhere else.*

**Fauna:** *No large native land mammals ever developed; coastal marine life includes whales, dolphins, and seals.*

**Population:** *About 3.5 million*

**Language:** *English and Maori are both official languages. English is more commonly used; Maori names often identify geographic features.*

you an ice axe, and lead you safely across an ice field. There's a relaxed feeling to tours here. Many guides welcome novices and are experienced in teaching them.

"There's bush [forest] in every backyard," said one longtime New Zealand resident. Children grow up walking barefoot on the beach near their homes, swimming in the surf, and playing hide-and-seek behind the trees. Much of the country's recreation, eating, and drinking takes place outdoors. In city or country, you'll find benches facing the water and tables under the trees. New Zealanders make excellent guides, whether in their home country or overseas; young New Zealanders are sought after as camp counselors. Among tour operators, health and safety standards, knowledge of natural history, and commitment to ecotourism are high priorities.

## NEW ZEALAND BASICS

New Zealand, an independent country linked historically with the British Commonweath, lies about 1,600 kilometers southeast of Australia in the Pacific Ocean—between 34 and 47 degrees south

Okarito Nature Tours

*A paddler gets a bird's-eye view of coastal rain forest and the
Southern Alps from Okarito Lagoon.*

latitudes. The country consists of twisted land forms and islands created by geothermal action. Perhaps 700 islands make up the entire archipelago, but only North and South Islands, along with much smaller Stewart Island, are inhabited. The country has a population of about 3.8 million, and about 80 percent of these people live in cities or towns.

About the size of Colorado, New Zealand is a compact country with a complex topography. It has 27 mountain peaks over 10,000 feet high, 6,200 miles of coastline, and lovely bays and beaches sheltered by rocky headlands. The major islands have lush green valleys and hills, with subtropical life forms in the north and subantarctic forms in the south. In some areas, 84 percent of the flora can be found nowhere else on Earth.

New Zealand lies at the juncture of two tectonic plates; geologic activity has moved, twisted, tortured, and scattered the land masses. Volcanoes still steam and occasionally erupt. Other natural features include reefs, geysers, caves, cliffs, waterfalls, glaciers, and fjords.

National parks and other reserves encompass 30 percent of the nation's land area, while historic and maritime parks protect rare archaeological sites and fascinating marine life. Two areas are UNESCO World Heritage Sites. Some regions have changed very little since the arrival of the Maoris.

# GEOLOGY

Sculpted by a series of ice ages and eroded by wind, rain, and waves, New Zealand has 270,534 square kilometers of land. It sits at the juncture of two tectonic plates—the Pacific and the Indian-Australian—and its major geologic features reach in general from southwest to northeast.

Many geologists believe that New Zealand was once joined to Australia, Antarctica, South America, and other land masses in the super-continent called Gondwanaland. About 70 million years ago, New Zealand separated from the rest of the continent and continued to develop in isolation, cut off from other land masses by the Tasman Sea and the vast Pacific Ocean. This long period of isolation allowed unique groups of plants to develop and enabled ancient species of fauna, like the large flightless moa (now extinct) and the tuatara, a reptile, to survive.

About 20,000 to 10,000 years ago, New Zealand's three largest islands were one land mass. During a series of ice ages, the ocean around New Zealand rose and fell. At different times the main islands were joined together, assumed different shapes, and were separated yet again by water. Some species of plants and animals survived the changes by migrating north during cooler periods. Other species died out.

Most of New Zealand's land surface is geologically young and still changing. Past volcanic eruptions have destroyed forests, created offshore islands, and joined islands to the mainland. Now and then, New Zealand still experiences volcanic eruptions and earthquakes. Ongoing erosion by ice, snow, rain, wind, and breaking waves continues to shape the land.

Geothermal forces have affected the two islands in different ways. On South Island, rocky material uplifted from the Alpine Fault has been pushed northward, creating unusual geologic formations. On North Island, which covers some of the Taupo Volcanic Zone, three volcanoes in Tongariro National Park are active, as is the offshore White Island volcano. Northeast of the island, five undersea volcanoes are active and at times send up plumes of black "smoke" (the color is from minerals) along the southern Kermadec Ridge.

## NATURAL FEATURES

Water is everywhere in this island nation. The country's irregular coastline is 15,811 kilometers long, and no place is farther than 70 miles from the sea. At 425 kilometers, the Waikato River on North Island is the country's longest. The Waikato, Whakatane, Whanganui, and other rivers flow from the interior highlands to the coasts. Also on North Island, Lake Taupo, 606 square kilometers in size, is New Zealand's largest freshwater lake—known for recreational trout fishing and boating. The smaller Lake Rotorua, at 83 square kilometers, became a magnet for early Maori tribes. Even smaller, lovely Lake Waikaremoana, 615 meters above sea level, offers perhaps North Island's greatest walk.

Mountains are another common feature on the landscape. On northern South Island, the Tasman Mountains, Richmond Range, and Kaikoura Range rise from 1,600 to 1,800 meters high. They shelter Golden Bay, Nelson, and Tasman Bay, along with the island-and-peninsula group known as Marlborough Sounds. Farther south, the Southern Alps, a rugged, off-center, and angled mountain chain, peak between 2,400 and 2,700 meters, running parallel to the Tasman Sea. Mount Cook, one of the Southern Alps, is the highest peak in the country. Near it, the Tasman Glacier, New Zealand's largest, stretches for 29 kilometers. Farther east, various lower and more central ranges enclose high-country lakes and, along with alpine mountains, separate the wilder, wetter, west coast from South Island's dryer eastern plains. Near Christchurch, the distinctive Banks Peninsula, with its sloping hills and elongated bays, was formed by volcanic action.

Southwest of Christchurch at Queenstown, Lake Wakatipu, with 293 square kilometers of surface, flows into the Kawarau River.

*Snow-covered alps feed west coast rivers and lush forests.*

Southwest of the Southern Alps are Fiordland's 1,000- to 2,000-meter mountains and ridges, broken by seawater inlets and layered with freshwater from frequent rains. East of the fjords are Lake Te Anau, New Zealand's second largest freshwater lake, and Lake Manapouri, a beautiful lake with several arms; the waters of Manapouri empty into the Waiau River. Farther south, Lake Hauroko—New Zealand's deepest lake at 452 meters—is the subject of Maori legends.

## CLIMATE AND WEATHER

New Zealand has a variable maritime climate, with generally mild temperatures and predominately westerly winds that often carry west coast rains. Rainfall may occur any time during the year; the average is between 640 and 1,500 millimeters. On the two main islands, mountain ranges trap moisture high on the western slopes and cast a rain shadow over the east.

7

Most of the country receives at least 2,000 hours of sunshine per year. Average temperatures range from 15 degrees Celsius in the far north to 9 degrees Celsius in the far south. Snow falls in winter on the mountaintops of North Island. Elsewhere on the island, the precipitation is rain. On South Island, winter snow (or spring or autumn snow) falls at high altitudes and in the interior.

In the south, the Southern Alps and west coast (including Fiordland) receive the most rainfall, while Nelson, Marlborough, Canterbury, and Otago get the least. In the north, the sunniest areas are Tauranga and Napier; in the south, Nelson and Blenheim. Yet average rainfall and temperature figures can be misleading, for New Zealand has a range of microclimates that vary with latitude, topography, and prevailing winds.

# FLORA

Lengthy isolation from other land masses, combined with a remote South Pacific location, delayed human habitation here until Maoris arrived in the fourteenth century. Thus, unusual species of flora and fauna developed and survived for centuries upon centuries without invasive competition. New Zealand's podocarp (conifer) forests, for instance, evolved from very early ancestors that lived about 190 million years ago. The country's beech trees trace their ancestors back about 135 million years. Both species have changed fairly little since ancient times.

## *Trees*

Kauri trees are conifers. The largest specimens of this native New Zealand species (*Agathis australis*) can grow more than 50 meters tall, with trunks more than 20 meters in diameter. The trees can live longer than 1,000 years. Known for their long, straight, smooth trunks topped by a canopy of branches and leaves, the kauris were, for a long time, the mainstay of the New Zealand timber industry, which began soon after settlers arrived. (Forests once covered most of the country. Forestry is still a major industry, with 27 percent of the land now forested.)

New Zealand has 17 species of podocarps, which grow mainly in the Southern Hemisphere. Among them, the tall kahikatea, a white pine, has scaly bark and can grow to 60 meters tall. The native pigeon likes to feed on its berries. The rimu, a red pine, has narrow leaves and red cones. There are four species of totara, a tree once favored by Maoris for building war canoes. The miro tree typically grows in shady lowland forests.

New Zealand's evergreen beech trees, related to oak and chestnut, dominated many forests before Europeans arrived. Today, five species of beech grow between certain latitudes and above or below certain altitudes. These are the hard beech, silver beech, red beech, black beech, and mountain beech.

The tawa tree, an important food source for birds, is the main native hardwood on North Island. The kamahi, a black birch with gray bark and dark green leaves, is the major native tree on South Island. In spring, tuis and other birds can be seen feeding on the nectar of the kamahi's yellow flowers.

The pohutukawa tree, found near the sea, displays flashy red blossoms in December. Northern and southern rata trees also have bright flowers, thus pohutukawas and ratas have become known as New Zealand Christmas trees. Maoris used the leaves of the nikau palm, which grows on both North and South Islands, as building material. The cabbage tree has spiky green leaves and yellow flowers, while the ponga (silver fern) tree resembles a feathered umbrella. When New Zealanders mention a tea tree, they could mean either a manuka or a kanuka—both are small, quick-growing species that serve as nursery trees for larger species. Manuka burns easily, even when wet, and is used to smoke salmon and other fish.

## Other Plants and Crops

Geology and lengthy isolation affected New Zealand's plant life as well. An estimated 84 percent of the country's flowering plant species are found nowhere else. During cooling periods that resulted from a series of ice ages, some species survived by migrating northward. During warming periods, more of the land area was covered by water, and some species died out. The Three Kings Islands, off Cape Reinga on North Island and closest to the equator, have become a haven for unusual plant species.

Before Europeans arrived Maoris used a variety of plants for food, clothing, and shelter. Flax and cabbage tree leaves were woven and used as clothing. *Pani* was the god of food plants; crops were planted with appropriate rituals. Maoris ate the roots of fern and cabbage trees and cultivated kumaras (sweet potatoes), taros, and yams. After Europeans arrived, the Maoris began growing potatoes and other new foods. During the nineteenth century, Maori farms grew a variety of crops and exported potatoes and grain. At one time, large Maori gardens on Waiheke Island helped supply food for the growing city of Auckland.

European settlers, curious to see what might grow in their strange new country, imported many plants. The English garden arrived with immigrants from Britain. Some imported species did not survive, others grabbed hold, and still others took over. The pretty yellow gorse, which covers many New Zealand hillsides, is actually a pest, crowding out more desirable species. Morning glory, honeysuckle, and jasmine; cotoneaster, lantana, and tree privet; periwinkle, African clubmoss, and Mexican daisy—all are introduced species that tend to crowd out native species. Many native plants are now found only in parks and reserves and at high altitudes in mountainous regions.

The tall native toetoe is a feathery beige grass that grows throughout the country. "Bush lawyer" is the common name for two native species of rambler rose that catch onto skin and clothing. Many species of clematis grow in New Zealand but only 10 are native. One of the natives has a showy climbing white flower that clings to trees, another has fragrant yellow blossoms. The kotukutuku, in some parts of the country called konini, is one of four native species of New Zealand fuchsia.

Orchids include epiphytes and ground orchids. One species of tree orchid has large white flowers with violet centers, another has creamy flowers. One ground orchid has tiny green flowers that blend almost imperceptibly into the textured foliage of forests. New Zealand also has 180 species of ferns, including the mamaku and ponga, large tree ferns.

Kumaras are still grown on both islands and often turn up on restaurant menus. The red-orange tamarillo, also called the tree tomato, has a tart flavor and adds brightness to sauces and salsas.

Many fruits commonly found in New Zealand—oranges, strawberries, grapes, mangoes, papayas, and passion fruit—are not natives. The kiwifruit, also called the Chinese gooseberry, came originally from the Yangtze River valley. New Zealand now produces about 19,000 hectares of kiwifruit each year.

# FAUNA

As with the flora, New Zealand's fauna developed during a long period of isolation before people arrived. The slow-growing tuatara, a fierce-looking reptile that survives on a few offshore islands, descended from the once-common rhynchocephalia, a group that became extinct about 100 million years ago.

The earliest Maoris discovered that the large flightless birds they called moas were easy prey, thus Maoris became known as moa-hunters. They ate moa meat, carved moa bones into tools and ornaments, and used the large moa eggshells for bowls. There were once more than two dozen species of moa; one grew up to three meters in height and weighed as much as 230 kilograms. Moas lived on the islands from about 15 million years ago until they became extinct, in about A.D. 1500. Maoris also brought with them a dog, called a *kuri*, which has become extinct, and a species of rat, the *kiore*, which has survived.

European whalers established stations along the coasts and hunted five different species of whales, including the giant southern right, the humpback, and the southern blue. Sealers found an abundant supply of New Zealand fur seals, along with elephant seals and sea lions.

During the latter half of the nineteenth century, New Zealanders formed societies dedicated to importing new species. Australian bell magpies, with their distinctive black-and-white markings, were imported during this period, as were red deer, white tail deer, and wapiti to be hunted for game. (The deer caused serious damage to forests and native species of trees.) In all, more than 130 species of birds, 50 species of mammals, and 40 kinds of freshwater fish have been brought into New Zealand.

In 1862, New Zealand governor Sir George Grey bought Kawau Island, converted an existing house into a mansion, and introduced many species of plants and animals. Grey planted the gardens and grounds with species from various parts of the world: rhododendrons from India, gum trees from Australia, oak trees from England, and olive trees from the Mediterranean. He also liberated a variety of exotic animals on the island, including zebras, monkeys, pheasants, and antelope. Wallabies thrived on the island, which is now part of the Hauraki Gulf Maritime Park. You can also see kookaburras, rosella parakeets, and peacocks there.

## *Birds*

Native birds are among the most interesting of New Zealand's life forms. They include the albatross; the kokako, a bird that takes off from high places and glides; the flightless brown kiwi; and the penguin, also flightless, which swims, feeds in the sea, and nests and rests on land. You'll also see mallards, gray ducks, brown teal (also called brown ducks), grey teal, and the New Zealand shoveler, which uses its bill to feed on small aquatic organisms. Gulls are commonly seen and include red-billed, black-billed, and black-backed species. Bellbirds, which inhabit forests, are known for the clarity of their calls. The kaka is a colorful parrot. The kakapo, a larger parrot, is increasingly rare. It cannot fly upward and stays mainly on the ground. The kea, a noisy inquisitive parrot with red and green feathers, inhabits the mountains.

There are three species of kiwi: the brown kiwi, little spotted kiwi, and great spotted kiwi. They can grow to be more than 30 centimeters tall. With their long pointed bills, they feed on worms, insects, and fallen fruit. Nocturnal birds, kiwis are seldom

Fiordland Travel

*Fiordland crested penguins in their nest.*

seen in the wild, but you can see them in zoos and kiwi houses equipped with special lighting.

The brown morepork, New Zealand's only owl, was given a name that resembles its call. Small colorful parakeets, called *kakariki* by the Maori, can be found on both main islands and several offshore islands. There are three species: red-crowned, yellow-crowned, and orange-fronted.

The pukeko, known as the swamp hen, is different from the weka, or wood hen. The pukeko, with its black, green, and red coloring, has declined in population with loss of habitat. The weka, which has brown and black (or gray, buff, or black) plumage, feeds at night on eggs, rats, and birds. The takahe, one of the country's most colorful birds, has a blue and green body and red markings above the beak. The bird, which is still quite rare, was thought to be extinct for about 50 years, until a colony was discovered near Lake Te Anau in 1948.

The tui, also known as the parson bird, is found in forests. It has a distinctive white tuft at the throat and what appears to be a lacy collar. The tui can imitate the cries of other birds, including the bellbird. New Zealand also has several species of warblers: the whitehead, yellowhead, grey, and fernbird, which makes its nest in swamps.

## Fish

New Zealand's nutrient-rich ocean waters support an array of commercial fish. Marine environments range from subtropical in the north to subantarctic in the south, from the shallow waters above the continental shelf to the deep waters of the Haukarangi Trough. Flounder, sole, snapper, John Dory, grouper, tarakihi, red and blue codfish, kingfish, and trevally are among the 30 inshore species.

Many deep-sea species inhabit the subantarctic waters between 40 and 55 degrees south latitude. Among them are the hoki, hake, southern blue whiting, warehou, oreo dory, and orange roughy. Tuna fish—albacore, yellowfin, skipjack, and bluefin—swim offshore and are also listed on restaurant menus. Marlin, known in New Zealand as billfish, can be found off the northeast coast during the austral summer.

New Zealand is also known for several kinds of shellfish. Rock lobster, an arrow squid, abalone (also known by the Maori name *paua*), and sea scallops are all harvested from natural habitats. Green-lipped mussels, oysters, and king salmon are farmed.

About 40 percent of New Zealand's freshwater fish comes from imported stock. Freshwater lakes have been stocked with trout and salmon since the nineteenth century, but salmon have not always thrived. Brown trout came originally from Europe, while the first rainbow trout came from California—by way of Tasmania. Although quinnat salmon have become well-established, especially on South Island east of the Alps, Atlantic and sockeye salmon have not adapted as well; many inhabit lakes that have no outlets to the sea.

## *Other Animal Life*

New Zealand has only two native species of mammals—both bats. A long-tailed bat, similar to those in Australia, and a short-tailed species, unique to the country, live in hollow trees and caves. New Zealand also has about 40 native species of bees. Butterflies include the common copper, red admiral, and a southern blue.

Among the spiders only the katipo is poisonous; the bite of the female can be fatal. The katipo can grow to be 25 millimeters across (including the leg length). It is black, with red or orange designs on its back. It can be found (not that you'd go looking for it) on beaches and under rocks, woodpiles, and plants, both on North Island and on South Island as far south as the Otago Peninsula. New Zealand has no other poisonous creatures.

Although New Zealand has no snakes, it has some 180 species of earthworms, including some very long thick ones. It also has more than 30 species of eels, including the largest freshwater eel in the world, which can grow to 1.5 meters in length and weigh up to 20 kilograms.

## HISTORY

A long narrative Maori poem, *Te Whakapapa o Te Ao Nei* (*The Origin of This World*), offers a history of New Zealand, beginning with nothingness, followed by powerful images of creation and growth. According to the poem, the world was formed during a long, stormy, and very dark night, when Rangi, the sky, united with Papa, the earth. The demigod Maui then fished up New Zealand's islands from the sea. The place was called Aotearoa—Land of the Long White Cloud.

Maori oral history, passed from one generation to the next, also describes intricate genealogies linking each Maori to ancestors who came from a mythical place called Hawaiiki. According to legend, the Maoris arrived in a group—in an event called the Great Migration— on one of eight large seagoing canoes: the *Aotea, Arawa, Tainui, Kurahaupo, Takitimu, Horouta, Tokomaru,* and *Mataatua.*

European missionaries began recording Maori stories in 1842, and anthropologists at one time supported the Great Migration theory. However, later research suggests that Maoris lacked the navigational skills to stage such a migration and probably arrived in small groups over a longer time period. Modern scholars have placed the Maori's arrival in the mid-fourteenth century, with the earliest canoes coming from the west and other groups migrating later from French Polynesia and the Marquesas Islands.

## European Settlement

The Dutch explorer Abel Tasman was the first European to visit what is now New Zealand. After sailing to Tasmania, while looking for a passage to South America in 1642, his party of two ships crossed the sea to sight the west coast of South Island. He named the islands Nieeuw Zealand.

More than a century later, Captain James Cook became the second European to "discover" New Zealand, and he claimed the land for Britain. Cook came to New Zealand in a barque called the *Endeavor,* accompanied by natural historians and an artist. He sighted the east coast of North Island in 1769, then spent several months sailing around both main islands and charting the coasts.

During a second voyage, in 1773, Cook sailed the *Resolution,* accompanied by Tobias Furneaux in the *Adventure.* This time they spent two months in the islands, setting up a blacksmith shop for making repairs—and brewing a little beer—in Dusky Sound on the west coast of South Island. Cook made a third voyage, again in the *Resolution,* in 1777, accompanied by the *Discovery.* He was killed in Hawaii on the journey home.

Cook and his associates were followed by whalers, sealers,

missionaries, and other pioneers. In the early nineteenth century, whalers frequented the port of Kororareka in the Bay of Islands. Most of the early ships were British and Australian. One estimate claims New Zealand had 200 whaling vessels in surrounding waters by 1839.

European attempts to settle the new land had begun earlier, amidst Maori intertribal wars. Maoris also clashed with white settlers. One of the most powerful Maoris was the tribal chief and army leader Te Rauparaha. Another chief, Hongi Heke (also spelled Hiki), used muskets to seek *utu* (revenge) against other Maori tribes. He even provided protection for early missionaries, believing their efforts to be positive. In 1820, accompanied by a missionary leader and another Maori chief, Hongi Heke sailed for England, where he met with King George IV. The historic route named for the chief, Hongi's Track, runs between Lake Rotoiti and Lake Rotoehu.

During early attempts at settlement, James Busby was appointed British resident. Captain William Hobson was sent to protect settlers and support British interests in the region, especially against the French. The British negotiated a formal agreement with the Maoris, the Treaty of Waitangi, signed by representatives of the Crown and a majority of the Maori chiefs. The treaty gave sovereignty over the land to the Queen of England, while reassuring Maori chiefs of their continuing rights to use traditional lands. Signed on February 6, 1840, the Treaty of Waitangi became the country's founding document.

Although nearly all the Maori chiefs had signed a Maori translation of the treaty, the document in the Maori language differed markedly from the English version. Early settlers took control of Maori lands without regard to the treaty's terms, and contention over land rights and other issues continued. Te Kooti (also spelled Kuiti) was a much-feared Maori guerilla leader—and an awesome fighter when cornered. His dispute with Europeans led to a Wairau Valley conflict, resulting in the death of Captain Arthur Wakefield and other Europeans in 1843.

New Zealand became a British colony in 1856. It was widely known that wealth could be made here, especially from the forests. Lumber from the smooth giant kauri trees was much in demand for buildings and ships' masts. Pastureland and farmland were cheap. In the mid-nineteenth century, gold was discovered in several regions; the central Otago mines turned out to be the most productive.

## *Twentieth-Century New Zealand*

After roughly half a century as a self-governing colony, New Zealand became a dominion in 1907. During World War I, New Zealand and Australian troops fought in Europe as ANZAC, the Australia and New Zealand Army Corps. ANZAC soldiers fought and died valiantly at Gallipoli, where the anticipated British support, for many reasons, was not forthcoming. When World War II erupted, New Zealand supported the Allies and fought in the Middle East, Italy, and the Pacific.

The country became fully independent in 1947. In 1952, New Zealand, Australia, and the United States signed a mutual security agreement called the ANZUS Pact. In 1954, New Zealand signed the South East Asia Collective Defense Treaty (forming SEATO) with Australia, Britain, France, the Philippines, Thailand, and Pakistan. Although SEATO was dissolved in 1977, the treaty still stands. The ANZUS agreement lasted until 1984, when New Zealand banned all nuclear-powered and nuclear-armed vessels from domestic ports. The United States claimed it could no longer continue the agreement because of the ban.

## *Continued Conflict*

Tension between Maoris and *pakehas* (whites) continues in the area of land claims. Recent Waitangi Day celebrations—commemorating the Treaty of Waitangi—have been marred by protests. In 1996, demonstrations became so disruptive that ceremonies were shifted from the Waitangi National Reserve to the capital city of Wellington.

Recently, Maori land claims have been allowed in court, but a NZ$1 billion cap was placed on such claims. In November 1998, Prime Minister Jenny Shipley, wrapped in a ceremonial feathered Maori cloak, made a formal apology to the Maori people for treaty violations. On Waitangi Day 1999, the prime minister spoke of reconciliation among activists, elders, and ministers.

## GOVERNMENT

New Zealand is an independent country associated with the British Commonwealth. A governor general represents the Queen. The country has a democratic system of government, modeled originally after the British parliament. The New Zealand parliament has 120 seats.

Since 1993, members of parliament (MPs) have been chosen by a mixed-member proportional election, similar to that used in Germany. Half the MPs come to power through general electorate votes, five are seated on the basis of Maori electorate votes, and the remaining members are chosen as a result of party votes. All citizens eligible to vote are required to register (and more than 80 percent of those eligible do vote). Each voter casts an electoral vote and a party vote. Maori voters and those of Maori descent may vote in the general electorate or the Maori electorate.

New Zealand has two main political parties. The Labour Party, formed in 1916 and currently led by Helen Clark, has had a history of shifting alliances with socialists and trade councils. The National Party was organized to promote good citizenship, self-reliance, and private enterprise. Largely opposed to government interference, the National Party has in general become more populist since it began as the National Political Federation in 1935.

In the capital city, Wellington, government buildings are clustered above one end of Lambton Quay. The nineteenth-century General Assembly Library has a large collection of valuable historic documents. Another building, constructed early in the twentieth century, houses the Legislation Chamber and facilities for conferences and other functions. British architect Sir Basil Spence designed a striking circular building known as The Beehive. It houses the offices of government ministers and administrative personnel.

In 1989, New Zealand was restructured into 22 regions for local governance. There are 14 city councils and several dozen district councils. Community boards serve as liaisons between local citizens and the councils.

# ECONOMY

From the beginning, New Zealand's economy has been closely tied to the country's natural riches. Early Maori inhabitants developed a lifestyle based on fishing and hunting and made shelter and clothing from natural materials.

Early trade between Maoris and Europeans was done by barter. Increasingly, British and other coins and currency came into use. In 1934, New Zealand's Reserve Bank finally acquired the sole right to issue currency. A portrait of Queen Elizabeth still graces New Zealand's twenty-dollar bill.

Early immigrants cleared forests of kauri and other valuable trees and used some of the land for agriculture. By the beginning of the twentieth century, more than 1 million hectares of kauri forest had been reduced to only 200,000 hectares. Pastureland for sheep and cattle was inexpensive. Wool and beef soon became important exports. After New Zealanders invented refrigeration late in the nineteenth century, dairy and meat products could be shipped to distant markets.

By 1900, Auckland had become New Zealand's main commercial and industrial center. Wellington, with its harbor on Cook Strait, was also involved in trade. Christchurch was the main commercial center on South Island's Pacific coast.

Formerly known for social welfare programs, including state-supported health insurance, New Zealand has more recently pruned such programs. Funding for academic research has shifted from the theoretical to the practical. Some industries resent government support for certain sectors—like tourism—and lack of government support for other sectors (usually the critic's own industry).

Though the country's economy has shifted from a rural to an urban emphasis, agricultural products continue to be an important part of the economic mix. New Zealand exports NZ$3.3 billion in dairy products every year, as well as NZ$2.9 billion in meat and animal products and NZ$2.5 billion in forest products. These products include butter, cheese, wool, wood pulp, and sawn timber.

New Zealand depends heavily on trade with Australia, Japan, the United States, the United Kingdom, and China, and is known for its involvement in high technology. Income also comes from foreign tourism, which creates NZ$4.7 billion in revenues a year.

# PEOPLE

New Zealand has a population of about 3.56 million, with about 1.1 million living in the sprawling Auckland area. This is the country's largest city, where the affluent live in houses with window walls and great bay views or in leafy urban neighborhoods nestled among the green volcanic hills. Wellington, New Zealand's capital city, set into hills above the harbor, has a population of about 325,000. Christchurch, on the Pacific coast of South Island, is the third largest urban area, with about 310,000 people. Flatter and more squared off than Auckland and Wellington, Christchurch is a city of parks and gardens. It has a port at Lyttelton Harbour, just north of the Banks Peninsula.

There is an ongoing rivalry between the more populous North Island and the less-settled and more scenic South Island. A North Islander might say, "South Island is very . . . *different* from North Island," while a South Islander might say, "The best way to see North Island is on an overnight train trip!" North Island has a higher percentage of Maoris in the population mix and greater cultural variety.

## Maoris and Pakehas

New Zealand is a land of immigrants—the Maoris, arriving in large seagoing canoes, were the first. The growth of the Maori population was at first held in check by intertribal wars and was later curbed by diseases brought in by Europeans. At one time, the Maori population dropped to about 40,000, but now about 545,000 New Zealanders claim Maori ancestry.

The majority of New Zealanders (79.6 percent) claim European ancestry. They are officially called *pakehas*, meaning non-Maori people. The greatest number of pakeha immigrants came from the British Isles, with others coming from Dalmatia, Germany, Bohemia, Poland, India, and China. More recent arrivals have migrated from Asia and from other South Pacific islands, including many from Western Samoa.

Although English is commonly spoken, English and Maori are both official New Zealand languages. Legal documents are bilingual, and most geographic features (Mount Tauranga, Lake Waikaremoana, the Kaikoura Ranges, for example) have Maori names.

Since the 1960s, there has been a renewed interest in Maori language and culture, among both Maori and pakeha social scientists, as well as non-academic Maoris. Maoris have compared genealogies, passed down through a rich oral history, and discovered ancestors in common with indigenous people in French Polynesia and Easter Island. Archaeologists, through studies of early Maori pa sites, food storage pits, middens, caves, and rock shelters, have determined that the early moa-hunters were Polynesian, not Melanesian. Since 1980, legislation has prohibited modification of archaeological sites without permission from the Historic Places Trust.

Although some Maoris can trace their lineage to early Maori kings, the majority of Maoris also have pakeha ancestors. In business and social life, Maoris and pakehas mingle daily. But racial tensions remain, with unbridged financial, educational, and employment gaps between the two groups. The Equal Opportunities Act, passed in 1977, prohibits discrimination on the basis of race, ethnic origin, religion, ethical beliefs, marital status, or sex.

Sally McKinney

*Les Lisle prepares his famous scones at the Mahinapua Hotel.*

The number of Maori-run tour companies has grown during the last decade; the companies offer natural history, soft adventure, and cultural tours in various combinations, especially in Northland and Rotorua. Several companies offer evenings on the *marae*—the open area in front of a Maori meetinghouse—featuring a traditional *hangi*, or feast, and entertainment.

## *Famous New Zealanders*

Inventiveness is a national trait among New Zealanders. As colonists in a remote and rugged land, New Zealanders had to be inventive to survive. Early in the twentieth century—before the Wright Brothers even got off the ground—New Zealander Richard Pearse fashioned a flying machine from bamboo and aluminum, powered it with a

# CONVERSATIONS WITH KIWIS

*In New Zealand the name kiwi can refer to a ground-bound bird, a round brown fruit, or a New Zealander. Kiwi International is the name of an airline, founded by a group of grounded pilots . . . so they could fly again!*

*Kiwis—the people—speak English, but, like the country's geology, flora, and fauna, Kiwi English evolved for a long time in isolation. Tune in to the Kiwis, and you'll hear unusual flourishes on all vowels. Because of a long association with the Commonwealth, some words have roots in British usage, for instance, motorway (freeway), windscreen (windshield), boot (trunk), push chair (baby stroller), nappie (diaper), and serviette (table napkin).*

*To shout means to treat another person, most often by buying the next round of drinks. A steinie is a Steinlager beer, and if you ask for a stubby, they'll bring a short bottle. The long black, short black, and flat white are all espresso drinks, while the All Blacks are the national rugby team. The Blues play for Auckland.*

*In kiwispeak, nicknames are common. Brekkie is breakfast, oaties refers to porridge or oatmeal, bikkie is biscuit (either a cookie or a cracker), ciggie is cigarette, a flattie shares an apartment, a bikie is a bike rider, and a yachtie belongs to the boating crowd.*

*Walking and hiking are called tramping in New Zealand, where trails are known as tracks. A wool jumper is a sweater, and a torch is a flashlight. A bach is a cottage or a cabin used for vacations. A motor camp means a campground, which is quite often a hodgepodge of lodging options. The outback means wilderness, the boondocks, a wild place beyond civilization's reach.*

homemade engine, and, in 1902, flew it a short distance in front of witnesses.

Adventure is another cultural theme. In 1936, Aucklander Jane (Jean) Gardner Batten became the first woman to fly solo from England to Sydney. She returned to Auckland by crossing the Tasman Sea in a single-engine plane. In 1953, Sir Edmund Hillary and Sherpa Tenzing Norgay became the first humans to stand atop Mount Everest. Other New Zealanders have invented refrigeration, the jet boat, and Velcro fasteners.

Wellington-born Katherine Mansfield (1888–1923), who became famous overseas, lived as a bohemian in London before returning to New Zealand after the death of her brother in 1915. The talented writer, remembered for "The Garden Party," "Miss Brill," and other stories, ultimately found New Zealand a rich source of material. Janet Frame, born in 1924, earned an international reputation for her short stories, nine novels, and an autobiographical trilogy titled *An Angel at My Table*. Ngaio Marsh, born in Christchurch and known for her mystery novels, was named for a native flower.

Author Keri Hulme, who first published *The Bone People* with the help of a women's collective, saw the novel become a best-seller in New Zealand through word of mouth. Eventually, in 1985, she received worldwide acclaim for the work. Hulme lives in the tiny remote village of Okarito on the west coast of South Island.

## Architecture and Visual Arts

New Zealand's architecture reflects the country's multicultural population, especially its Maori and British heritage. Early Maoris built large wooden meetinghouses, decorated with symbolic carvings. They lived in small square houses called *whares*, which had open verandas and thatched roofs. Some early European settlers built similar homes from available materials. Others, especially those from Britain, tried to replicate what they had known in Europe. Small Episcopalian churches were made from kauri wood shipped from one coastal port to another. Stained-glass windows and marble were imported from overseas. Scottish immigrants to Dunedin created massive stone buildings in the style of their homeland.

The British influence, especially the Victorian and Edwardian periods, shows in historic urban villas—a few in disrepair, others lovingly restored as residences and B&Bs. As in England and Australia, many shops face covered sidewalks. What seems to be an alley could lead to an appealing arcade—a cluster of shops with a shared atrium. You'll also notice an "outback" influence on architecture—wrap-around verandas on blocky buildings with steep-pitched roofs.

South Pacific style reveals itself in the use of corrugated material for roofs. Once made of metal, the roofs have recently been reinterpreted in bright plastic. The country's rather mild climate and the proximity to ocean beaches have also prompted the design of California- and Mediterranean-style buildings.

The country's large cities all have public and private art galleries. The Auckland City Art Gallery, the oldest in New Zealand, opened in 1888. During London Fashion Week in 1999, several New Zealand clothing designers, exhibiting under the labels Karen Walker, Zambesi, World, and Nom D, caught the attention of a jaded fashion press with their edgy separates, playing luxurious stretch wool and other fabrics against exposed female skin.

## PERFORMING ARTS

New Zealand's Dame Kiri Te Kanawa, now based in London, is known worldwide for her operatic performances in soprano roles. The novel and film *Once Were Warriors* won international acclaim and is being made into a musical. Neil Finn and the band Split Enz are New Zealanders, though based in Australia. A New Zealand group called The Feelers has won national awards. Talented Maori cultural choirs also perform internationally.

Australians began crossing the Tasman Sea early in the twentieth century to make movies here. An early New Zealand silent, *The Romance of Hinemoa*, was distributed throughout the world. The New Zealand Film Commission was established in 1978 to encourage the industry.

Westerns and commercials have been made in the high country around Queenstown. Forest scenes for *Willow* were shot near the small airport at Milford Sound. Filmmaker Peter Jackson is making *Lord of the Rings*, a film trilogy based on the J.R.R. Tolkien written trilogy, using New Zealand's magical rain forests and eerie volcanic landscapes as locations. Extras from New Zealand's armed forces will take part in battle scenes, fighting to save Middle Earth. *The Fellowship of the Ring*, the first of the three films, will be released summer 2001.

New Zealand films have been screened widely overseas. They include *Smash Palace*, in which the hero expresses built-up tensions in unexpected destruction; Geoff Murphy's *Good Bye Pork Pie*, a story about military aviators; Vincent Ward's imaginative film *The Navigator*; *Once Were Warriors*, a violent film dealing with the issues facing urban Maori males; and Jane Campion's unsettling work *The Piano*. Campion also filmed *An Angel at My Table*, based on the Janet Frame novel.

# CUISINE

Agriculture is a major industry (more than half of New Zealand's land area is used for farming and ranching), and restaurants serve fresh local ingredients. Menus are developed around New Zealand beef and lamb, and fish caught offshore or pulled from freshwater lakes. Salmon, snapper, trout, cod, orange roughy, tuna, and tarakihi all commonly appear on menus, along with crayfish, clams, crabs, scallops, oysters, mussels, and eel. "Whitebait" often refers to one of several small white fishes. Cervena, which is farm-raised venison, is also served, along with wild venison and other game animals.

The east coasts of the main islands are used for fruit growing, from the oranges near Kerikeri to the kiwifruit in Poverty Bay to the stone-fruit orchards in Otago. Vegetables you might encounter here include kumara (sweet potato), beetroot (beets), courgettes (green squash and zucchini), pumpkin (yellow squash), aubergine (eggplant), capsicum (sweet pepper), silverbeet served cooked or raw, and rocket, which is used in salads.

Although New Zealand cuisine has a meat-and-potatoes heritage, meals have become more sophisticated as Pacific Rim, Mediterranean, and American (Californian and southwestern) influences have grown. Fruits, vegetables, chicken, seafood, salads, and whole-grain breads are featured in lunches and dinners. Vegetarian dishes are tasty and popular, even with meat eaters. Nearly every menu has some veggie options, and a few very good restaurants serve only vegetarian meals. You'll find rows of cafés in major urban neighborhoods; Auckland has the most cosmopolitan choices. In rural villages, however, the only source of prepared food might be a fish-and-chips shop. The "chips," of course, are not potato chips but French fries.

New Zealand offers several regional specialties. On South Island, the village of Havelock is known for its green-lipped mussels, farmed offshore. Kaikoura is known for crayfish, whitebait is popular on the west coast, and the southern port of Bluff is known for oysters.

The traditional "Kiwi breakfast" is a platter loaded with fried eggs, bacon or sausage, fried potatoes, and a grilled half tomato. For "brekkie," light eaters often choose a cereal called Weet-Bix, topped with sweetened canned fruit, then milk. Morning tea break might include a huge muffin with a "flat white" coffee—espresso topped with foamy hot milk. A "short black" is an espresso without milk, and a "long black" is a double.

Your New Zealand lunch might be a sandwich, perhaps a meat, fish, or veggie combo on whole-grain, pita, or panini bread. Seasoned hot chicken or seafood served on cool salad greens is another option. Fruit juices and espresso drinks are popular accompaniments. Muffins and desserts are usually fresh and very good; you may have a choice of sweet or savory muffins.

Dinner, the main meal of the day, begins with a starter (soup or appetizer) course. However, some starter plates can be filling enough to stand in for the main. The main course itself is usually a plate piled with meat or fish, rice or potatoes, and cooked vegetables. Salads are usually ordered separately. The unofficial national dessert is Pavlova (also the national dessert of Australia). Named for Russian dancer Anna Pavlova, it was supposedly created in her honor while she was on tour. The dish has a soft meringue base, a layer of green kiwi and other bright fruits, an optional hefty scoop of ice cream, and a high mound of sweetened whipped cream—you might as well skip the meal!

"Bikkies" are tea biscuits (refers to both cookies and crackers). In rural areas the evening meal is often called tea, even when tea is not served. It might consist of a plate of roast hoggit (mutton), browned potatoes, and carrots or peas, with everything smothered in gravy.

The Cobb and Co. chain, named after an early interurban bus service, has restaurants throughout New Zealand. Although Cobb and Co. serves many traditional foods, it also has lighter options, including meatless dishes. The Robert Harris chain has come up with a classier version of the traditional take-out lunch counter. It's more like a cafeteria for elaborate sandwiches. Robert Harris also serves fancy coffee drinks and various teas, along with fresh tasty muffins and good soups.

Wine making in New Zealand goes back to the nineteenth century, although a few colonists made wine before then. In 1902, an Italian immigrant set up a government research center for wine-making, although the industry didn't really take hold until later in the century. West Auckland, Hawkes Bay, and Marlborough on South Island are among the nation's several wine-making regions. New Zealand is known internationally for its light fruity whites. Recently, a few wineries have been turning out very good reds.

Captain James Cook was the first person to make beer in New Zealand. The country now produces 400 different beers and holds an international beer-judging competition. NZ and DB are the main breweries. Microbreweries include Mac's, of Nelson. Licensed restaurants can sell beer, wine, mixed drinks, and liqueurs. BYO restaurants allow you to bring your own wine and beer; there may be a charge for corkage.

A non-alcoholic option, Auckland-made Ch'I is a blend of sparkling mineral water and healthy herbal extracts, including ginseng, aloe, and Gotu-kola. New Zealand health enthusiasts consume Spirulina, made from green seaweed.

# TOURISM

Warm hospitality, world-class scenery, and well-run soft adventure tours make New Zealand a very appealing destination. The New Zealand Tourist and Publicity Department, organized in 1901, is the oldest such department in the world. The New Zealand Tourism Board, formed in 1991, tries to maximize the country's long-term potential as a tourist destination, with overseas offices in countries that represent major markets: Australia, the United States, Japan, the United Kingdom, Germany, Singapore, Canada, Hong Kong, and Taiwan. Nearly every village throughout the country has an information center affiliated with the Visitor Information Network (VIN). VIN centers bear a distinctive logo.

# WHEN TO GO

New Zealand's summer runs from December 21 to March 21. The peak holiday and school vacation period runs mid-December through early January, and the Easter holiday, another peak in domestic travel, falls toward the end of summer. Summer in New Zealand means great beach weather, though it also means more crowds.

The winter season—ski season—runs from June 21 until September 21. The main North Island ski resorts are located on the slopes of volcanoes—known for their occasional eruptions (it's not smart to visit then). During winter, Auckland and North Island, especially the west coast, receive heavy rainstorms brought by westerlies crossing the Tasman Sea. Expect wind and cold. And while there is little snow, there is also little central heating. Many soft adventure tours and cruises operate on North Island throughout winter, although operators usually reserve the right to cancel tours in bad weather.

On South Island, Queenstown ski resorts stay busy during winter. Other winter adventures depend on the activity and the altitude. At southern, coastal, and sea-level destinations, outdoor activities continue year-round. However, tour operators reserve the right to cancel for inclement weather or rough seas.

During spring (September, October, November), flowers bloom, and the lambs gambol in New Zealand's luminous green pastures. Spring, however, can be very rainy—and in the alpine environments of South Island the rain will be snow. Don't hike on Mount Aspiring in spring—unless you know how to build a snow cave. In Fiordland, you can wake up and see snow on the mountaintops even in spring.

Autumn can be lovely, with leaves turning colors, especially on South Island. This is harvest season, and orchards gleam with ripe fruit. It can also rain during autumn and get very cool at night. Yet you can still enjoy adventure activities—if you are prepared.

# ORIENTATION AND TRANSPORTATION

New Zealand has international air terminals at Auckland, Wellington, and Christchurch. Most international visitors arrive at Auckland, with many planes coming from Sydney, Singapore, Hong Kong, Tokyo, Los Angeles, London, and Frankfurt. Wellington has mainly trans-Tasman connections to Australia. Christchurch has flights to Australia, Japan, and other countries.

Domestic air routes link cities and towns, including Auckland, Rotorua, and Wellington on North Island and Nelson, Queenstown, Christchurch, and Dunedin in the South. On a clear day, the scenery from the air can be stunning. You might see Mount Taranaki on North Island or the snowy Southern Alps on South Island.

A network of paved (and some unpaved) roads offers access to most nature destinations. However, some parts of South Island (Kahurangi National Park and most of Fiordland, for instance) have no roads. You can rent cars, camper-vans, motorbikes, and bicycles in Auckland and other cities, or buy them for a longer trip and sell them before you leave. Bus networks—large and small—serve both main islands. Local transportation options include vans and taxis. Even in remote areas, vans (and sometimes small boats) usually

Destination Northland Limited

*Autumn is an ideal time for adventure or quiet reflection at
Cape Maria van Diemen.*

# THE AUTHOR'S TOP DOZEN PICKS

*So much to see, so little time. Suppose I have enough money and unlimited time, but must choose a mere dozen favorite nature adventures in New Zealand. What will I choose?*

*Certainly, I'd go snorkeling or diving at the world-class Poor Knights Islands, accessed from Tutukaka on North Island's east coast. Next, I'd travel farther north, where I'd enjoy a stroll across the lovely Waitangi National Reserve, with its huge, memorable* **waka** *(Maori seagoing canoe), historic buildings and meeting-house, and hilltop views of the Bay of Islands. Next, I'd head for the lush west coast rain forests, where I'd spend ample time marveling, gazing, and meditating before Tane Mahuta. Known as "the Lord of the Forest," this giant tree is an awesome presence, the greatest kauri of them all. Returning to Auckland and Waitemata Harbour, I'd take a leisurely nature cruise on the* Te Aroha, *an ancient renovated trading scow. The operators, who describe the craft as a "stress-free zone," call at Tiritiri Matangi Island, among others in the Hauraki Gulf. At this nature sanctuary, I'd not only see rare native birds in a natural setting, I'd also awake to birdsongs at dawn. After that adventure, I'd head for Tongariro National Park for the challenging Tongariro Crossing—a one-day walk. This adventure involves scrambling over the saddle between Mount Ngauruhoe and Mount Ruapehu, following the Red Crater's rim, skidding down a sand ridge, gazing at the*

provide transport to and from the Great Walks—the country's world-class hiking trails—and other tramping tracks.

Companies like the Magic Traveller's Network and Kiwi Experience operate large buses to nature sites. Buses pick up passengers at their lodgings in the morning and drop them off at new places at the end of the day. Helpful driver-guides offer commentary along the way and play passengers' favorite music. Although most are young

*Emerald Lakes, and passing steamy Ketetahi Hot Springs, a site sacred to the Maoris.*

*On South Island, I'd head down the west coast, opting to paddle around the Okarito Lagoon. This experience combines a close look at rain forest and bird life with splendid views of the snow-crested southern alpine range. Mount Cook National Park, accessed east of these mountains, encloses New Zealand's highest peaks—there I'd take climbing lessons or do day hikes while gawking at stunning mountain scenery. I'd then head farther south to Fiordland where I'd board an adventure cruiser on Doubtful or Milford Sound. Such small-boat cruises combine paddling, hiking, and snorkeling with healthy meals and a good sleep in a cozy bunk at night. In the same region, I'd either walk the entire Milford Track or spend at least a day exploring magical beech rain forest. From there, I'd proceed to the Otago Peninsula where I'd marvel at the wonderful yellow-eyed penguins as they cross the beach at dusk. Next, I'd head north to Kaikoura where I'd take a nature cruise to observe whales, dolphins, seals, sharks—anything that surfaces in Pacific waters. Finally, I'd head back to Nelson to take yet another look at Abel Tasman National Park. After exploring the estuaries in a kayak, I'd wrap up the journey with lunch at the Awarua Cafe—for there's no nature experience quite like a leisurely outdoor meal: delicious food, a glass of wine, and the cheep-cheep of birds.*

people, passengers represent a range of age groups and come from various social backgrounds and foreign countries. Most are sociable, though late-night party lovers tend to sleep on the buses. Passengers have the option of staying an extra day or more in locations they select, boarding the next bus that comes around. Less rigid than lock-step package tours and bus lines, these networks also offer services such as stops at food markets and banks. One price covers transportation and the various nature stops along the way. (Look for more details in the Appendix.)

Seaplanes, ferries, and cargo boats are options for reaching islands and exploring bays. Some tour operators have special transport rates; they're traveling a certain route in any case and will drop you off on the way.

## HOW TO USE THIS BOOK

This book is divided into eight destination chapters; each begins with an introduction that orients you to the region, capsules its history, tells you what flora and fauna you might see there, and lets you know how and where to find certain sights and attractions. You'll also find practical suggestions about getting to and from the region and for getting around.

Next, you'll learn about top nature sites and activities in the area's most appealing settings. For the most part, you'll learn about eco-sensitive ways to explore, such as walking, climbing, paddling, pedaling, and snorkeling.

Then you'll find suggestions for tour operators and outfitters—specifically those who have excellent reputations, provide access to the most appealing natural areas, limit—or minimize—the use of motors and fossil fuels, and keep resources within the local community. A growing number of New Zealand tour operators are of Maori descent. When possible, Maori companies are featured.

Finally, you'll find listings of commercial and Department of Conservation (DOC) campgrounds, accommodations, and restaurants. Among the lodging choices are B&Bs in renovated historic buildings and some eco-sensitive operations. Cafés and restaurants were chosen for their proximity to activities, their fresh and tasty food, and their New Zealand character. A few of the cafés feature vegetarian food entirely; nearly all restaurants in the book offer vegetarian options. Note that all prices are given in New Zealand dollars.

To conclude, this book will guide you to some of the best nature experiences in New Zealand. The information comes from my visits to each region, participation in activities, listening to tour operators, meeting with people from tourism offices and the DOC, and, especially, listening to other travelers describe their favorite trips and tours. Unlike a guidebook researched in a high-rise office, the information comes from a stack of notebooks, the pages ruffled by winds, the scribbled ink notations blurred by rain. I try to provide you with background so you can appreciate what you see, offer practical help in planning your trip, and encourage you to tread lightly . . . wherever you go.

*Lyttleton Harbour near Christchurch*

Paul Thompson/Leo de Wys

# CHAPTER 2

# Conservation and Responsible Tourism

As nature tourism has grown in popularity, the term *ecotourism* has been used all too loosely to describe any number of activities that involve travel and the environment. In one country, visitors on "eco-tours" doze in reclining seats on crowded buses that belch smoke as they whiz past scenery. In another country, visitors on an "ecotour" race, jump, and skid around in four-wheel-drive vehicles, destroying the fragile desert environment. In yet another country, visitors enjoy a low-impact nature experience. But nearby villagers and the struggling host island country receive few benefits—the tour company takes home all the profits. In yet another country, eco-travelers pay dearly to do sweaty work on valuable projects that sustain the local economy and enhance the environment long-term.

At its best, ecotourism enhances the environment while doing it no damage and contributes to the local and national economy. At its worst, ecotourism is a buzzword used to entice visitors into taking tours that divert resources from local and national economies and also damage the environment.

In the Adventures in Nature series, *eco-travel* refers to travel and tourism that focuses on natural attractions, the environment, natural history, and local culture. Books in this series will help eco-travelers make choices that at the best help preserve the local environment and culture and at the least do not add to its deterioration.

## ECO-TRAVEL IN NEW ZEALAND

This book is designed to heighten awareness of environmental issues in the small but complex country known as New Zealand, where the land is still being formed, the islands are slowly shifting, and unique species of plants and animals need help to survive. The book will examine conflicts between development and conservation and will suggest strategies for greater harmony. It will also explain how eco-travelers can contribute to solutions rather than exacerbate problems.

As a travel guidebook, this book makes a serious effort to feature low-impact eco-friendly options, not only in the areas of soft adventure, tour operators, and outfitters but also in lodging and dining choices. Whenever possible, we recommend small, local, and regional businesses. We also offer a smorgasbord of eco-travel options for people of different cultures, backgrounds, budgets, and tastes.

## ECO-SENSITIVE CHOICES

Wherever you travel, it's important to weigh decisions involving time, energy, and money; to decide which of many choices will sustain the local economy; and to determine how best to tread lightly on— or even enhance—the unique environment you explore. As an eco-traveler, you are challenged to direct your dollars in appropriate ways. The money you spend for food, lodging, and nature tours will be passed on to the local farmer, printer, and gas station attendant. In the same way, ecotourism can nourish and sustain the community and the environment long-term through the construction of eco-sensitive lodging, the practice of organic agriculture, the sale of local handicrafts, and environmental education. Fortunately, New Zealand already has many such practices in motion.

New Zealand offers visitors an array of nature travel options, and many are kinder to the environment than others. Therefore, much of the future of nature travel in New Zealand will depend on which businesses you choose to support. Here are questions you might ask in New Zealand (and elsewhere) before choosing a tour company, lodging, or restaurant:

- Does the business employ local people, treat them with respect, and pay them an appropriate wage?
- Does the business feature traditional materials in its building, use heritage themes in its decor, or somehow showcase traditional culture? Will you enjoy a *New Zealand* experience here?
- Does the business use a portion of its income for wildlife or conservation projects? Which projects? Have the results been effective?
- Does the business purchase local or regional foods? Has food such as shellfish been harvested in season, according to quotas that sustain the population?
- What sort of wood does the business burn in its fireplace? Does the business use eco-sensitive cleaning materials? How are sewage and other waste discharged?
- Is the owner of the business also the manager? Does he or she live in the local community? Is the owner enthusiastic about nature—or about increasing his or her own wealth because of your enthusiasm?

## THE ECO-TRAVEL EXPERIENCE

Eco-travel is about expanding your horizons—about reaching beyond your own comfort and self-interest. You might currently enjoy vacations in luxury resorts. But resort hotels, in addition to being expensive and wasteful, can also be boring and bland. Sealed windows and air-conditioning systems shut out tangy sea breezes and mute the serenade of birds in nearby trees. A more eco-sensitive lodging choice can be more pleasurable.

An eco-traveler who becomes sensitive to environmental issues is no longer at the center of a nature experience—the focus is outward. On a day hike through coastal rain forest, for instance, you might walk through rain all day. At some level of discomfort, you'll be challenged to understand nature's cycles—the way rain nourishes waterfalls and the relationship between rocks, mosses, lichen, and trees. If you focus outward, on your surroundings, you'll more fully appreciate the intricate web of life and renew your love of nature.

*Eco-minded travelers enjoy "bushwalking" on Stewart Island.*

Tourism Southland

Fortunately, New Zealand's ecotourism industry offers a range of choices for visitors with various income levels, backgrounds, and tastes. This guidebook suggests such an array of tours, restaurants, and lodgings and then lets you make your own decisions. In the Christchurch chapter, you'll read about a very expensive yet quite eco-sensitive wilderness lodge set amid stunning mountain scenery. The Northland chapter describes an inexpensive—and also very eco-sensitive—lodge with cabins set among forests, ponds, and luxurious plantings. In the Dunedin chapter, you'll learn about an expensive expedition to remote subantarctic bird colonies. Yet other adventures in that chapter are more or less free—once you know where to find them. The book also describes an intricate network of buses, hostels, cafés, and services for backpackers and other budget travelers.

## NEW ZEALAND'S TOURISM HISTORY

From the time the Maoris arrived in their great canoes, New Zealand's oral literature has described Aotearoa's lush scenic beauty and its volcanoes' awesome power. Before human habitation, about 78 percent of New Zealand's land area was covered with forests, with about 14 percent in the alpine zone.

With the arrival of humans, native species were hunted down, and forests were burned. European whalers, sealers, and loggers were links in a system that generated wealth at the cost of the environment. During the colonial era, British settlers imported an array of new species, as an experiment to determine which exotics would grow.

# EDUCATION FOR RESPONSIBLE TOURISM

*You can learn about conservation issues, increase your eco-sensitivity, and have fun, all in a modern museum setting. Mount Bruce National Wildlife Centre, located on North Island, 30 kilometers north of Masterton on SH 2, conducts threatened plant and bird breeding programs run by a well-informed staff. During a visit to the center, you can see threatened native birds like the takahe, saddleback, stitchbird, and kokako. You can watch kaka, eels, and brown trout (an introduced species) while they feed. Through hands-on exhibits, you can learn more about the issues involved in saving threatened wildlife. On a bush walk through a remnant of native forest near the center, you can see how the rimu, rata, kamahi, and other plants grew before the forests were burned and logged. The center is open daily year-round. Contact the center by phone at 06-375-8004.*

Women enjoyed imported roses in their gardens, while men went out to hunt and fish.

The focus of tourism in New Zealand has always been on nature. By the late 1870s, the Pink and White Terraces, considered one of the natural world's greatest wonders, were attracting tourists from overseas. Early in the twentieth century, visitors were escorted through Waitomo Caves by Maori guides and taken on horseback past geysers, craters, and mud pools. By 1900, the Milford Track was open. The first tourist office in the world opened in New Zealand in 1901. Soon visitors from overseas were gazing at the splendid Remarkables Mountains from the deck of a Lake Wakatipu steamer and enjoying houseboat accommodations on the Whanganui River.

Increased interest in conservation of the country's stunning landscapes—and the tourism they fostered—led to the Scenery Preservation Act of 1903. By 1920, New Zealand had set aside for the future at least half the land now organized into parks and reserves. However, with trout (an introduced species) flashing below the surface of mountain lakes and deer (also introduced) standing in the dappled shadows of the forests, New Zealand had also become a sportsman's paradise.

Tourism is still an important segment of New Zealand's economy and a major source of foreign exchange. Over the last 30 years, though, the tourism emphasis has shifted from extractive fishing and hunting to active yet benign pursuits that explore the natural environment in more sensitive ways.

## DEPARTMENT OF CONSERVATION

The DOC administers the majority of publicly owned land in the country—about 30 percent of New Zealand's land area. The land is protected for scenic, scientific, historic, and cultural reasons. The National Parks Act of 1980 provides for public entry and access to the land.

In all, the DOC administers 13 national parks, 20 forest parks, and about 3,500 reserves. Additional private reserves are protected by covenants. The DOC also administers New Zealand's two World Heritage Areas: Tongariro National Park on North Island and Te Wahipounamu on South Island, which includes Fiordland National Park and other public lands. The DOC administers many offshore islands and more than a million hectares of marine areas and marine mammal sanctuaries. The department also manages more than 500 historic places.

According to legislation, the soil, water, and forests in New Zealand's national parks are to be maintained in their natural state, with some exceptions. The DOC is allowed to provide accommodations for staff and visitors, build tracks for hiking, and construct roads, service buildings, and parking lots for visitors. The DOC may also arrange for private companies, such as Abel Tasman National Park Enterprises, to provide transportation, guides, and other visitor services. However, some national parks, for example, Fiordland, are so vast and remote that they have seen little development.

Almost all of New Zealand's foreshore and seabed is government-owned, including margins at the edges of rivers, lakes, and the seashore. These 20-meter-wide margins are known as the Queen's

Chain and date from Queen Victoria's time. Although they are publicly owned, the public does not have the right to reach these margins by crossing private land. For instance, to reach a penguin colony nesting in a margin on the beach, tour operators might have to obtain permission from a landowner to cross a sheep pasture. The government also owns most riverbeds and lake beds, although some, like Lake Taupo, are Maori-owned.

The DOC is also in charge of developing strategies for biodiversity in New Zealand. The department runs programs to increase numbers of indigenous species, improve habitats, and reduce numbers of certain introduced species. Efforts include 140 bird programs, 146 plant programs, 32 programs for indigenous freshwater fish, and 86 programs for invertebrates, amphibians, reptiles, and bats. During one recent budget year, the DOC carried out sustained possum control over a 1.3 million-hectare area. The 1996–97 DOC budget was around NZ$163 million, more than half of it used for conservation management.

The DOC maintains a head office, regional and conservancy offices, and a network of field centers around the country. It employs about 1,400 permanent staff members and several hundred temporary and seasonal workers. DOC field offices hold stores of useful information about public lands. Large topographic maps decorate office walls and often show appealing tour routes. Visitors can select from racks of free brochures or purchase brochures, including trail descriptions and maps, for a small cost. The offices also sell books on many natural history topics. If staff members are not overly busy, they'll often share information from their personal travel experiences or tell you about special little-known nature sites. The staff can also book lodging for you in the DOC's network of 960 backcountry huts and tell you about local outfitters, small boats, and vans that will take you to and from trailheads and nature areas.

## NORTH ISLAND NATIONAL PARKS

Tongariro National Park, established in 1887 and given to New Zealand by the Maori people, was the first national park in the country. Tongariro has three volcanoes that are periodically active and often covered with snow: Mount Ruapehu, Mount Ngaurahoe,

## SWIMMING WITH SHARKS

*On dolphin- and seal-swimming tours, operators must be licensed, and the animals are protected by the DOC. On shark-swimming tours, however, it's swimmers who need protection.*

*On one tour that operates off Kaikoura, a locked cage protects anyone "swimming with sharks." The tour operator communicates with nearby dolphin-swimming operators, stays clear of dolphin swimmers, and locates blue and mako sharks without altering their feeding patterns.*

*Sharks do occasionally attack swimmers in the water off Pacific beaches, so be aware before you swim in the ocean.*

and Mount Tongariro. Urewera National Park, along with adjacent Whirinaki Forest Park, contains the largest area of native forests on North Island. The scenic trail around Lake Waikaremoana is North Island's one Great Walk. Egmont National Park surrounds and includes the lovely conical Mount Egmont, first named by Captain James Cook and also known by its Maori name, Taranaki. Whanganui National Park, which borders the Whanganui River, is in an area rich in history.

## SOUTH ISLAND NATIONAL PARKS

Kahurangi National Park, established in 1996, is New Zealand's second largest park. Kahurangi, which means "a treasured possession" in the Maori language, is known for its remoteness, stunning scenery, and unique plants, animals, and rock formations.

Abel Tasman National Park, the smallest national park, has crescent sand beaches, tidal estuaries, aquamarine bays, and a backdrop of low forested mountains. Nelson Lakes National Park encloses a rugged mountain area that extends south from the lovely lakes

Rotoiti and Rotorua. Paparoa National Park, on the west coast, includes the unusual Pancake Rocks at Punakaiki on the coastal highway. Arthur's Pass National Park, in the heart of the Southern Alps, straddles a divide. Westland National Park has a spectacular range of environments, from the alpine heights and glaciers of the Southern Alps, to rivers and lakes, to the estuaries and lush rain forests of the Tasman coast.

Mount Cook National Park has the country's highest mountain (3,754 meters), and the Tasman, the longest glacier. The park offers stunning scenery and many challenging activities. Mount Aspiring National Park has complex glaciated environments and New Zealand's highest peak outside Mount Cook National Park.

Fiordland National Park, New Zealand's largest at 1,251,924 hectares, is also one the largest national parks in the world. Uniquely scenic, it includes mountains and glacial lakes, rain forests, waterfalls, and fjords. Marine environments within the fjords, most of them not protected, combine freshwater and seawater and contain unusual life forms like black coral trees.

Sally McKinney

*Franz Joseph Glacier in Westland National Park*

43

## OTHER PARKS AND RESERVES

Forest parks include coastal forests (including stands of native bush), mountains, tablelands, and grasslands. These parks provide recreational activities and may allow fishing and hunting.

Reserve areas are organized into various categories. *Scenic reserves* include caves and thermal regions. *Nature reserves*, established primarily for preservation of species, include many offshore islands. *National reserves* are protected for their natural beauty or scientific or ecological value. They may also be protected as breeding places for endangered species. *Scientific reserves* are involved in research; public access may be prohibited. *Historic reserves* may enclose Maori rock drawings or historic buildings. *Recreation reserves* often have campgrounds. *Wildlife reserves* are proclaimed over certain areas without affecting ownership of the land. *Marine reserves* and *marine parks* protect habitats; none of the marine resources contained there may be extracted.

## GUIDELINES FOR NATURE ACTIVITIES

The DOC publishes the New Zealand Environmental Care Code (printed on recycled paper). The code has 10 basic tenets:
1. Protect Plants and Animals. Treat New Zealand's forests and birds with care and respect. They are unique and often rare.
2. Remove Rubbish. Litter is unattractive and harmful to wildlife and can increase vermin and disease. Plan your visits to reduce rubbish and carry out what you carry in.
3. Bury Toilet Waste. In areas without toilet facilities, bury waste in a shallow hole, far from waterways, tracks, campsites, and huts.
4. Keep Streams and Lakes Clean. Because soaps and detergents are harmful to water life, do your washing far away from the water source. Drain dirty water into the soil, which will filter it. If you suspect that drinking water may be contaminated, boil it for at least three minutes, filter it, or chemically treat it.
5. Take Care with Fires. Portable stoves are less harmful to the environment and more efficient than campfires. If you do build a fire, keep it small, use only dead wood, douse it with water, and make sure ashes aren't smoldering when you leave.

6. Camp Carefully. Leave no trace of your visit.
7. Keep to the Track. By keeping to the track, where one exists, you lessen the chance of damaging fragile plants.
8. Consider Others. People visit the backcountry and rural areas for many reasons. Be considerate of other visitors.
9. Respect Our Cultural Heritage. Many places in New Zealand have a spiritual and historical significance. Treat these places with consideration and respect.
10. Enjoy Your Visit. Enjoy your outdoor experience. Take a last look before leaving an area—will the next visitor know that you have been there?

In addition to these general guidelines, look for more specific guidelines in each park or reserve. For example, on Kapiti Island, a nature reserve, the number of visitors is regulated by a permit system. Human needs are seen as secondary to the conservation of plants and animals. You'll be encouraged to pick up any litter dropped earlier by other people, along with any of your own. Fires are not allowed, and smoking is allowed only on the beach—with permission of the conservation staff.

## SAVING ENDANGERED SPECIES

Despite increased environmental awareness, more than 500 of New Zealand's plant and animal species are threatened. Introduced weeds are crowding out native plants. Introduced animals—possums, stoats, rats, and others—are consuming native vegetation and destroying native fauna. The clearing of forests and drainage of wetlands have damaged habitats. Over-harvesting has reduced the diversity of marine ecosystems.

The DOC is responsible for ensuring the survival of endangered species and the ecosystems they inhabit. The department places species in three categories, according to a checklist of factors, to determine those most in need of conservation action. This list includes 159 plant species, 98 invertebrate species, and 146 vertebrate species, including 10 fish species and 98 bird species. In addition to this "urgent" list, 408 species fall into several additional categories.

These include species that haven't been seen for a while and might be extinct, those about which there is little information, those that are endangered in New Zealand but not elsewhere in the world, and those of cultural importance to the Maori.

In 1993, New Zealand signed the Convention of Biological Diversity, joining more than 150 countries in an effort to prevent the further loss of vital flora, fauna, and genetic resources. In general, the convention aims to conserve existing biological diversity; assure that the use of species, genetic material, and living systems can be sustained long-term; and share the benefits from genetic resources fairly and equitably.

## PRESERVING NATIVE FLORA

The destruction of New Zealand's native flora literally began at home. Native trees like rata and maire were burned as firewood. After the destruction of mature forests, large stands of fast-growing tea trees (manuka and kanuka), which play a sheltering role in colonizing slow-growing forests, were also used as firewood. In the Auckland region, where central heating is uncommon and rainy winters can be quite cool, tea tree wood is hauled from forests to feed Auckland fireplaces more than 100 kilometers away.

The Royal Forest and Bird Protection Society has started a campaign with the slogan "Don't put native trees up your chimney." The group suggests burning introduced species rather than native trees and even specifies alternative types of firewood: eucalyptus, macrocarpa, radiata, wattle, she oak, willow, and poplar.

New Zealand has hundreds of invasive weeds, including woody trees and shrubs, creepers and climbers, and herbs and groundcovers. Not only do these weeds invade private gardens but they also tend to take over and eventually destroy native plant communities in forests, wetlands, and coastal areas. Some of these invasive plants even migrate to offshore islands.

A campaign on North Island targets invasive weeds. Another campaign educates gardeners and homeowners about old man's beard (*Clematis vitalba*), a vine that rapidly takes over trees and shrubs, blocking out light, and produces up to 100,000 seeds a year.

Gardeners are instructed to cut the vines, prevent their contact with the ground, dig out seedlings, and pull new plants out by the roots. Other problem plants that compete with or smother native species include gorse, blackberry, boxthorn, and honeysuckle.

## PRESERVING NATIVE FAUNA

Because New Zealand's native birds and other wildlife species evolved in the absence of large predators, they were extremely vulnerable to rodents like the kiore, a Polynesian rat brought by the Maoris, and other rats and mice that arrived with European settlers. Over the years, ferrets, stoats, weasels, goats, pigs, and possums, along with pet cats and dogs gone feral, have reduced populations of native birds, lizards, and insects. These animals have also transported diseases.

Plans to protect dwindling numbers of native species are multi-faceted. They include the killing of introduced predators like possums and rats; the relocation of endangered animals to offshore island reserves, where they are protected from competition, introduced animals, and fires; increased screening of arriving visitors and imported automobiles and machinery; and widespread education about endangered species. The cloning of certain species could offer an additional strategy.

The Kokako Recovery Plan is one of many efforts to assist threatened and endangered species. The kokako, a native species of the wattlebird family, has declined in numbers and is now endangered. Only a few of the birds remain in New Zealand in scattered and remote locations on the main islands. Known for their beautiful song, kokakos have light blue and steel gray feathers that blend into olive. They are vegetarians, feeding mainly on fruits, leaves, shoots, and berries. The birds have always been weak flyers, a fact that has made them vulnerable to predators. They also reproduce slowly, with the female incubating one to three eggs for about 24 days. Both parents bring food to the nestlings.

Kokakos have declined from loss of habitat, mainly due to logging. Predators such as possums and rats feed on eggs, chicks, and even adult kokakos. Possums and other browsing animals compete for their food supply. Their slow cycle of reproduction has also been a handicap.

The recovery plan is designed to increase the population until kokakos are self-sustaining and no longer endangered. The program involves research into the causes of the decline; management techniques such as radio-tracking, predator control, replanting, and fencing; and the establishment of a self-sustaining but captive population. New Zealand researchers have also met with Peter Sharp, head of the Reproduction and Development Division at the Roslin Institute in Edinburgh, Scotland, to discuss possible kokako clones. Sharp is known worldwide for cloning Dolly the sheep. He claims that the institute's experiments with chickens, if successful, could lead to the cloning of kokakos, if current habitat management and other strategies fail.

Another population recovery program involves the toutouwai, the North Island robin. These songbirds—no longer found on the mainland in the wild—have been released into Auckland's Wenderholm Regional Park, with its lush habitat of native bush along with regenerating forest.

The famous flightless kiwi is a fast-running ground bird with poor eyesight, a keen sense of smell, and nostrils at the tip of its beak. Loss

Steve Vidler/Leo de Wys

*A spotted kiwi guards her eggs.*

of habitat (especially from the clearing of native forests), predation by dogs, inadvertent kills in possum traps, road kills, attacks by other animals, and entrapment in artificial holes have all contributed to the kiwi's decline. In response, the Bank of New Zealand, the DOC, and the Royal Forest and Bird Protection Society have launched the Kiwi Recovery Programme, with the goal of ensuring the kiwi's survival on the mainland.

Some bird species are declining not only because of predators and loss of habitat, but also because of urban noise. Car alarms and sirens from fire engines and ambulances are making the songbirds tone deaf. Some birds actually imitate these artificial sounds instead of making their traditional calls. As a result, birds suffer a reduced ability to attract mates and to defend territory with calls. Tuis, grey warblers, silvereyes, and other native songbirds have all been affected.

Historically, marine mammals have been vulnerable to human predators, and certain species continue to be so, including the endangered Hector's dolphin and Hooker's sea lion. Seals, whales, and dolphins are now protected by the Marine Mammals Protection Act passed in 1978. Whales are protected in a large expanse of the South Pacific, and an additional protected area is being considered farther north.

## REDUCING PEST POPULATIONS

Introduced grazing animals have done major damage to New Zealand's forests. Goats, wild pigs, rabbits, possums, rats, sheep, and cattle threaten native populations. Deer have been a problem for many decades.

In the nineteenth century, organizations patterned after the Societe Zoologique et Botanique D'Acclimatation in Paris introduced deer, pheasants, and other exotic species into New Zealand. Sport hunting did not keep the deer population in check, and by the early twentieth century the problem was known as "the Deer Menace."

In the 1930s, under the leadership of George Yerex, the Department of Internal Affairs waged a deer-hunting campaign using military strategies and organization. The department hired an army of deer-cullers to fight the so-called menace. Widespread unemployment during the Great Depression motivated hunters to work hard for low wages—not to mention bounties for deerskins and tails. By 1938, hunters had killed more than 100,000 deer. Eventually, the campaign included the culling of other introduced animals, including wild goats, pigs, and chamois.

Possums, specifically the Australian brush-tailed possum, were introduced to New Zealand in the mid-nineteenth century in an effort to launch a fur industry. Fruit farmers and conservationists warned of the damage the animals could do, but scientists declared them harmless. Soon the animals had become a menace. They took over orchards and gardens and gnawed on young plants and willow trees.

Another campaign was mounted, and farmers proceeded to trap, poison, and skin the animals for bounties. The campaign was marred by a general distrust of poisons, concern about poisonous residues in water, and accidental human poisonings. The campaign continues with safer methods, with the cost of possum research and control in New Zealand at an estimated NZ$50 million per year.

Boaters must be vigilant about keeping rodents in check, especially near offshore island nature reserves. They are advised to set out poisonous bait or traps, load and offload supplies during the day when the animals are less active, and anchor offshore at night to reduce the chance of rodents boarding.

New Zealand's Ministry for Biosecurity monitors unwanted biological invaders. A phytoplasma carried by introduced plant hoppers has been killing the country's native cabbage trees and spreading to other native plants. First limited to northern North Island, the disease has now spread across Cook Strait to South Island. (A similar disease has been attacking strawberries and other fruits in Australia.) Asian gypsy moths and white-spotted tussock moths arrive in New Zealand in the form of egg masses attached to automobiles, machinery, and shipping containers. The moths threaten forests, gardens, parks, vineyards, and orchards. Other invading insects blow in from Australia, carried by the wind, or stow away in the luggage of unsuspecting visitors.

Immigrant mosquitoes also arrive with travelers and stow away in cargo shipments. Although mosquitoes are not a problem in most of New Zealand, the odd one does fly in at night and buzz around, especially near attractive indoor lights. Mosquitoes breed well in New Zealand's climate, and greater numbers could increase the risk of such diseases as malaria and dengue fever.

The issues around imported species are not always clear-cut. Consider the question of rainbow lorikeets imported from Australia. They inhabit stands of bush on Auckland's north shore and a few other places. The birds are also prized as pets—a hand-raised rainbow lorikeet sells for around NZ$200. One radio station even gives a daily report with descriptions of missing pet birds.

However, the DOC claims the birds are aggressive, may harbor disease, and can drive out tui, kaka, and other native birds by taking their food, nesting sites, and territory. The department has been catching lorikeets—giving some to bird lovers and killing others. Many people don't want the birds killed, however. Homeowners appreciate their bright colors and happy chatter in the garden. Some people claim the birds make wonderful pets, while others believe the birds should not be caged.

# PROTECTING NEW ZEALAND'S WATERS

In New Zealand, a maritime nation surrounded by the South Pacific Ocean and the Tasman Sea, water quality and the sustenance of marine life are of utmost importance. For commercial fishing, an offshore Exclusive Economic Zone (EEZ), about 20 times the size of New Zealand's land area, extends between 25 and 55 degrees south latitude. Reaching deep into the Southern Ocean, the zone is the fourth largest maritime territory in the world. While some coastal waters are degraded and polluted, most of the EEZ remains pollution-free.

The zone is home to 80 to 100 different species of fish and shellfish that are caught and sold commercially, generally from the shallower locations. A Quota Management System is used to sustain the fish populations long-term. Under this system, catch limits are reassessed annually. Commercial, recreational, Maori, and environmental groups are involved in the process, which is carried out by a group called MFish.

Yet the EEZ is a vast area, and regulatory officials can't monitor everything that happens there. An estimated 40 percent of the commercial fish caught in the zone bypass New Zealand's regulatory (and taxation) systems and are processed overseas. Some violators run a

# FUR SEAL VIEWING

*Although hundreds of thousands of fur seals were killed during the early nineteenth century, New Zealand's fur seal population is now increasing. The seals can be seen basking on rocks and swimming at scattered locations along the coasts of the main islands.*

*The males, which are larger than the females, can grow up to 1.8 meters long and weigh up to 140 kilograms. Although usually playful in the water, they can be aggressive on land, especially when they are cut off from water, their pups, or what they perceive as their territory.*

*On DOC-licensed seal-swimming cruises, tour operators will give you guidelines for encountering seals in the water. When you encounter seals in other situations, the DOC gives this advice:*

- *Keep your distance; go no closer than five meters.*
- *Do not cut off their escape route to the water.*
- *Do not stand between adult seals and their pups.*
- *Do not feed the seals or pick up the pups.*
- *Seals can bite and may harbor parasites or disease.*
- *If a seal seems to be sick or injured, or if you see someone harassing one, contact the DOC.*

lucrative black market in native paua shellfish, considered a delicacy in expensive overseas restaurants.

Marine reserves have fairly restrictive policies for fishing and boating. Guidelines for "boaties" cruising the Bay of Islands change according to season (more people visit in summer), drinking water supply, and availability of a trash collection barge. Fires are prohibited, and recycling is strongly recommended. Boaties are encouraged to release toilet wastes into deep water, far out to sea.

Also in the Bay of Islands, laws and rules about amateur fishing and the gathering of shellfish are fairly complex. Daily limits are set per individual and cannot be shared. Certain equipment—some kinds for catching finfish, others for taking shellfish—is clearly prohibited. Scuba equipment cannot be used to take paua, for example, and rock lobsters cannot be captured by puncturing their exoskeletons.

In Fiordland, responsible fishing means catching fish with barbless hooks for easy release and returning undersized rock lobsters to locations where they can find shelter. For more details on the regulations, consult the skipper of a diving or fishing boat, or get the latest "Amateur Fishing Information" brochure from a Ministry of Fisheries office.

Water quality is an important issue, especially in Auckland, a sprawling city inhabited by roughly one-third of New Zealand's population. Seawater from Auckland's bays washes onto the city's many beaches and fills tidal pools. In summer, high E . coli bacteria counts sometimes prevent swimming at East Bay beaches (Mission Bay, Kohimarama, and St. Heliers). People are also cautioned not to swim at urban beaches within two days of a rainstorm, because the city's overflowing drainage system discharges raw sewage.

City administrations have for too long ignored the region's aging sewage systems. By now, solutions to the discharge problem have become very expensive, but are finally being implemented. In addition to a NZ$360 million long-term plan for a new system, the Auckland Regional Council also faces renovation costs of NZ$165 million during the next 20 years.

Also in Auckland, a Hauraki Gulf Marine Park bill, under consideration, would create special status for assorted land and marine environments in the greater Hauraki Gulf, require periodic environmental quality reports, and enable diverse government officials to cooperate more easily on environmental quality issues.

## OTHER ENVIRONMENTAL PROBLEMS

Although New Zealanders sometimes call their country GodZone ("God's own"), the islands are not a paradise. The thinning ozone layer over Antarctica has brought increased ultraviolet radiation to New Zealand, in levels that peak during spring.

New Zealanders generate more than 3 million tons of solid waste a year; industrial wastes account for more than half of this figure. People do recycle, and production systems have been streamlined to generate less waste and emissions. Yet the total amount of waste is still increasing, and waste management systems are less than ideal.

## CONSERVATION ORGANIZATIONS

Many private and nonprofit organizations are active in conservation efforts. The World Wild Fund for Nature is prominent in New Zealand. Projects include supporting the Southern Ocean whale sanctuary; backing research on fur seals, black robins, and pilot whales; and assessing the impact of whale and dolphin watchers on Hector's dolphins and sperm whales. Contact World Wild Fund for Nature at P.O. Box 6237, Wellington, 04-499-2930, for more information.

The Royal Forest and Bird Protection Society, known as Forest and Bird, has been operating in New Zealand since 1923. The

*Seal-swimming tours follow strict guidelines about protecting New Zealand fur seal populations.*

organization works to protect native forests, threatened species, the country's maritime heritage, and the environment in general. Efforts include grassroots organization, public debates on environmental issues, and lobbying decision-makers. Forest and Bird helped create Kahurangi National Park, the South West New Zealand World Heritage Area, and the Kermadec Islands and other marine reserves. Contact Forest and Bird at P.O. Box 631, Wellington, 04-385-7374, or at its Auckland field office, Level 2, Emcom House, 75 Queen St., Auckland, 09-303-3079.

Other organizations include the Queen Elizabeth II National Trust, which works to enhance New Zealand's open spaces, and the New Zealand Natural Heritage Foundation, which educates people about the country's natural history. The Yellow-eyed Penguin Trust (P.O. Box 5409, Dunedin) creates penguin reserves, plants trees, and protects breeding sites.

The New Zealand Native Forests Restoration Trust, in alliance with several other organizations, works to save forests. Contact the group at P.O. Box 80-007, Green Bay, Auckland. Native Forest Action works to stop the logging of native forests. Contact them at P.O. Box 836, Nelson, 03-545-6040, nfa_office@ts.co.nz.

New Zealand Wilderness Volunteers, an offshoot of the New Zealand Wilderness Trust, runs community education and grassroots projects. Project volunteers pay for packages that include food, travel, and accommodations at wilderness locations. They work without pay for one week or more, on projects such as planting trees, controlling possums, or monitoring endangered species. Work hours are 8 to 4; volunteers also help with cooking and cleaning. Packages run about NZ$155 for one week, NZ$120 for each extra week, and NZ$520 for four weeks.

# ECO-SENSITIVE BUSINESSES

Many New Zealand businesses have increased their environmental awareness during the last few years. Tour operators are one example. New Zealand Nature Safaris, for instance, will give you a true ecotourism experience. The company offers small guided safaris in four different regions. Tours last from 4 to 10 days and include cook-

# PROTECTING MAORI TREASURES

*The 1993 Convention on Biological Diversity recognizes the right of indigenous communities such as the Maori to use certain plants and animals for cultural purposes. At times, Maori interests dovetail neatly with conservation programs. For example, a pair of saddlebacks, birds known to the Maori as tiekes, escorted early arrivals on a canoe from Cuvier Island. Over the years, this species became increasingly rare, especially on the mainland. Eventually, only one colony remained, so increasing the population of saddlebacks became a DOC goal. When conservation officials recently released 40 of the birds into the Cuvier Island habitat, the act had special meaning. For Maoris, the birds are tonga—spiritual treasures.*

*At other times, conservation programs are at odds with Maori tradition. After a Northland flood in early 1999, residents of the village of Panguru found valuable native tree trunks among the debris that had washed down from the hills. The minister of Maori affairs, convinced that the timber belonged to the people, had portable sawmills brought into the village so residents could use the timber to rebuild their homes. However, the DOC claimed that it owned the trees. Amid much anger and controversy, the Department ruled that the timber could not be used for building.*

ing out, vehicle-based camping, and some overnight stays in huts. Experienced guides (seven men and one woman), all New Zealanders, take you where other tours don't—with the emphasis on nature. Tours depart weekly and involve hiking through alpine terrain, rain forests, coastlines, and caves. Depending on the region, you might encounter keas, kotuku (white herons), penguins, seals, or dolphins. You'll learn how to walk through rivers (without falling down), read maps, paddle a kayak, abseil (rappel) down a rope, and make tasty meals over a campfire. Yet this is not a marathon; a couple of active days with a lot of hiking might be followed by a visit to a natural hot pool—heaven for tired muscles. The emphasis will be on learning about the natural world, not on hitting this year's trendiest nature sites.

Tours include a North Island Safari and three options for South Island: an Arthur's Pass tour (oops, seven hours of hiking in one day on this one), a West Coast Wilderness Adventure, and a Secret South Safari. Tours depart weekly in summer from Auckland, Nelson, Queenstown, and Christchurch.

The company asks that you be reasonably fit, bring some enthusiasm, and expect an international sampling of companions. No group is larger than 11 people, and though most participants are under age 40, you don't have to be.

The operators will provide you with an equipment list and a detailed itinerary (printed on recycled paper). Costs run from NZ$300 to NZ$800 per tour, plus a food kitty of about NZ$15 a day and occasional kayak rental or other fees. For each passenger booked, New Zealand Nature Safaris donates NZ$10 to the New Zealand Wildlife Research Fund. For more information contact New Zealand Nature Safaris, 52 Holborn Dr., Stokes Valley, 6008, 0800-697-232, fax 04-563-7324, nzns@globe.co.nz, www.nzsafaris.co.nz.

Another eco-sensitive business is Budget Bins, the largest New Zealand–owned trash removal company in the country. Owner Peter Luxford saw an opportunity to enhance his business after the Auckland Regional Council raised its rates for trash removal. Luxford countered by hiring more workers and directing them to separate components of the trash. They divided waste into metals that could be sold as salvage, vegetable material that could be used as compost, and concrete and other materials that could be used in private land-fills. Customers, city officials, and environmentalists appreciated the way these recycling efforts helped the environment. Budget Bins has become a NZ$10 million operation.

Organic farming is growing rapidly in New Zealand. Nearly 600 food producers and processors are licensed to use the Bio-Gro label, a symbol that shows compliance with internationally approved standards for organic production. The standards also include the humane treatment of livestock. Because the costs of meeting the standards are high, Bio-Gro foods are perhaps 10 to 15 percent more expensive than conventionally grown foods.

Organic food exports are also growing, with large markets in North America, Japan, and Europe. Free-range eggs from New Zealand are now sold in supermarkets in California. Milton Vineyard and a few other wineries also use organic methods. The organic products industry expects exports to reach NZ$65 million by the year 2000.

# FUTURE STRATEGIES

The Resource Management Act of 1991 outlined a plan for the use, distribution, and preservation of New Zealand's natural and physical resources, including its air, rivers, lakes, coastal areas, thermal areas, forests, farms, and buildings. The legislation requires people to ana- lyze the environmental impact of all proposed building projects and provides for community involvement in decisions.

Here are some goals of the Resource Management Act. You might keep them in mind as you travel around New Zealand:
- Preserve the natural character of the coastal environment.
- Protect outstanding natural features and landscapes from inap- propriate development.
- Protect significant habitats for indigenous flora and fauna.
- Maintain and enhance public access to and from coastal marine areas, lakes, and rivers.
- Respect the culture and traditions of the Maori and their relation- ships with ancestral lands, water, and sacred sites.

In an attempt to take a long-term view of the country's environ- mental goals, New Zealand has targeted the following priority issues:
- managing the resources of land, water, and air
- protecting habitats and biological diversity
- managing pests, weeds, and diseases
- sustaining fish populations
- managing the environmental impact of energy services and transportation

- managing waste, contaminated sites, and hazardous substances
- reducing the risk of climate change
- restoring the ozone layer

Reaching these goals will involve the cooperation of government, private industry, individuals—and visitors.

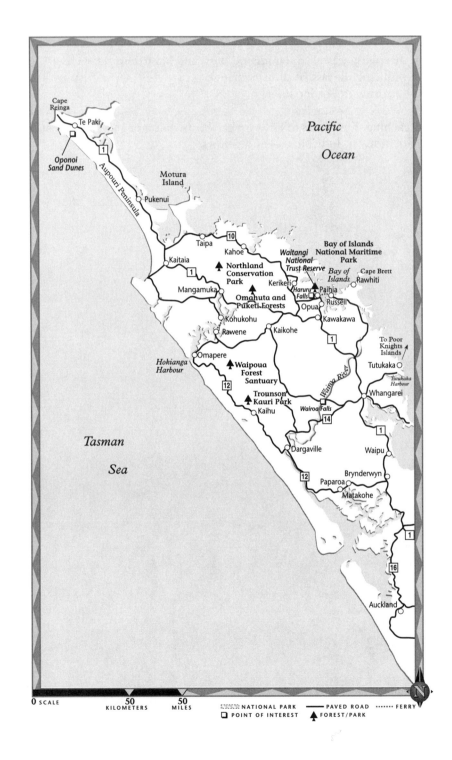

Cape
Reinga

Te Paki

Oponoi
Sand Dunes

**1**

*Aupouri Peninsula*

Motura
Island

Pukenui

Taipa

Kahoe

**10**

Kaitaia

▲ **Northland
Conservation
Park**

Mangamuka

**1**

Kerikeri

*Waitangi
National
Trust Reserve*

**Bay of Islands
National Maritime
Park**

*Bay of
Islands*

Cape Brett

Rawhiti

▲ **Omahuta and
Puketi Forests**

Kohukohu

*Haruru
Falls*

Paihia

Opua

Russell

Rawene

Kaikohe

Kawakawa

**1**

*Pacific

Ocean*

To Poor
Knights
Islands

*Hokianga
Harbour*

Omapere

▲ **Waipoua
Forest
Sanctuary**

*Tutukaka*

*Tutukaka
Harbour*

**12**

▲ **Trounson
Kauri Park**

Kaihu

*Wairoa Falls*

**14**

*Waiora River*

Whangarei

**1**

*Tasman

Sea*

Dargaville

Waipu

**12**

Paparoa

Bryderwyn

Matakohe

**1**

**16**

Auckland

0 SCALE

50
KILOMETERS

50
MILES

⌗ NATIONAL PARK    ▬ PAVED ROAD    ∙∙∙∙∙∙ FERRY

▢ POINT OF INTEREST    ▲ FOREST/PARK

N

# CHAPTER 3

# Northland Region

Whether you come to see majestic kauri trees, paddle through shady mangrove estuaries, or peer through a dive mask at the face of an eel, the subtropical Northland has great appeal. It took millions of years for this region to develop into what it's become. During the cooling and warming of the ice ages, when seawater alternately covered then exposed this land, Northland acquired distinctive land forms inhabited by unusual plants and animals.

Migratory seabirds nest in the west coast sand dunes near surf-washed beaches. Rare brown kiwis wander about patches of tangled bush. Gnarled pohutukawa trees, rooted in rocky cliffs, frame east coast beaches. The Bay of Islands has more soft adventure tours than anyone could imagine, and the region's small size allows for day trips to the west coast from Paihia.

Northland's network of highways is the key to reaching the most appealing natural areas, whether you travel by car, RV, or public bus. Follow SH 1 northwest of Auckland onto the Northland isthmus and you'll encounter three loops of major highways. Beyond Brynderwyn Junction, you can follow part of the first loop toward tiny Tutukaka Harbour or head west toward the region's tallest and oldest trees.

Travel farther and you'll reach Paihia, historic Russell, the Waitangi Reserve, and the Bay of Islands, long popular with New

Zealanders as a summer holiday destination. Beyond Kawakawa, the third highway loop links the more secluded bays and beaches of the east with the bush-covered central hills. Farther northwest, the highway continues to Cape Reinga.

## HISTORY, CULTURE, AND CUSTOMS

The Bay of Islands, Hokianga Harbour, and the Aupori Peninsula played major roles in Maori history. Evidence of early Maori habitation abounds: terraces, middens, and fortifications known as *pas* can be seen throughout Northland. Maoris were living on both coasts when Captain James Cook arrived in New Zealand in the mid-eighteenth century; many Northlanders have Maori ancestors. Europeans sailed into the harbors at Kororareka (now Russell), Karikari, and Hokianga, then explored upriver by boat. As early European settlements grew, coastal trading and riverboats extended the reach of commerce.

Business ventures often exploited the region's natural riches. Most of the native forests, dominated by massive kauri trees, were depleted or burned. Whales were hunted offshore, and the brown fur seals you now see sleeping on coastal rocks were once clubbed to death. Remnant populations of kauri trees and marine mammals can still be seen. Fortunately, today's visitors hunt with cameras only.

Northland has retained its historic rural character—you may need to adjust to a slower pace. In Northland, people don't fret if they miss the ferry boat; there's usually another one coming along soon. If a passenger doesn't show up for a tour, the driver may go find him. So if your gourmet dinner hasn't yet been served, relax and sip a drink while you wait. In fact, a sunset dinner in a special restaurant might be your entire evening's entertainment. In Northland, far from movies, theaters, and nightclubs, there's often nowhere else to go!

## NATURE AND ADVENTURE ACTIVITIES

Although this region lacks New Zealand's highest mountains, deepest caves, and most stunning scenery, its mild climate means greater comfort throughout the year. The warm Auckland currents enhance water activities along both coasts.

On the more-developed east coast, tour operators offer organized nature adventures. You can have memorable independent adventures on both coasts, but before you set out, get good information and equipment. Despite occasional bouts of wind and rain, many visitors travel Northland on bicycles. The region has great spots for picnics and some gorgeous campsites.

On the wilder rainier west coast, the surf rolls in from the Tasman Sea before spilling onto wide sandy beaches. Beach hikes, sliding down sand dunes, bush walks, camping, and bird-watching are the main activities here. Sea kayakers favor the irregular and scenic east coast, with its open and sheltered beaches and bays, inlets and estuaries. Hiking tracks ascend rocky headlands for stunning views, then drop down into forests and lovely coves.

## FLORA AND FAUNA

Along the sand hills, in tall clumps of toetoe, and on grassy cliff faces of the coast, you'll find seabirds such as red-billed or black-backed gulls, white-fronted terns, and pied or spotted shags tending their nests. Among coastal saltwater marshes with their borders of mangroves, look for kingfishers, stilts, and banded rails.

Kauri trees still dominate some patches of forest. In Northland, you'll also find nikau palm, rimu, kowhai, totara, kahikatea, pohutukawa, and cabbage trees. Walk softly, walk quietly, and walk alone, and you could encounter a stately wood pigeon with its sheeny blue-green feathers, a brown morepork, a fantail bird, a weka, or a tui . . . at least you'll hear them. Cruise along Northland's Pacific coast, and you might see a sperm whale, a pod of orcas, some common dolphins, or the distinctive bottle-nosed dolphin.

## VISITOR INFORMATION

New Zealand's official network of visitor information centers, identified by a distinctive logo, is very helpful, as are DOC offices. For more information you can phone Tourism Northland in Paihia, 09-402-7683; Whangarei Visitors Bureau, 09-438-1079; Bay of Islands Information Office, 09-402-7426; Kataia Information Office, 09-408-0879; Dargaville Information Centre, 09-439-8360; Hokianga Information Centre, 09-405-8869; and Kaikohe Information Centre, 09-401-1693.

Stock up on cash before traveling in rural areas. Banks and ATMs can be scarce; small businesses rarely take credit cards. The smaller the town, the more likely that shops—even food shops—will be closed evenings and Sunday.

Subtropical Northland does not have major seasonal changes. However, you might experience spring, summer, and fall weather all in one day! Carry drinking water, a sun hat, warm clothing, rain gear, long pants, an energy snack, sun block, and insect repellent on daily outings and cruises. Sand flies are a nuisance at many beaches and some outdoor cafés.

## GETTING AROUND

Buses, rental cars, and RVs travel a network of good roads in Northland. The major public bus lines are InterCity at Sky City Complex, Hobson Street Terminal, Auckland, 09-639-0500, and Northliner at the Downtown Airline Terminal, 86-94 Quay St., Auckland, 09-307-5873; ask about travel passes and discounts for seniors, students, Youth Hostel members, and so on. Kiwi Experience and the Magic Traveller's Network, Ground Floor, Union House, 36 Queen St., Auckland, 09-358-5600, provide transportation to many nature sites.

Cars and RVs are usually rented in Auckland, driven around a loop, and returned there. Make sure you're recovered from jet lag before challenging Auckland traffic.

## NATURE AND ADVENTURE SIGHTS FROM WHANGAREI AND TUTUKAKA HARBOUR

### Poor Knights Islands

For a time, seagoing Maoris inhabited the Poor Knights, which were named by Captain James Cook. Now incorporated into the **Hauraki Gulf Maritime Park**, the environment is protected as a nature reserve above the water and a marine reserve below the water. You'll soon discover why Jacques Costeau once named this destination one of the five best dive sites in the world.

The Poor Knights are distinctive because the warm Auckland current creates near-tropical conditions on the lee side of the two largest islands and nearby smaller islets, sea stacks, and rocks. The islands themselves, formed centuries ago by dynamic volcanic action, total 267 hectares. The highest point rises to 240 meters. In some places, the cliffs extend some 90 meters below sea level.

Millions of seabirds breed in this rugged habitat, including Buller's shearwaters and nine species of petrel. The rare Poor Knight's lily, with its fuzzy red blossoms, grows abundantly amid flax and the feathery toetoe. Insects called the giant tree weta and the giant cave weta live here, along with tuataras, geckos, and skinks. However, most likely, you won't be walking around among these creatures; landing permits are issued only to scientific researchers.

The easiest way to reach this world-class dive site (and nature and marine reserve) is by a 32-kilometer motorboat ride across Pacific waters. Boats depart from Tutukaka Harbour, about 30 kilometers east of Whangarei via the Ngunguru Road.

A number of tour operators offer diving excursions to Poor Knights. If necessary, these companies will pick you up or arrange transportation from Whangarei. Sightseers and snorkelers are welcome on dive excursions, as are beginning divers. Boats operate most weekends throughout the year and depart daily from late October through late April.

On a typical dive outing, you might explore 2 of more than 10 well-known sites. Among the options are **Nursery Cove**, a maze called the **Labyrinth**, the **Landing Bay Pinnacle**, the **Blue Maomao Arch**, and the **Gardens**, which features seawood, tunnels, and a domed cave. Descend into the depths and you might see rare black coral or a sleek manta ray. You'll see anemones, starfish, and sea cucumbers, and schools of fish including pink and blue maomao, the crimson cleaner, green or yellow wrasse, and black angelfish. Visibility may extend to 15, 20, or even 30 meters.

Aqua Action is a PADI-certified operation with a dive shop and

Sally McKinney

*Hilltop view from Urupukapuka Island*

equipment for rent. Full equipment packages cost NZ$150; snorkeling packages cost NZ$95. The shop is on Marina Road in Tutukaka, 0800-689-222 or 09-434-3867, fax 09-434-3884, aquaaction@xtra.co.nz.

Kevin Butler of Knight Diver Tours has more than 20 years of diving experience and dives with his clients. Contact Knight Diver Tours, 30 Whangarei Heads Rd., Whang-arei, 0800-766-756, phone /fax 09-436-2584, mobile 025-999-611.

Knight Line Charters offers ecotours, along with snorkeling, diving, and sea kayaking at Poor Knights. A permit from the DOC allows the company to give you close encounters with dolphins and whales. Contact Knight Line Charters, P.O. Box 404, Whangarei, 0800-288-882, fax 9-434-3704, mobile 025-810-826, knightline@ xtra.co.nz.

*Details: Contact Hauraki Gulf Maritime Park, Ferry Building, Quay St., Auckland, 09-379-6476.*

## NATURE AND ADVENTURE SIGHTS FROM PAIHIA AND THE BAY OF ISLANDS

### Bay of Islands

During the eighteenth century, great kauri forests covered these islands, and large herds of whales could be found in the surrounding waters. The giant trees were soon cut down, with some timber used in local construction and large quantities shipped overseas. Whalers based in the port of Kororareka (now called Russell) rapidly reduced the whale population. Early in the twentieth century, the bay became known for its bountiful supply of big game fish. The bay's current status—Bay of Islands National Maritime and Historic Park—has changed visitors' activities.

Each island has a special appeal. **Moturoa Island,** a bird sanctuary, has a walking track linking the island's four beaches. (You can get a pamphlet about the track from the BOI office in Russell.) **Okahu Island Scenic Reserve** is a snorkeling and diving site. **Urupukapuka Island** has high green hills dotted with grazing sheep, and lovely beaches and bays with wooden piers reaching into clear pale water. Author and adventurer Zane Grey used Urupukapuka's Otehei Bay as a base for big-game fishing during the 1920s; a restaurant there now bears his name. Camping is permitted on the island; follow DOC guidelines.

About a thousand years ago, a thriving Maori community inhabited Urupukapuka, living on fish, shellfish, and sea eggs, along with kumara and other garden crops. On a Urupukapuka Island archaeological walk, you'll see evidence of ancient pas on the headlands, flat-terraced areas where clusters of houses once stood, underground storage pits, and slight ditches that were probably garden drains. Allow five hours or more to complete the loop trail. If you have less time, choose either a north loop walk with more spectacular scenery but fewer archaeological sites or a south loop with more sheltered bays and more sites.

The Bay of Islands itself, with its 800 kilometers of coastline, subtropical climate, and secluded beaches, provides a scenic setting for kayakers. Banded rails nest in the sedges, stilts probe the shallow seawater for tasty morsels, and red-billed gulls soar overhead. The **Waitangi River delta,** just north of Paihia, especially appeals to kayakers for its various inlets, some of them shaded by gnarled mangrove branches. (In the Maori language, Waitangi means "weeping water.") Head farther upriver and you'll encounter the impressive **Haruru Falls.** It's fun to explore the islands beyond Russell and Tapeka Point by kayak. Formed long ago by volcanic action, most of the islands have often-deserted sand beaches, sheltered lagoons, and even caves.

Several outfitters offer guided day tours, overnight camping, and equipment rental. Coastal Kayakers, 09-402-7730, www.nzinfo.com/seakayak/coastalkayakers.htm, offers half-day, full-day, and two-day guided tours and independent rentals year-round. Three-day trips run November through May. A one-day guided tour takes paddlers to deserted **Motumaire Island.**

Sailboats offer another eco-sensitive way to experience the coast and islands. From November to April, the *R. Tucker Thompson*, a schooner that resembles an early sailing ship, offers six-hour bay cruises daily. Visitors may help with the sailing or lean back, relax, and savor scenic views of the many islands. The NZ$75 per adult price includes a barbecue lunch. Most tours pass **Black Rocks Scenic Reserve**, an island group formed from dark molten lava, Moturoa Island, and Motuarohia Island, once visited by Captain Cook.

Other operators offer cruises on smaller sailboats: *The Gungha*, 0800-478-900; *She's a Lady*, 09-402-8119; and *Straycat*, 09-402-6130. At Paihia's Charter Pier, 09-402-7143, fax 09-402-7142, options include sailing lessons, flotilla charters, skippered charters, and bare-boat sailing (no skipper). If you opt for a motorized cruise, choose a full-day tour with a leisurely pace that will allow you to explore several islands.

The King's Bay in a Day cruise (NZ$75), departing from Paihia takes you to the **Hole in the Rock**, a natural tunnel through Piercy Island, and other sights. In addition, the captain will look for dolphins—or orca whales or whatever else is out there—then cut the engine for excellent wildlife observation and photography. The stable catamarans have outdoor decks fore and aft. The six-hour Fullers Cream Trip, P.O. Box 145, Paihia, Bay of Islands, 09-402-7421, reservations @ fullersnorthland.co.nz, is similar to King's. Cruises operate October to April daily. The adult price is NZ$65.

Several companies offer marine-mammal-watching tours. Common and bottle-nosed dolphins can be seen year-round. Under certain conditions, you're allowed to climb into a net bay while the dolphins swim beside you. Orca whales visit seasonally, and the bryde's whale is a semi-resident. Occasionally, you might see minke, pilot, or humpback whales. Although each trip is unique, you will usually encounter seabirds and fish and, at times, seals or little blue penguins.

Prepare for the day by wearing a swimsuit under your clothing. Bring warm clothes to counter chill winds and rain. DOC guidelines insist that boats stay a specified distance from the mammals and allow swimmers in the water only under certain conditions. Whether you swim or not, it's great fun to watch dolphins glide to the surface, slip under the water, and leap and twirl above it. A pod of orcas makes a memorable sight, as does a surfacing humpback whale.

In 1991, Dolphin Discoveries, P.O. Box 400, Paihia, Bay of Islands,

# THE ORIGINAL *RAINBOW WARRIOR*— WHERE IS IT NOW?

*In 1985, the Greenpeace vessel* Rainbow Warrior, *which had been protesting nuclear testing by France in the South Pacific, was bombed by French terrorists. The well-placed first bomb sank the ship in Auckland Harbour; the second bomb accidentally killed photographer Fernando Pereira. Two agents, ultimately linked to the French General Directorate for External Security, were tried and pleaded guilty to manslaughter. Although given long sentences, they were eventually released to the French government, which soon set them free. The damaged* Rainbow Warrior *was later floated to the Cavelli Islands, then sunk for use as a dive site.*

*About 30 meters under the sea, the ship now has a peaceful resting place. With the bowsprit facing west, the boat lists a bit to starboard. It has acquired a softer look, with a covering of bright living sea creatures: barnacles, soft sponges, and anemones that radiate purple, yellow, and blue.*

*Most divers explore only the exterior of this controversial wreck. Those who are especially qualified may explore within. Depending on conditions, divers may encounter yellow-black triple fin, leatherjackets, blue maomao, crested blenny, scorpion fish, kingfish, or moray eels. Two dive boats based in Paihia (see Tour Operators) take divers to the Cavelli Islands site. Nearby on the coast, a* Rainbow Warrior *memorial stands at Matauri Bay.*

*Ten years after the tragic bombing, the French resumed nuclear testing, and Greenpeace sent* Rainbow Warrior II *to protest.*

09-402-8234, fax 09-402-6058, was the first company on North Island to be licensed by the DOC to run marine-mammal tours. The company uses a catamaran with toilets and hot showers, offers easy access to the water, and has video cameras in the hull for underwater viewing.

Fullers Northland, Maritime Building, Marsden Rd., Paihia, 09-402-7421, fax 09-402-7831, reservations@fullers-northland.co.nz, offers a Dolphin Encounters tour on a catamaran driven by jet propulsion, not propellers. Through an underwater microphone, you can listen to dolphins communicating.

Bay of Islands Heritage Tours, Maritime Building, Marsden Rd., Paihia, 0800-423-657 or 09-402-6280, fax 09-402-6808, sales@dolphinz.co.nz, offers a dolphin swim and whale watch. The excursion includes Maori history and legends of the sea. "Our family has been in the bay for over 900 years," claims this Maori tour operator.

Keep in mind, says Dolphin Discoveries, "All marine mammals and other wildlife seen on this tour are wild and free. When we encounter them we are entering their world—it is a privilege, not a right, and we must respect this."

The tour operators claim a 90 percent success rate for dolphin viewing and will take you out again free of charge if no dolphins appear during your cruise. Depending on the operator, coffee, tea, hot showers, wet suits, and snorkeling equipment may be included.

**Details**: *Bay of Islands Maritime and Historic Park Visitor Centre, The Strand, Russell, 09-403-7685.*

## Rakaumangamanga Track/Cape Brett Walkway

This winding 20-kilometer route runs between Rawhiti and the Cape Brett Lighthouse, crossing seven hills of great significance to the Maori. Fit experienced hikers can walk the trail in eight hours. Some hikers choose to spend the night at the Cape Brett Hut and return the following day; overnight lodging can be arranged through the DOC. Another two-day option is to return to Rawhiti by water taxi. A third possibility combines a water-taxi ride from Rawhiti to Deep Water Cove, a five-hour hike to and from Cape Brett, and a water-taxi return.

To the Maoris, the seven hills on the cape represent the great *wakas*, the seagoing canoes that brought them to New Zealand during the Great Migration. A Maori proverb sums up the appeal of the walkway: "Walk the valleys of our ancestors/learn the history/marvel [at] the beauty." Pohutukawa trees, with their lavish display of red summer blossoms, once flourished here; Maoris knew this place as the Crimson Cape.

Follow the track and you'll see native and regenerating bush growing on DOC and Maori trust land. As you walk, stunning sea views alternate with forest scenery. Occasionally, ancient pas and wahi indicate Maori habitation in centuries past. You'll also learn about possum and control and regenerating native forests.

From Rawhiti to **Pukehuia**, the trail ascends the steep side of a mountain. Although well-marked, the track varies from narrow to wide, and it's rough going—not a smooth walkway. Beyond Pukehuia, the trail turns toward the cape, then follows the backbone of the rugged peninsula between the Bay of Islands and the Pacific Ocean. About one-third of the way to the cape, you'll pass through the gate of an electric fence designed to keep out marauding possums. This fence crosses the entire peninsula. You'll encounter the Waitui Stream. Beyond it, a spur leads down to a campground at Deep Cove, but the main trail continues to the lighthouse.

**Cape Brett Lighthouse**, with its catwalks and ladders, stands 14 meters high. A few people lived here early in the twentieth century, and the lighthouse was staffed for 70-some years, until the signals were automated in 1978. **Cape Brett Hut**, former home of the assistant lighthouse keeper, now sleeps 21 trampers. Facilities include bunks and mattresses, a gas range, running water, and composting toilets.

Water-taxi travel usually involves a landing at **Deep Water Cove**, where marine life thrives. When the sea is calm, a Cape Brett landing may also be possible. Water-taxi trips also include visits to the Hole in the Rock and Cathedral Cave on Piercy Island. Kaimarama Bay Tours, 09-403-8114, boat phone 025-538-743, operates a water taxi. Costs range from NZ$20 to NZ$90; ask about group discounts.

*Details: For track fees and hut bookings, contact the DOC Visitor Centre, P.O. Box 134, The Strand, Russell, Bay of Islands, 09-403-7685, fax 09-403-7649. Adults pay NZ$8 per night for the hut and a track fee of NZ$15.*

## Russell

Walk along the strand in the shade of pohutukawa trees, and you'll see little to remind you that this quiet village was once a notorious whaling center. At one time, 30 or more grog shops served whalers eager to make the most of their shore leave. The **Duke of Marlborough**, a renovated historic building now offering rooms and meals, was the first licensed pub in New Zealand.

Begin your tour of Russell by strolling southeast on the strand past "The Duke." You'll walk by a customs house that dates from the 1870s, when this was a busy port. Beside it, notice the elderly Moreton Bay fig tree, planted by an early customs official. The pohutukawa trees that border the beach usually burst with showy red blossoms during the Christmas season.

Small boats call here at Kororareka Bay (from a Maori word meaning "sweet broth of the penguin"). Beyond Pitt Street, note the impressive **Pompallier Building**. Formerly used by Roman Catholic missionaries, this is one of two important historic structures (the other is a church) that survived the sacking of Russell by Maoris in 1845.

Turn onto Pitt Street and you'll find the headquarters of the **Bay of Islands Maritime Park**, 09-403-7685. Here, you can orient yourself to the region by studying the exhibits and huge maps. Beyond, at the

*Once a notorious whaling center, the quaint town of Russell is now a jumping-off point for adventurers.*

corner of Pitt and York Streets, the **Russell Museum**, P.O. Box 68, phone/fax 09-403-7701, contains artifacts from the whaling period and a scale model of *The Endeavor*, Captain Cook's ship. (Cook named the Bay of Islands.) At the museum, you can purchase leaflets for NZ$1 on historic walks in Russell and the Maritime Heritage Trail.

Continue walking northwest up York Street and you'll reach Flagstaff Road. It's a steep climb uphill, but you'll be rewarded with stunning views. Stand atop **Flagstaff Hill** (also called Maiki Hill) and look southwest across the bay toward Paihia and low coastal hills, south to Opua and the car ferry crossing, and east toward a few of the 150 islands in the bay. The crest of a hill hides Long Beach, at the edge of Russell on Oneroa Bay. Look back the way you've come and you'll see Russell, with its red roofs, white villas, and green trees spread across the hills.

Although the original flagstaff was raised as a symbol of peace, it was cut down four times by Maori warriors. The present flagstaff was erected in 1847. Twelve days of the year you can look up at the historic flag of the Maori Confederated Tribes rippling in the wind. After enjoying the hilltop views, follow a forest path, marked with a sign, and descend the hill through dense bush to return to the Strand.

The Maritime Heritage Trail map lists 32 historic sites, from early Maori pas and homesteads to trading posts and isolated settlements. Begin the tour by taking one of the frequent ferries—the *Bay Belle, White Ferry*, or *Blue Ferry*—from Russell Wharf across the bay to Paihia. In summer, a ferry crosses about every 20 minutes. From the ferry deck you can see distant headlands that shelter curved beaches, rocky islets, and, here and there, the sites of early Maori pas.

At Paihia you can rent various types of motorized boats for an hour, a half-day, or a day. At Charter Pier, 09-402-7127, charter.pier@ voyager.co.nz, you can rent a 40-horsepower boat and explore the inner harbor at whatever speed you choose. Prices start at NZ$60 an hour with a NZ$200 deposit; fuel is extra.

Many boaters go past Russell and Tapeka Point to the islands beyond. You'll find the river deltas and inlets of the inner harbor layered with history. With enough time you can cruise past Opua into the **Waikare Inlet**, where many narrow peninsulas reach into the water. The Kawakawa and other rivers bring water into the inlet from surrounding bush-covered hills. Large portions of the high ground are included in forest reserves.

*Details: Bay of Islands Visitor Information Centre, Ferry Terminal, Marsden Rd., P.O. Box 333, Paihia, Bay of Islands, 0900-363-463 or 09-402-7345, fax 09-402-7314, paivin@nzhost.co.nz. For a water taxi call 09-403-7123.*

## Waitangi National Trust Reserve

Other guidebooks list this historic location among their "must see" sights, but few mention the natural beauty of this 506-hectare setting. The early treaty house, an impressive war canoe, and an ornately carved Maori meetinghouse stand on manicured green hills, with splendid views that extend to the Bay of Islands.

Stop first at the visitors center, which stands in a lush setting of coastal bush. Follow the footpath toward the beach and you'll come upon a striking red Maori *waka taua*, a war canoe 35.7 meters long. Capable of carrying 80 paddlers and up to 55 passengers, this canoe was built for the centennial celebration of the Treaty of Waitangi, signed on February 5, 1840. During the 1990 Waitangi Day celebration, a large fleet of recently built waka assembled near Hobson Beach.

From the canoe house, follow **Nias Track**, which runs along the beach where Captain William Hobson landed after sailing from Sydney to negotiate the treaty. Continue walking up Flagstaff Hill and you'll see the historic treaty house on the left, set against a flower garden. Nearby, you'll see a large pohutukawa tree planted by Queen Elizabeth II in 1953 and a Norfolk pine planted by the early resident's wife.

The original three-room house, built mostly of kauri wood, was prefabricated in Sydney and brought across the Tasman Sea by James Busby in 1833. As the British resident, Busby's mission was to support British interests amid land disputes, lawlessness, and growing tensions between Maoris, traders, missionaries, and seamen. With the Treaty of Waitangi, eventually signed by more than 500 Maori leaders, the Maoris ceded their sovereignty to the Queen of England. In return, the Maoris were guaranteed possession of traditional lands, forests, fisheries, and other properties.

Walk across the lawn to the elaborately carved whare runanga, a traditional Maori meetinghouse and a tribute to Maori ancestors. On the walls, elaborately carved wooden panels alternate with patterned

*Visitors explore native culture at Waitangi National Reserve.*

woven fabric. The ceiling features painted crossbars. Here and there, note the inlaid paua-shell eyes. Unlike the standard whare runanga, typically dedicated to the ancestors of one tribe, this meetinghouse represents tribes from all parts of New Zealand. Stop a while and listen to the birds outside and the short sound-and-light show.

Within the reserve you'll also find a golf course, unusual pillow lava rocks, and a six-kilometer walking track that leads through regenerating native bush, mangrove trees, and tidal estuaries to Haruru Falls. The **Mangrove Walk Haruru Falls Track** begins west of the coast road, north of the parking lot, and west of the visitors center. About 280 meters of this track is boardwalk, an excellent way to examine the coastal bush, mangrove trees, salt marsh, and mudflats. While you walk, you might hear tui birds sing or encounter fantails. If time permits, walk all the way to Haruru Falls, the upper limit of the Waitangi River estuary. Some hikers arrange a return ride (in a rental car or taxi) from the falls via the Blackbridge/Paihia Road.

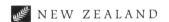 

*Details:* Waitangi National Trust, P.O. Box 48, Paihia, Bay of Islands, 09-402-7437. Bay of Islands Information Centre, Ferry Terminal, Marsden Rd., P.O. Box 333, Paihia, Bay of Islands, 09-402-7345, fax 09-402-7314.

## NATURE AND ADVENTURE SIGHTS FROM MATAKOHE

### Kauri Forests

The kauri tree is a conifer found only in New Zealand. With their great size, fine grain, and relatively hard wood, these massive trees were once the focus of the North Island economy. Majestic kauri forests once dominated the island, but today only a few forests remain. The largest remaining kauri has a height of 51.5 meters, a trunk 13.8 meters around, and an age of about 2,000 years. New Zealand has organized the scattered pockets of kauri forest into the Northland Conservation Park. Supporters are now seeking national park status for these lands.

Begin your kauri experience with a visit to the **Kauri Museum** on Church Road in Matakohe, 09-431-7417, fax 09-431-6969, kauri @xtra.co.nz. There you'll see a kauri slab 22.5 meters long; a collection of kauri furniture; displays showing how the logs were felled, cut, and transported; early photographs of pioneer life; and an exhibit of valuable and beautiful kauri gum.

Beyond Matakohe, some splendid kauri forests—including some of the largest living specimens—can be seen in various ways. The nearest forest is **Trounson Park**, an island of kauri trees and home to the threatened brown kiwi and the kukupa (pigeon). A 40-minute loop trail links the highlights of Trounson.

It's easy to access the **Waipoua Forest** with a car. The forest includes Tane Mahuta (the largest living kauri tree), Te Matua Ngahere (the second largest), the Four Sisters (four kauri trees), and the Yakas Kauri-all a short walk (15 to 30 minutes) from the parking lots along Highway 12. For a longer walk follow the six-kilometer Yakas Track from the Te Matua Ngahere parking lot. It leads past the Yakas Kauri to the Waipoua River and takes about three hours.

Farther north, the **Puketi** and **Omahuta Forests** offer several trails through a large tract of native bush. On the **Waipapa River Track**, 20 kilometers long, you will follow the river through the heart of the Puketi Forest, a mixture of hardwoods, podocarps, and kauri trees.

Kauri Country Safari, Devon Grove, Matakohe, 0800-246-528 or phone/fax 09-431-6007, mobile 025-880-826, kauri.country@xtra. co.nz, can extend your geographic reach. Guide Jason Smith, whose ancestors were early settlers, takes you in a four-wheel-drive vehicle past scenic farmland once covered with kauri forests. From a hilltop you can imagine the forests that once stretched from the Tasman Sea to the Pacific Ocean. Smith, who studied conservation in England, will challenge you to use all your senses. You'll walk through groves of kauri (and rimu, totara, and kahikatea) trees and learn how shrubs, ferns, mosses, lichens, and epiphytes each play a role in the kauri forest ecology.

***Details***: *Waipoua Forest Visitor Centre, SH 12 between Dargaville and Hokianga, 09-439-0605, fax 09-439-5227. Kerikeri Field Centre, Landing Rd., P.O. Box 128, Kerikeri, 09-407-8474. DOC Northland Conservancy Office, P.O. Box 842, 149-151 Banks St., Whangarei, 09-438-0299.*

## TOUR OPERATORS

**Paihia Dive and Charter Ltd.**, a dive shop on Williams Rd., P.O. Box 210, Paihia, Bay of Islands, 09-402-7551, fax 09-402-7110, uses a 40-foot launch to reach *Rainbow Warrior*, volcanic rock reefs, kelp forests, and other dive sites. The company offers PADI-certified dive courses, dive and snorkeling excursions, and equipment rental.

**Dive North**, Bay of Islands Information Centre, Paihia, 09-402-7345, 09-402-7730, or 09-402-7311, divenorth@xtra.co.nz, takes small groups to the *Rainbow Warrior* and other sites in the *Diversion*.

**Alma Working Museum**, P.O. Box 27, Rawene, 0800-726-925 or phone/fax 09-4057704, provides travel on the last large-deck coastal scow still afloat, built in 1902. The 78-foot cruiser explores the sand dunes at the entrance and the upper reaches of Hokianga Harbour. The tour is a good value at NZ$20.

**Northern Exposure Tours**, 0800-573-875 or 09-402-8644, mobile 021-588-098, takes clients from Paihia on an all-day excursion to the Waipoua Forest and the Opononi Sand Dunes at Hokianga Harbour. You walk with a guide into forests dominated by the west coast's largest kauri trees, swim at Omapere, see harbor vistas, and bathe in Ngawha hot pools.

# CAMPING

## *Commercial Campgrounds*

**Ngunguru Motor Camp**, Waters Edge, Papaka Rd., Ngunguru, R.D. 3, Whangarei, phone/fax 09-434-3851, is located on an estuary four kilometers from Tutukaka Harbour. The camp has rental cabins, on-site RVs, and campsites. Guests can walk to town or to the wide Pacific beach. The camp rents sea kayaks, canoes, Windsurfers, and dinghies and can arrange a kayak trip on the Ngunguru River.

**Russell Holiday Park**, Longbeach Rd., Russell, 09-403-7826, fax 09-403-7221, is affiliated with Top 10 campgrounds. The park offers a mixture of motel units, tourist flats, cabins, and backpacker bunk rooms, plus tent and RV campsites. A 10-minute walk from the wharf in central Russell, the camp offers views of the bay.

**Bay of Islands Holiday Park**, Lily Pond, Puketona Rd., P.O. Box 393, Paihia, phone/fax 09-402-7646, stands beside the Waitangi River. This camp has 200 tent sites and 100 power sites, plus rental RVs, tourist flats, cabins, and a 66-bed lodge. You'll also find a communal kitchen, laundry facilities, TV room, playground, sports equipent, a freshwater swimming area, and sociable campfires on cool evenings.

**Twin Pines Tourist Park**, Haruru Falls, Puketona Rd., RD1, Paihia, phone/fax 09-402-7322, enquiries@twinpines.co.nz, offers tent sites, power sites, cabins, and tourist flats. Accomodations include a communal kitchen, dining room, and barbecue facilities or dine at the café/bar/microbrewery on the premises, open seven days a week.

**Kauri Coast Holiday Park**, Trounson Park Rd., Kaihu, phone/fax 09-439-0621 (32 kilometers north of Dargaville on SH 12), offers an array of tent and powered campsites, cabins, flats, motel rooms, and backpacker bunks. Some campsites are located on the river. Children enjoy a playground and trampoline; mountain bikes can be rented. Ask about guided night tours of the forest where you'll see glow-worms and nocturnal kiwis.

*Hikers on the Cape Brett Walkway*

## DOC Campsites and Huts

In the Bay of Islands, camping is available on the south side of **Urupukapuka Island;** in summer the camp collects modest fees. Campers will find a water supply and shower facilities on Cable Bay and Urupukapuka Bay, but no toilets. Bring your own portable toilet and screen, with biological (not chemical) additives. For more information contact Russell Field Centre, 09-403-7685.

**Trounson Kauri Park**, set in lovely kauri forest, can be reached via SH 12, 40 kilometers beyond Dargaville. You'll camp in the heart of Waipoua Forest, in a beautiful riverside setting. At the nearby information center, you can learn more about the forests and get maps of walks. You might see the kukupa here, along with brown kiwis and the North Island robin, reintroduced in 1997. Contact the Waipoua Visitor Centre, 09-439-0605.

**Cape Brett Hut**, DOC, P.O. Box 134, The Strand, Russell, 09-403-7685, fax 09-403-7649, is located at the end of the Cape Brett Walkway. The hut sleeps 21 people and has freshwater and gas stoves.

79

Campers should bring utensils and bedding and must carry out all refuse. Hikers pay a track fee and hut fee to gain access.

**Puketi Forest Hut**, DOC, Kerikeri Area Office, Landing Rd., P.O. Box 128, Kerikeri, 09-407-8474, fax 09-407-7938, next to the Puketi campsite, is a 24-bed hut with hot water, stove, and refrigerator.

For **Waipoua Forest** cabins, contact the DOC, Waipoua Forest Visitor Centre, Private Bag, Dargaville, 09-439-0605, fax 09-439-5227. Smaller cabins have either two or four beds; users pay per bunk. A larger two-bedroom cabin has cooking facilities.

# LODGING

**Pioneer Luxury Apartments**, Marsden Rd., P.O. Box 423, Paihia, Bay of Islands, 0800-272-786 or 09-402-7924, fax 09-402-7656, pioneer @xtra.co.nz, offers two-bedroom temperature-controlled apartments. Each apartment has a king-size bed, private balcony with a gas barbecue, bath with a spa tub and hair dryer, fully equipped kitchen, washer, dryer, and ironing board. Breakfast comes with a daily newspaper. Outside there's a swimming pool and hot tub. Each apartment sleeps four people comfortably. Apartments rent for NZ$175 to NZ$260.

**Nautilus Resort**, P.O. Box 217, Puketona Rd., Paihia, 0800-186-0661 or 09-402-8604, fax 09-402-6247, offers two-bedroom apartments and smaller studios. Expect king-size beds, spa baths, daily maid service, and cooking facilities. Breakfasts can be ordered in. You'll also enjoy a swimming pool, tennis court, and boat parking/washing area. Walk about 200 meters and you'll be at the beach.

**Peppertree Lodge**, 15 Kings Rd., Paihia, phone/fax 09-402-6122, was built for backpackers. Its owners have traveled the world themselves. This well-run lodge in Paihia opens to an outdoor courtyard. A window wall encloses a dining area with a plush lounge above it, useful for reading and quiet games. The large kitchen has electric ranges with enclosed burners, cooking pots, a set of matching dishes, and wineglasses. Small dorms sleep one to four people, have showers and toilets, and get daily cleaning. Owners Wendy and Phil and the other staff work hard to keep the quality high. Thoughtless guests cause the only occasional flaws by leaving unwashed dishes.

**Centabay Lodge**, 27 Selwyn Rd., Paihia, 09-402-7466, fax 09-402-8145, centabay@xtra.co.nz, is high on the list of backpackers' dorms. The owner-operated lodge has various accommodations: studio units with kitchens and baths, double/twin rooms with adjacent baths, and double/twin rooms with shared facilities. A 10-minute walk from central Paihia, the lodge is inexpensive and offers kitchen privileges. Guests can relax in communal lounges, with or without TVs, videos, and music, or in an adjoining garden.

Farther out, the **Ash Grove Motel**, Ash Grove Cir., Haruru Falls, P.O. Box 213, Paihia, Bay of Islands, 09-402-7934, fax 09-402-6279, offers mid-priced lodging in a rural setting. You can choose from studio or one-bedroom motel units on a 1.3-acre site with a swimming pool and garden. Rates range from NZ$60 to NZ$120.

The luxurious and expensive **Orongo Bay Homestead**, Aucks Rd., RD 1, Russell, Bay of Islands, 09-403-7527, fax 09-403-7675, orongo.bay @clear.net.nz, stands amid 17 acres of green lawns, organic gardens, natural springs, and native forest. The grounds are a sanctuary for the endangered brown teal duck. Built around 1860, this renovated historic home with sea views was the first American consulate in New Zealand. Guests can book one of two guest rooms or two suites. The uniquely decorated guest quarters have names like the Oyster Bay Room and the Consul's Suite. By prior arrangement, award-winning chef Michael Hooper prepares gourmet dinners. The homestead's fine wines and champagnes can be brought up from an extensive cellar.

For lodging near Matakohe, consider the **Old Post Office Guest House**, Oakleigh Rd., P.O. Box 79, Paparoa, 09-431-6444. The small yet charming sleeping rooms have the ambience of an early New Zealand home. The backyard deck and lawn offer a lovely pastoral view. The owners cook a tasty breakfast, shuttle guests to and from the Kauri Museum, and serve evening conversation with biscuits and tea. There are bush walks nearby, and guests have complimentary use of canoes on the Paparoa River. The owners, who live on the premises, also offer backpackers' quarters and tent sites behind the building at lower rates.

**The Tree House**, RD 1, Kohukohu, Hokianga, 09-405-5855, fax 09-405-5857, can be accessed by ferry from Rawene. You could call this a backpackers' retreat—which it is—but that doesn't do justice to the lavish plantings of native and exotic trees, the extensive research done by the eco-sensitive owners, and the lovely wake-up serenades by resident songbirds. Located on the north shore of historic Hokianga Harbour, the lodge's cabins (on a pond) and dorm rooms with decks flow into an artfully planted forest. Walk the hilly nature trail, and you'll pass manuka, piriri, and totara trees. Depending on the hour, you might encounter a tui, some fantails, or the nocturnal morepork. The site is many miles, however, from certain necessities. The closest food shop is in Rawene, a ferry ride across the harbor, though owners Phil and Pauline Evans sell some food and take credit cards. Only environmentally safe cleaning products are used. The kitchen, toilet, and shower facilities drain into a subsoil effluent system—one that's low-tech (without pumps or electricity) and requires zero maintenance, the Evanses claim. The Tree House is a lovely place, it's inexpensive, and it's a favorite among eco-travelers.

# FOOD

**Bistro 40**, facing the bay in Paihia, 40 Marsden Rd. 09-402-6066, serves only seafood in a traditional, homelike setting. Oysters, scallops, calamari, king prawns, salmon, and game fish, prepared with herbs, spices, and sauces, are brought to small tables. The fish of the day can be ordered four different ways—depending on your taste. The fresh seared game fish comes with cashews, bamboo shoots, and herbs. Other seafood dishes make use of phyllo dough and fettucine. Open daily for dinner only.

Also in Paihia, come to **Caffe Over the Bay**, upstairs, The Mall, Marsden Rd., Paihia, 09-402-8147, david.sandra@xtra.co.nz, for espresso, light meals, a glass of Sauvignon Blanc, a spicy snack—whatever you choose, whenever you choose it. The inexpensive to mid-priced café roasts its own coffee beans and offers a great view of the harbor. You order at a counter, then fresh-cooked food is brought to your table. The balcony breakfast—steaming plates piled with sausages, apples, potatoes, scrambled eggs, smoked salmon, and bagels—is popular with locals. A hearty pureed soup, eaten with toasted garlic bread, makes a tasty lunch. Desserts are tempting, and dinners can also be had here—perhaps fresh fish with mango salsa, steamy potatoes, and a side salad.

Mall in central Paihia, opens for lunch and dinner. You'll find good, hot, well-seasoned, and no-doubt familiar dishes here like spring rolls, sweet and sour pork, egg foo yung, and fried rice. The inexpensive food can be eaten at nearby tables or carried off to the beach.

**The Tides** on Williams Road, Paihia's main street, opens at 11 for lunch, then serves dinner from 6 to 11. The menu changes often. Expect dishes like a green salad with maple-smoked duck, tasty pork spareribs with a tamarillo glaze, or pan-fried snapper with a white-bean and sun-dried tomato stew. Note that hours may be reduced in winter. Phone ahead, 09-402-7557, to make sure the restaurant is open.

You'll find good food, a pleasant atmosphere, and prompt service at the **Quarterdeck**, located on the Strand in Russell, 09-403-7761, fax 09-403-8411. It's near the wharf so you can watch ferries come and go, framed by pohutukawa trees. The chefs make an imaginative seafood chowder, a lavish seafood platter, tua tua fritters, and a vegetarian dish of the day. Food combinations are comfortably familiar, including dishes like beef filet with bacon and mushrooms and king prawns with garlic and chilis. Prices are rooted in the real world, and the polite and helpful waitstaff adds to the experience.

In Rawene, turn right at the ferry dock and walk along the water to reach the **Boatshed Gallery and Cafe**, Clendon Esplanada, Rawene, phone/fax 09-405-7728. Inside the renovated boat shack, which perches above the harbor, you'll find espresso and breakfast that might include a black raspberry muffin, some muesli, yogurt, and fruit. Check the blackboard for a shifting menu of lunch specials, priced at NZ$10 or less, and note the Pacific Rim influences. The menu might list a smoked chicken and papaw salad on crispy noodles with curry dressing or fresh pasta with salmon and a creamy dill sauce. Desserts are awesome, perhaps a chocolate almond and coffee liqueur cake topped with fresh fruit and whipped sweet cream.

**Blah, Blah, Blah** on Victoria Street in central Dargaville serves New Zealand nouvelle. You can order breakfast, lunch, or dinner from a giant menu that changes often. Choices might include pancakes with grilled banana and maple syrup, salmon on fresh foccacia bread with field greens and tomatoes, or venison with kumara and date fritters. Espresso drinks are good. For dessert, try the kumara pecan pie. Prices are low for such good food.

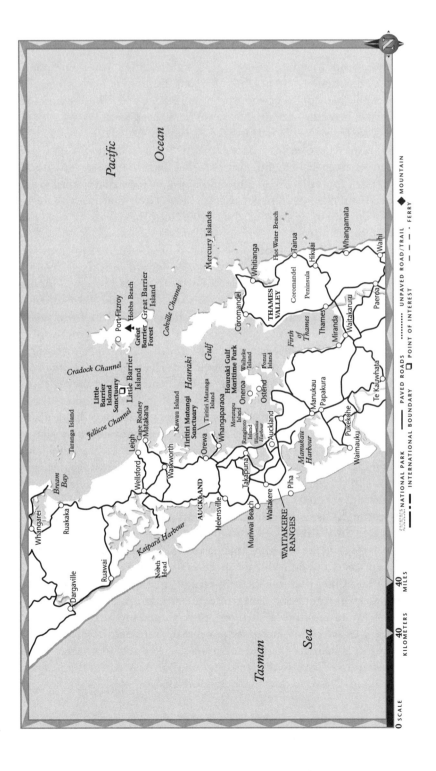

# CHAPTER 4

# Auckland and the Hauraki Gulf

Some visitors fly into Auckland, take a whirlwind bus tour, then rush to Rotorua the following day. They may not realize that you can stroll across black sand beaches on Auckland's wild west coast, hike the rugged Waitakere Ranges, camp on an island where Maoris once farmed, cruise to island nature sanctuaries to observe rare birds, climb to the edge of volcanic cones, paddle a sea kayak past tidal pools on a deserted beach, or discover fossils formed from marine creatures when the land was ocean floor.

With a population of more than a million, Auckland sprawls over green volcanic hills between two harbors, Waitemata and Manukau, and extends onto peninsulas. Downtown Auckland (facing Waitemata Harbour) makes a good base for exploring. Climb up One Tree Hill for views of the city and the twisted isthmus formed by lava that rose from the sea.

The city has four major boroughs. Manukau City sprawls east of Auckland International Airport, and Waitakere City reaches west. North Shore City includes historic Devonport and North Head, plus the Takapuna beach community beyond. Auckland itself (the central city) includes urban neighborhoods oriented to the north and the busy harbor.

The suburbs spread north and south along the Hauraki Gulf

Coast, a meandering shoreline of beaches, headlands, and bays. On the gulf coast you'll find marine reserves with good beaches, snorkeling, and diving at Long Bay and Cape Rodney (Okakari Point).

The inner Hauraki Gulf Islands can be reached quickly and easily by ferry, yet they offer a feeling of remoteness. Rangitoto, the youngest volcano in the region, has unusual regenerating plant life. Motukorea has many early Maori archaeological sites. Waiheke, though partly inhabited, has walking trails, a bird reserve, and mountain bike and kayak rentals. On Tiritiri Matangi, farther north, you can find rare birds in their natural habitat. On Kawau you'll find wallabies and kookaburras once brought from Australia—and running free.

The outer gulf islands, also accessed by boat, lie within 100 kilometers of the downtown. Rugged Great Barrier Island, named by Captain James Cook, has campsites near a variety of natural areas and several hiking trails. Spectacular Little Barrier Island, with its seaside cliffs and often cloud-covered mountain, has dense bush and a variety of rare species.

Northwest of Auckland, along the Tasman coast, you'll find black sand Muriwai Beach and a colony of migratory gannets. Piha Beach farther south has a dramatic setting, surrounded by hills. Southeast of Auckland, along the Firth of Thames, you'll find Miranda, a refuge for migratory wading birds.

## HISTORY, CULTURE, AND CUSTOMS

Maoris traveled to this region in boats several hundred years ago and settled in the Hauraki Gulf. Tiritiri, Motutapu, Motukorea, and the Great Barrier Islands have evidence of early habitation: pas, storage pits, and midden sites.

At the time of Maori arrival, tangled bush covered much of the land. Rangitoto was sometimes active. Most travel was done by water: in sailing ships, smaller boats, and canoes. Scattered settlements where Auckland now stands were linked by rough tracks. Eventually, Maoris sold the large triangular tract that would become the city of European colonists.

With its good harbor and fertile soil, Auckland became New Zealand's capital for a time; this designation shifted eventually to

Wellington. With about one-fourth of the nation's population, Auckland is still the country's economic center. City residents have varied backgrounds, from Maori to European to Asian.

Central Auckland has many neighborhoods. Parnell and Ponsonby, perched on hills, flank the downtown office towers that run from Aotea Square along Queen Street to the waterfront.

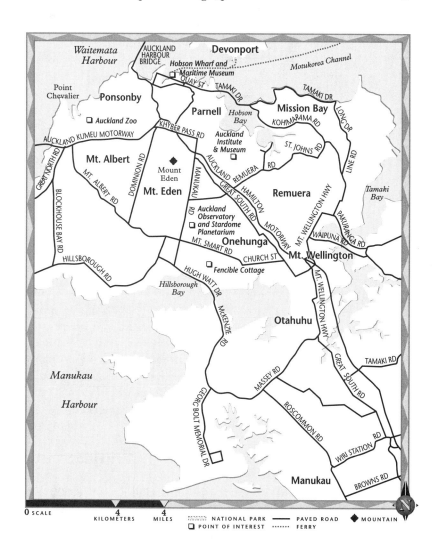

87

*Pohukatawa trees overlook the Hauraki Gulf from Waiheke Island.*

Sally McKinney

Devonport, across the harbor, along with Mission Bay, Kohimarama, and St. Heliers, have their own beaches and bays, plus great views of the downtown skyline.

The city's Maori heritage and its unique natural setting have strongly influenced the urban culture. Contemporary artwork shows turbulent volcanic shapes rising from lush green foliage and surreal boats on aquamarine bays. Motifs inspired by nature, and drawn from the Maori tradition, have been incorporated into modern design. The sea and sky have inspired such musical works as *Aotearoa* and *Waterlands*.

Concerts, live theater, art galleries, movie houses, and museums are all part of the urban mixture. The community holds an international film festival during the rainy New Zealand winter. Locals run in and out of theaters, grabbing quick cappuccinos between downpours before heading indoors for yet another foreign film. Summer mornings mean walking the dog, jogging, or breakfast at an outdoor café. Summer evenings often bring tea on the beach: a swim, a picnic on the grass, some Chardonnay, and a view of sailboats on the horizon.

Despite the city's growth and residents' varied backgrounds, most people are cordial to strangers. But in recent years crime has increased, and Auckland residents no longer leave their doors unlocked.

## NATURE AND ADVENTURE ACTIVITIES

Auckland, which straddles a narrow isthmus, claims about 1,000 kilometers of coastline. The east coast beaches are best for swimming or general lying about, and can be found along the North Shore and the East Bays (from Mission Bay to St. Heliers). The tidal flats around the harbors are good for fishing, bird-watching, and searching for wee creatures in tidal pools. Windy and wild, the west coast is great for bush walking and observing migratory shorebirds. Beaches are known for their scenic beauty, dark ironsand, and pounding surf. West coast waterplay involves the risk of riptides: swimmers sometimes drown.

The Hauraki Gulf Maritime Park, administered by the DOC, offers appealing natural settings for mainland bush walking, island walking and tramping, mountain biking, diving, camping, and bird-watching. In Auckland regional parks you can find nature trails in pockets of bush, Maori archaeological sites, extinct volcanic cones, and scenic beaches. Some regional parks have campsites.

Within city center, you can rent bicycles and protective headgear, in-line skates, kayaks, Windsurfers, and sailboats in a range of sizes. You may not need a car. Some nature areas can be reached via public transportation, and tour operators will take you from city center to beaches and bays, pockets of forest, hiking trails, bird reserves, rocky cliffs, vineyards, and wineries.

Transport to the Hauraki Gulf Islands is usually by water (or air); ferries and tour boats leave from the Ferry Building or nearby wharves along Quay Street. Some bicycle riders begin their North Island tours on ferries to the North Shore or the Coromandel—to avoid city traffic.

## FLORA AND FAUNA

The hills above Auckland's beaches and bays, once covered with podocarp and broadleaf forest, are now studded with suburban homes. Pockets of forests can still be found on private land and in public parks. In the larger mainland reserves, in the Waitakere and Hunua Ranges, a few regal kauris still stand, along with rimus, kahikateas, totaras, ratas, and tawas.

Plant life on the inner islands has seen much destruction by humans, who have also introduced many non-native species. On nearby Hauraki Gulf islands, pohutukawa trees frame wooden wharves and crescent beaches. Some stands of forest remain; others are regenerating.

On the outer island, Great Barrier, early logging operations removed much of the kauri, yet large areas of native forest remain. Neighboring Little Barrier has changed little since the time of Captain Cook, who gave the island this name. Little Barrier has perhaps the best remaining indigenous forest in the region and species that range from pohutukawa, manuka, and kanuka along the coast to kauri, beech, rata, and tawa on the higher slopes to subalpine mosses and ferns above 600 meters.

Warmed by the East Auckland Current, water in the Hauraki Gulf shifts about 10 degrees Celsius between summer and winter. There are two high tides and two low tides each day. Prevailing southwesterly winds account for fairly calm inner waters, but northeasterly storms churn up very rough seas.

Many intriguing creatures inhabit the coastal waters of the gulf: heart urchins, bristleworms, striped shellfish, gorgonian fans, golf-ball sponges, starfish, scallops, and crayfish. Look for them in marine reserves. In the outer gulf waters, migrating humpback whales, orca whales, common dolphins, and bottle-nosed dolphins can sometimes be seen.

The Hauraki Gulf has more than 100 species of fish. Marlin and tuna inhabit the region in summer. Schools of kingfish and kahawai move quickly from place to place. Below the surface you might see banded blennies, red mullet (also called goatfish), or red moki, especially near rocky reefs, along with snapper and blue maomao.

Kiore and brown rats inhabit some islands. Hochstetter's frog, discovered during the nineteenth century by gold miners, lives near freshwater streams on Great Barrier Island. An array of insects live on various gulf islands: bush wetas, orange spotted ladybirds, stick insects, and darkling beetles. The largest insect, a giant wetapunga that grows to 100 millimeters long, is essentially harmless. Reptiles include the tuatara, which no longer lives on the mainland but inhabits about two dozen offshore islands. There are no land snakes.

Little blue penguins occasionally swim in Waitemata Harbour. Shags, terns, gannets, dotterels, herons, gulls, and petrels also live in the region. Certain migratory species come from Siberia, Alaska, and New Zealand's subantarctic region. The weka and brown kiwi have been released into the Waitakere Ranges. Several species at risk have been relocated or released into the Little Barrier Island sanctuary.

# VISITOR INFORMATION

Visitor Information Centres, linked to New Zealand's Visitor Information Network, can be found at Auckland's international and domestic airline terminals, New Zealand Cup Village at the corner of Quay and Hobson Streets, Queen Elizabeth Square south of the Ferry Building at 1 Queen Street, and Aotea Square at 24 Wellesley Street West. Open seven days a week, these centers have helpful staff, offer free maps and brochures, and also function as travel agencies—with bookings for selected tours, lodging, and transportation.

The Auckland Visitor Centre is also located on Wellesley Street, 09-366-6888, fax 09-366-6893, reservations@aucklandnz.com, www.aucklandnz.com. While you're downtown, you can visit the DOC office in the Ferry Building on Quay Street, 09-379-6476, fax 09-379-3609, for information on the region's natural areas.

# GETTING AROUND

You can get bus, train, and ferry information for the city of Auckland (this includes Devonport and Waiheke Island ferries) by phoning RIDELINE at 09-366-6400.

The Downtown Airline Terminal offers airport shuttle services. The complex also has small information/booking offices, including bus service between Auckland and other cities. Newman's Coachlines and Mount Cook Landline have booking offices in this complex.

The large InterCity terminal, 09-358-4085, operates from the base of the Sky Tower block. The Downtown Bus Terminal on Commerce Street, 09-366-6400, operates an information kiosk during the busiest weekday hours, with more limited hours on weekends.

AirBus at 09-275-7685, fax 09-275-9394, offers ground transport from Auckland International Airport. The bus runs to the city center from the international, domestic, and Ansett terminals daily between 6:20 a.m. and 10:00 p.m. It runs to the airport from the city center daily from 5:10 a.m. to 8:50 p.m.

InterCity Coachlines operates from the Sky City Terminal; use the Hobson Street entrance. InterCity is a major operator with widespread bus routes plus a network of affiliates on South and North Islands.

For rail service to Wellington and other cities, call TransScenic Train Journeys at 0800-802-802. For ferry transportation from Auckland, Sea Link at 0800-485-387 or 09-373-4036 takes passengers and cars. Gulf Trans, a motorized barge that operates from Wynyard Wharf, carries up to 85 passengers plus motor vehicles. Call 09-373-4036 for information.

## NATURE AND ADVENTURE SIGHTS

### *Coast to Coast Walkway*

Leafy neighborhoods have replaced the dense sea of fern trees that once covered Auckland's hills and valleys. Yet you can still hike the nine-kilometer route Europeans once traveled from Waitemata Harbour to Onehunga Beach. Along the way you'll find hilltop views of sailboats in the bay, bright containers stacked on busy wharves, squat historic buildings sheltered by sleek office towers, pocket gardens, red-roofed homes, geological oddities, and the remnants of Maori terraces, storage pits, and pas.

The route is marked with signs and arrows. With maps in hand, begin walking at the historic **Ferry Building** on Quay Street, then pass the neoclassical **Chief Post Office** at the foot of Queen Street before turning up Customs Street to **Emily Place**. This former headland, once known as Point Britomart, was the site of early government buildings. The city of Auckland was founded here in 1840.

Continue south along Princes Street, a segment of road extended in 1872, past several late-nineteenth-century buildings. Well-to-do merchants once built homes here in what has become a heritage area. You'll pass **Albert Park** and a remnant of stone wall that formerly encircled the Albert Barracks.

From Princes Street, head along Alfred Street, cross Symonds Street, and follow Grafton Road to the **Auckland Domain**, developed on an 81-hectare reserve donated to the city in 1845. The domain, with its formal gardens, statuary, and playing fields, now covers 136 hectares. The domain's Centennial Drive, built in the late 1930s over the protests of environmentalists, is lined with native trees and maintained as a walkway. Paved roads, footpaths, and unpaved tracks now link the **Auckland Museum**, **Winter Garden**, **Domain Nursery**, stands

# AUCKLAND MUSEUMS

- The **Auckland Institute and Museum**, located on a hilltop within the Auckland Domain, 09-377-3932, fax 09-379-9956, has an impressive collection of Maori displays, including a carved meetinghouse and a large war canoe. Maori cultural performances take place daily. Browse the retail shop for hand-crafted gifts.

- The **Auckland Observatory and StarDome Planetarium** is located within the One Tree Hill Domain, 09-624-1246, fax 09-625-2394, infoline 09-625-6945, www.stardome.org.nz. The StarDome features 3,500 stars and covers the solar system, moon and sun, comets and clusters, nebulae and galaxies. Choose from afternoon or evening shows Tuesday and Thursday through Sunday. During a separate one-hour session, subject to weather conditions, you can look at the sky through a 50-centimeter telescope. Times are Tuesday, Thursday, and Saturday evenings.

- An expert diver who wanted to share his experiences with the public developed **Kelly Tarltons Underwater World and Antarctic Encounter**, 23 Tamaki Dr., 0800-805-050 or 09-528-1994. Underwater World takes you through transparent tunnels to observe schools of colorful fish, shellfish, stingrays, moray eels, seahorses, and sharks swimming above and around you. In the nearby Antarctic Encounter, you'll see colonies of live penguins moving about in real snow and ice, view exhibits related to Robert Scott's 1911 expedition, and take a Snow Cat ride across a frozen landscape. The cost is NZ$18 per adult.

- The **Auckland Zoo**, Motions Rd., Western Springs, 09-360-3805, infoline 09-360-3819, is involved in breeding programs for the survival of the tuatara, brown kiwi, and other native species. More than 600 animals can be seen representing every continent. In the New Zealand Aviary, you can see native bird species in a bush environment.

of totara, and clusters of special plantings. Explore the domain and you'll see a palisade around a large totara tree; the memorial honors Potatau te WhereWhere, a Maori leader who engineered peace among various competing tribes. Memorials and sculptures are here and there. Limestone concretions, shaped like spheres, have been brought into the domain as natural sculptures.

The walkway continues along Park, Mountain, and Clive Roads, then loops around volcanic **Mount Eden**. The Maoris named it Maungawhau (Mountain of the Whau Tree) for a species that once covered the mountain's slopes. Deep in the crater, the Maoris believed, lived the god of volcanoes. Although Auckland's volcanoes are now considered extinct, the volcanic field remains active.

The summit of Mount Eden, 196 meters high, is the southern point of the triangular tract purchased from the Maoris in 1840. The northern side of the triangle, along Waitemata Harbour, reaches from Cox's Creek to Hobson Bay. While walking around Mount Eden, you can see **Te Ngutu**, the ceremonial entrance to an early pa site, and a lava pinnacle used by Maoris as an altar.

*A view of downtown Auckland and the Sky Tower from Mount Eden*

The route continues along Owens Road and Marama Avenue, passes through **Melville Park**, and follows Kimberley Road to the statue of Sir John Logan Campbell, who gave his **One Tree Hill** estate to New Zealand's people. Continue walking into **Cornwall Park**, which adjoins One Tree Hill Domain. One Tree Hill, known to Maoris as Maungakiekie—the mountain of the climbing plant, still has the scarps and terraces of an early Maori fortress. The legendary totara tree that led to the name One Tree Hill disappeared in 1855; an obelisk, a talisman of the kumara god, has replaced the tree. Like Mount Eden, One Tree Hill was also the site of an early European settlement.

Continue walking south along Manukau Road, Symonds Street, Quadrant Road, and Normans Hill Road, and you'll soon pass several early buildings: the **Royal Oak Hotel**, now used as offices; **Fencible Cottage**, replica of a pioneer home; and **Jellicoe Park**, site of an early military post that was one of a chain used as defense against hostile Maoris. The walkway ends at Beachcroft Avenue. Here, on what was Onehunga Beach, Maoris once came in canoes to barter and trade with resident Europeans.

*Details: Obtain maps at Auckland's Visitor Information Network offices: Aotea Square, 24 Wellesley St. W. or Queen Elizabeth Square, 1 Queen St. For more information about Auckland's parks and gardens, call 09-379-2020. Call RIDELINE, 09-366-6400, for a schedule of city buses that access the parks, including the trail end at Onehunga.*

## Great Barrier Island

North Island's largest offshore island, 100 kilometers northeast of Auckland, is a rugged wonderland of forested volcanic mountains, scenic bluffs and ridges, historic relics, beaches, headlands, inlets, and bays. On the west coast, bush-covered hills overlook snug harbors visited by yachts and cargo boats. On the east coast, the Pacific Ocean rolls onto crescent white sand beaches, and freshwater creeks flow into tidal wetlands. A winding road—Highway 1—links scattered settlements. Port Fitzroy, Whangaparapara (site of an early whaling station), and Tryphena are west coast island settlements. The remote northern forest wilderness, Te Paparahi, is seldom visited—it has no roads.

The barrier's proximity to Auckland, isolation (electricity comes from generators), and variety of terrain and wildlife habitats give it unusual appeal. You can cross the Hauraki Gulf to reach the island by ferry, seaplane, or cargo boat (the journey itself is an adventure). The ferry ride lasts two hours.

You'll arrive at an island with maybe 1,300 inhabitants and an appealing remoteness. The DOC administers more than 60 percent of Great Barrier Island; remaining land belongs to private landholders or Auckland city reserves. You can book DOC backcountry huts or pitch a tent on a DOC campsite. Campgrounds and huts are located near the best natural areas, and early logging roads provide a network of hiking trails.

Walk through dense forest to the top of **Mount Hirakimata**, 621 meters high, and you'll be rewarded with great views of Little Barrier and other gulf islands, with the great Pacific Ocean to the east. This volcanic mountain and other high places are the main nesting sites for the New Zealand black petrel.

In **Great Barrier Forest**, once dominated by kauri, you can find unique species of rata, hebe, and daisy. Although much of the kauri has been logged, these magnificent trees can still be found near **Te Kirikiri Bay** and the **Harataonga Recreation Reserve**. Much of the island's regenerating forest is dominated by kanuka. Although Great Barrier once had problems with feral cats and other pests, the island has stayed free of ravaging possums; thus, more than 50 species of threatened native flora thrive.

On the east coast, you can see brown teal, a nocturnal duck; dotterels and rails; and migratory godwits and oystercatchers in the Whangapoua estuary. This sheltered tidal bay, and the marshy Kaitoke Creek farther south, are important regional wetlands.

Sally McKimney

*Dolphins surface near the Te Aroha.*

Follow a trail inland from Whangaparapara Harbour, and you'll crisscross a stream, climb up and then descend a steep hill, and come upon **Kaitoke hot springs**, where you can bathe in a hot pool (test it for hot spots before jumping in). Then walk on to Whangaparapara Road, about three kilometers from the starting point.

Another trail begins at Windy Canyon, follows a ridge, and leads to **Mount Hirakimata**. Surrounded by kauris, silver pines, and monoaos, you might see or hear many species of native birds. The trail then heads west, takes you downhill, passes early kauri dams, and follows Kaiarara Stream to Kaiarara Bay on the gulf side. You'll also find a mountain bike track running from Whangaparapara Road to Kairara Bay.

The **Great Barrier Forest Track** is a four-day loop walk. You can book bunks in basic DOC huts at Whangaparapara and Kaiarara. There are DOC campgrounds at Akapoua (near Port Fitzroy), Whangaparapara Harbour, the Whangapoua wetland (near the settlement of Okiwi), Harataonga Beach, Awana, and Medlands, where you'll camp beside a lovely crescent beach.

*Details: For information or to book huts, contact the DOC information center in the Ferry Building on Quay Street in Auckland, 09-379-6476, fax 09-379-3609, or the field center in Port Fitzroy, 09-429-0044.*

*Fullers, also in the Auckland Ferry Building, 09-367-9111, infophone 09-367-9117, provides transport to Great Barrier Island by ferry or plane. GulfTrans, 09-373-4036, operates a car and passenger ferry from Wynyard Wharf on the Auckland waterfront. Great Barrier Airlines, 0800-900-600 or 09-275-9120, provides service to the island from the Auckland Airport (domestic terminal).*

## Hauraki Gulf

The Hauraki Gulf, buffered by Great Barrier Island and partly enclosed by the Coromandel Peninsula, extends north to Cape Rodney. About 800 kilometers of land borders the gulf. In all, the scattered Hauraki Gulf Islands have about 450 kilometers of shoreline. Cook named Great Barrier, and more than 100 Hauraki Gulf Islands have names. Yet many islets, sea stacks, and rocks remain nameless. Beyond Pakatoa, you'll find rock islets favored by gannets and spotted shags.

The Maoris, who first explored the gulf by water then settled here in the fourteenth century, named the gulf Hauraki, which means "Winds from the North." European adventurers explored the gulf in sailing ships. Sailboats and nature cruises will let you experience the gulf firsthand. Standing on the deck of a ship, you will experience the wind, sea, and sky. Gulls will soar above you on salt-air thermals; dolphins will swim below in water so clear you can anticipate the next leap and snap photos when they surface.

Begin your sailing experience with a visit to the **New Zealand National Maritime Museum** on Hobson Wharf, between the Viaduct Harbour and Princes Wharf, P.O. Box 3141, Auckland, 09-373-0800, fax 09-377-600, jollyroger@wave.co.nz, www.hmu.com/maritime_museum. Inside, innovative displays teach you about maritime history. Exhibits cover Polynesian and European maritime adventures, as well as those of New Zealand. You'll hear presentations by live actors, listen to sea stories, and browse among examples of maritime art. Other exhibits describe New Zealand's historic involvement in the America's Cup competition.

Outside in the marina you can see historic boats from the permanent collection, along with traveling exhibits of notable sailing ships. The museum offers a luncheon heritage cruise on the *Ted Ashby*, a traditional ketch-rigged sailing scow. Character actors provide narration as you cruise past the Harbour Bridge and Westhaven Marina and enjoy a boxed lunch. A shorter cruise on the *Ted Ashby*, without lunch, departs twice daily.

In summer, the impressive tall ship *Soren Larsen* offers three- or six-day cruises on which you can help the crew and learn about sailing—or not, depending on your mood. On summer weekends you can board the *Soren Larsen* for shorter coffee cruises, day sails, or a special Valentine's Day dinner cruise. For more information contact Tallship Soren Larsen, P.O. Box 310, Kumeu, 0800-SORENLARSEN or 09-411-8775, http://squaresail.q.co.nz.

On Pride of Auckland yachts—one is an 18-meter sailing catamaran, others are monohulls—you can also view Auckland (the City of Sails) from the water. Pride of Auckland Co. Ltd. is based at the New Zealand National Maritime Museum. Contact them at 09-373-4557, fax 09-377-0459, pride.of.akl@xtra.co.nz. Cruises run NZ$40 to NZ$80.

Adventure Cruising Company, Hobson Wharf West, P.O. Box

338, Auckland 1, phone/fax 09-444-9342, boat phone 025-948-166, adventure_cruise@clear.net.nz, www.ecotours.co.nz, offers nature cruises on the *Te Aroha*. Climb aboard and enter an official "stress-free zone." The coastal trading scow, refitted for passenger comfort and operated by people who grew up on boats, visits the best nature areas in Hauraki Gulf. Cruises last one to five days; overnight trips cost from NZ$165 to NZ$595. Bring sunblock, a swimsuit, rain gear, warm layers, and sturdy footwear for nature walks ashore. Meals are quite good, the boat has a small bar, and cabins are cozy. Your hosts, Dee and Mike, are witty, charming, and experienced.

*Te Aroha*'s itinerary varies. One day you might join a geologist for a fossil hunt on Waiheke or Motukorea. Another day you might visit a gannet rookery, explore the tidal pools on a deserted beach, climb to look at volcanic cones, or hunt colorful saddlebacks with a camera. The *Te Aroha* calls at remote natural areas where tourists don't go. One of them is **Tiritiri Matangi**, an open sanctuary. On selected longer cruises, the *Te Aroha* calls at **Little Barrier**, a wildlife sanctuary with 100-meter cliffs and a volcanic mountain 722 meters high that is often hidden in clouds.

If you want a sailing experience that goes beyond raising the odd mainsail, consider sailing instruction. Several sailing schools in the Auckland area offer lessons and courses. Rangitoto Sailing Center, also based at the New Zealand National Maritime Museum, P.O. Box 3141, 09-358-2324, fax 09-377-6000, mobile 025-626-562, offers courses and individual lessons, along with sailing adventure holidays. Courses run NZ$250 to NZ$325. One involves learning to sail in the sheltered Waiheke Channel and accommodation at the Pakatoa Island Lodge.

Barry Littlewood's Westhaven Sailing School, 63 Speight Rd., Kohimarama, Auckland, 09-575-5051, mobile 025-329-300, gives instruction on the 37-foot *Notre Dame*, a keel yacht that's more forgiving to beginners than smaller sailboats. The school emphasizes building your confidence while increasing your competence. You will learn by setting the sails, tacking, jibing, luffing, reefing, and the rest. Yachting New Zealand, 09-303-2360, yachtingnz.org.nz, has information about sailing clubs.

**Details:** *Contact the Auckland Visitor Center, 09-366-6888, fax 09-366-6893, reservations@aucklandnz.com.*

## Rangitoto Island

The great Maori epic poem *Te Whakapapa O Te Ao Nei* explains the origin of this world: "The earth shook, shivered and leapt until the earth's skin was rent and fire gushed forth," states one passage. "The mountains rose up, fire and lava spewed out. . . . That is the origin of the volcanoes in Tamaki Makau Rau."

Rangitoto is the youngest of the Auckland regional volcanoes, and this low basaltic cone is an awesome presence in Waitemata Harbour. About 600 years ago, Rangitoto was formed through a series of eruptions. Magma from deep in the earth formed an explosive reaction with groundwater, spewing out fire, along with clouds of ash and steam. Red hot lava flowed down the slopes, hardening into rock. During the most recent eruption, probably about 200 years ago, the Maoris who lived in the area watched the eruption in awe.

Rangitoto now supports regenerating forest and an array of plant life. More than 200 species of native trees and plants grow here, along with more than 40 types of ferns and several kinds of orchids. Fantails, grey warblers, silvereyes, and moreporks live among the canopy of

Sally McKinney

*The vintage* M.V. Kestrel

pohutukawa trees, with mingimingi, koromiko, and puka growing below. Black-back gulls nest in fields of dark broken scoria and inhabit two rookeries. Populations of possums and wallabies, animals brought from Australia that once threatened Rangitoto's bird life, have been reduced.

For visitors, Rangitoto has rest rooms, telephones, a small shop, a barbecue area, and a saltwater swimming pool. There is no lodging on the island, although neighboring Mototapu Island, linked by a causeway, has campsites. You can reach Rangitoto via a 30-minute ferry ride from the Ferry Building in Auckland. Be sure to bring food, water, sunglasses, sunscreen, a hat, and rain gear in a daypack. Wear rugged boots or sturdy shoes as protection against rough scoria.

The ferry lands at Rangitoto Wharf. If you choose, you can board an open-air, four-wheel-drive road train for a guided loop tour past pohutukawa forest and lava rocks. You can then explore the volcano's crater and summit by walking a 900-meter boardwalk and climbing some steps. You'll get wonderful 360-degree views of the Auckland skyline, Waitemata Harbour, and other Hauraki Gulf Islands from the summit. Board the train again and ride past scenic **McKenzie Bay**, an early lighthouse, and more trees. See unusual fan-shaped kidney ferns and a grove of kowhai trees before returning to the wharf.

By delaying your return, you can take a self-guided walking tour that begins with a climb to the 259-meter summit. Along the way, see many regenerating pohutukawas, the dominant tree in a series of successions that begins with mosses, lichen, and algae. Because the rocky volcanic slopes are highly porous, not covered with soil, reach high temperatures, and retain little permanent water, regenerating plants that root in humus in the cracks have taken unusual forms. Mangroves grow above the lava. Alpine lichen grow on the volcano at nearly sea level. Pohutukawa trees have formed hybrids with northern rata. Astelia and Kirk's daisy, epiphytes that normally cling to the branches of trees, grow on the ground.

Just before the summit, a spur trail to the right of the main path leads to lava tunnels and caves. With enough time, you can walk downhill to the wharf at the end of Islington Bay; note the causeway that links Rangitoto to Motutapu Island. A coastal track from the wharf skirts the bay and returns to Rangitoto Wharf.

*Details:* Maps are available from the DOC office in the Ferry Building. If stranded on Rangitoto, phone the DOC at 09-307-9279. A conservation officer lives on Motutapu and can be reached at 09-727-674.

Fullers Volcanic Explorer tour, 09-367-9111, fax 09-367-9116, information 09-367-9102, operates two or three times a day year-round and costs NZ$35 per adult. It includes the ferry crossing and return and the two-hour guided safari.

## Tiritiri Matangi

North of Auckland and four kilometers off the Whangaparaoa Peninsula, this 220-hectare island has become an open sanctuary for wildlife. Once mostly covered by bush, the island was damaged by farming and, through years of human habitation, some areas were reduced to grassland.

Conservationists have put a huge effort into replanting a mix of native trees to provide a rich and varied habitat for bird species, isolated from predators. Since 1984 more than 200,000 trees have been planted, many by volunteers. After stands of pohutukawa were established, taraire, kohekohe, and puriri could then grow in the shade. Rare birds—the saddleback, takahe, parakeet, North Island robin, whitehead, little spotted kiwi, and brown teal—have been introduced, even though some are not native to the island. Scientific experiments are carried out here as well.

Within guidelines, visitors can explore this island, find native flora and fauna and, at times, observe rare species living in the wild. Although you can access the island from the Whangaparaoa Peninsula, there's a ferry from Auckland three days a week. You'll cruise past Devonport and North Head, through the Rangitoto Channel, and pass the Hibiscus Coast before reaching the island.

Climb onto the pier. The conservation officer will greet you, explain conservation policies, and answer any questions. Pets and fires are not allowed on the island, and smoking is allowed only in a limited area. You must carry out all trash and stay on the trails. Bring binoculars, a camera, a swimsuit and towel (in summer), a sun hat, rain jacket, and a warm jacket (in winter). The island has no food service.

It's only a 10-minute coastal walk from the wharf to **Hobbs Beach,** where boxes placed beside the track provide shelter for little blue penguins. In spring and at night, penguins nest here or take shelter.

For a longer walk, follow the **Wattle Track** through a gully where wattle trees thrive—a habitat favored by many native birds, including the saddleback, tui, bellbird, whitehead, and robin. This track leads to a vintage 1865 lighthouse, 20.5 meters tall, which now operates by solar power.

From the lighthouse, follow the **Ridge Track**. It takes perhaps half an hour to walk the track, along the island's backbone, for great panoramic views, access to other tracks, and a look at some of the replanting being done here. Shorter tracks accessed by the Ridge Track lead to **Pohutukawa Cove** and the Tiritiri Matangi pa site. You can also reach the penguin nesting area from the ridge.

Evidence of early Maori habitation, especially pas and kumara storage pits, can also be seen on the west coast; the **Kawerau Track** provides access from the ridge. From the northern end of the Ridge Track, the **Ngati Paoa Track** loops past the site of an early Maori pa and leads to Northeast Bay, where there once was a Maori village. Adventure Cruising Company, P.O. Box 338, Auckland 1, phone/fax 09-444-9342, operates nature cruises that include Tiritiri Matangi. One tour includes overnight accommodations on the *Te Aroha*, the Tiritiri evening birdsong chorus, and a guided bird walk at dawn.

*Details: Island conservation officers can be reached at 09-479-4490. Gulf Harbour Ferries, P.O. Box 496, Whangaparaoa, Hibiscus Coast, 0800-424-5561 or 09-424-5561, fax 09-424-5510, provides transport to and from Tiritiri Matangi on Thursday and Sunday, plus Saturday in summer. Ferries depart from Pier 3 next to the Ferry Building in Auckland or from Z Pier, Gulf Harbour Marina, Whangaparaoa Peninsula. On request, Gulf Harbour Ferries will provide a box lunch.*

## *Waiheke Island*

If your take on nature involves sipping a cappuccino in the shade of a tree, consider a visit to Waiheke Island. The largest of the Hauraki Gulf Islands, this is a great place to unwind and experience nature without working at it very hard. Its green hills, underlined by pale sand beaches beside aquamarine bays, give it great natural beauty.

Generally sunnier and a few degrees warmer than the rest of Auckland, Waiheke is only a 35-minute ferry ride from the city.

There are bays on both sides of the irregular, 92-square-kilometer island. Its 7,000 residents and a weekend influx of visitors that can reach 30,000 support many restaurants and cafés. The island has a subtropical climate, and many activities take place outdoors. **Oneroa**, the largest village, is spread across a ridge. On a fine day, you can sit on the deck of Vino Vino overlooking Oneroa Bay, sip a Cabernet Sauvignon, and watch small birds waiting for crumbs.

Waihekeans have fought to keep the island from becoming just another Auckland suburb. The locals recycle glass, aluminum cans, tins, plastics, and paper. On the western third of the island, homes cling to hillsides. Here you'll find seven communities between Matiatia Bay and Oneroa Beach. Oneroa, the main village, has a tourist office, cafés, shops, banks, and post office. **Ostend** has scattered shops and cafés and a great Saturday market. **Onehunga**, near the beach, has the most visitor lodging, the fewest food shops and cafés, a wonderful beach, and proximity to the bird reserve.

Beyond these communities, you'll find much to explore. The island has more than 40 kilometers of beaches. Some are sandy and good for swimming, others are sheltered by rocky headlands—better for kayaking and snorkeling. The more exposed north coast has great scenery and lovely sand beaches. The more sheltered irregular south coast offers intriguing stands of mangroves, mudflats, and shellbanks.

**Whakanewha Regional Park** consists of 270 hectares of land, with forested hills dominated by kohekohe and taraire trees, a beach with shells and sand, and a wetland visited by bitterns, banded rails, and spotless crakes. The park has picnic areas and campsites behind the foreshore.

Near Onetangi Beach the Royal Forest and Bird Protection Society has created a reserve with hiking trails. In the forest, consisting largely of taraire and pohutukawa, there are also puriri, rewa rewa, kohekohe, matai, tawa, and kanuka trees. The forest in Woodlands Bay has the diversity found earlier on North Island coasts. At **Omaru Bay** the forest has yet another mix, dominated by taraire and tawa. **Te Matuku Bay** combines mangroves, mudflat, shellbanks, and regenerating native bush. **Tawaipareira Creek** has stands of cabbage trees, and **Awaroa Bay** has a wetland of raupo and mangrove.

Sally McKinney

*Waiheke Fruit and Vegetable Market in Oneroa village*

Maoris occupied the island for 1,000 years; Waiheke has more than 50 pa sites. At one time, Maori farms on Waiheke were an important food source for Auckland. You'll still find olive orchards, vineyards, and 25 boutique wineries on the island. Some of New Zealand's best red wines come from Waiheke, with its hot dry summers, stony soils, and skilled resident wine makers. Some wineries have tasting rooms.

Fullers' Island Explorer tour, 09-367-9919, combines ferry transportation with a bus tour of the island. Fullers' winery tour, including ferry transportation, costs NZ$55 per adult. An all-day bus pass and ferry ticket costs NZ$30 per adult. It's also fun to plan your own day and move about at whatever pace you choose. After lingering over breakfast, you might explore the ridges by mountain bike—to get your bearings and great photos. For lunch you could have a picnic or enjoy Chinese take-out. In the afternoon you might paddle around deserted inlets in kayaks or ride horses along the beach. One evening you might dine at an island winery. Another you might have a more casual meal, then join the locals at the beach for full-moon drumming.

To outfit these adventures and others, Wharf Rats Trading Company at Matiatia Wharf, 09-372-7937, rents mountain bikes for NZ$25 per day and NZ$15 per half-day. Ross Sea Kayaking Adventures, P.O. Box 106-037, Auckland, 09-372-5550, fax 09-372-2211, offers full-day and half-day guided tours, plus two- to three-day camping and kayaking adventures. Owner Ross Barnett has 25 years of experience. Shepherd's Point Riding Centre, 91 Ostend Rd., Ostend, Waiheke Island, 09-372-8104, offers lessons and beach and farm rides. Operators Mary and Mike Richards also offer a three-hour combination ride/hike to Cascade Falls. Waiheke Rental Cars, Matiatia Wharf, Waiheke Island, 09-372-8635, rents cars, jeeps, utility vehicles, motorbikes, and scooters.

*Details: Waiheke Visitor Information Centre, 2 Korora Rd., P.O. Box 96, Oneroa, Waiheke Island, waiheke@iconz.co.nz, can book tours and lodging, including campsites in the Whakanewha Regional Park. Its "Waiheke Island Walkways" brochure gives details about 14 walking tracks along coastal ridges, beaches, and bays. Call ParksLine at 09-303-1530 for additional Whakanewha Regional Park information and campsite reservations.*

*The Fullers' Waiheke Ferry, 09-367-9919, runs several times a day from the Auckland Ferry Building. The cost is NZ$23 per adult round-trip. Pacific Ferries Ltd., 09-303-1741, mobile 021-993-633, operates slower, cheaper, and more traditional passenger ferry service on the* Lady Wakehurst. *Subritzky Shipping, 09-534-5663, carries vehicles and passengers.*

## TOUR OPERATORS

**Bush & Beach Wilderness Experience**, Shortland St., 0800-423-224 or 09-478-2882, bbl@bushandbeach.co.nz, www.bushandbeach.co.nz, offers half- and full-day tours from Auckland to and from west coast beaches and forests. Tours include visits to Muriwai Beach, stands of ancient kauri trees, and the gannet colony. Tours operate daily except Christmas, in whatever weather comes at you (the company furnishes rain gear). Tours can be combined with lodging in the Waitakere rain forest. The cost is NZ$60 to NZ$90, plus lodging.

**Auckland Adventures Ltd.**, P.O. Box 87-023, Meadowbank, Auckland 5, 09-379-4545, fax 09-379-4543, auckland-adventures@acb. co.nz, www.acb.co.nzadventure/, combines mountain bike adventures with west coast wilderness tours and Auckland sightseeing. The cost is NZ$55 to NZ$75.

**Ecotrails,** P.O. Box 490, Whangaparaoa, phone/fax 09-424-5820, mobile 025-280-8749, benfatto@xtra.co.nz, offers half- and full-day loop tours that involve visits to regional parks and marine reserves. Led by an expert in natural history and environmental issues, the tours involve a four-wheel-drive vehicle and guide service. They may include bush walking, mountain biking, horseback riding, snorkeling, diving, swimming, bodysurfing, or fishing. Lunches include local foods— wine, cheeses, and seafood. The guide can also accommodate special diets. A deluxe tour, for NZ$225 or NZ$349, includes preferred activities and a lavish meal. The standard tour price for a small group (minimum two adults, maximum six) is NZ$99.

**Tuatara Tours Ltd.**, P.O. Box 8757, Meadowbank, Auckland, 058-882-827 or 09-520-1143, fax 09-520-1147, mobile 025-291-7957, offers personalized tours, including bush walks and longer hikes. The full-day Outdoor Odyssey combines learning about native species with hikes to the Waitakere Ranges, kauri trees, black sand beaches, and sand dunes. The cost is NZ$80 per adult.

**Off the Beaten Track**, 136 Horseman Rd., RD 2, Waitakere, Auckland, 09-810 8686, fax 09-810-8689, is operated by a retired police officer with extensive regional search-and-rescue experience. They feature hiking in easy to rugged terrain, picnics and barbecues in scenic settings, and farm visits. You can learn bush craft, survival techniques, and first aid from this experienced guide before undertaking longer trips on your own.

**Auckland's Highlights and Specialty Garden Tours**, led by horticulturist Mike Maran, 3 Edith St., Point Chevalier, 09-846-5350, fax 09-846-5315, mobile 025-784-779, combines Auckland sightseeing with visits to private city and country gardens and regional botanic gardens. Tours include visits to exotic flower gardens, stands of native bush, and native ferns displays. The cost is NZ$49 to NZ$89 per adult.

**Kiwi Scene Tours**, 32 Wood Bay Rd., Titirangi, phone/fax 09-817-2180, blends visits to wineries with beach and nature activities.

**The Little Adventure Company**, P.O. Box 32 384, Devonport, Auckland, 09-445-1451, mobile 021-631-376, jamie@littleadventure.co.nz, www.littleadventure.co.nz, runs kayak tours beginning on the beach next to the Devonport ferry dock. You'll paddle past historic and natural sights, early Maori sites, Devonport's ornate wooden villas, volcanic North Head, Rangitoto, and Motutapu Islands.

**Auckland Volcanic Experience**, offered by geologist Murray Baker, GeoTours, P.O. Box 11-600 Ellerslie, Auckland, phone/fax 09-525-3991, mobile 025-860-771, murray@geotours.co.nz, http://kiwipages.co.nz/geotour.html, has one- and two-day tours from Auckland to examine scenic geologic features on the Coromandel peninsula: extinct volcanoes, lava rock formations, quartz reefs, honeycomb cliffs, and Hotwater Beach.

**Bike Auckland City** is a 50-kilometer bike route that loops around the city. Contact Transport Planning, Private Bag 92516, Wellesley St., Auckland 1, 09-379-2020, for more information or pick up the route map and brochure from any tourism office. For a shorter route, pedal from downtown on the paved 12-kilometer route past the Mission Bay, Kohi, and St. Heliers cafés, beaches, and bays.

**Adventure Cycles,** 1 Fort Ln., P.O. Box 91-296, Auckland 1030, 09-309-5566, fax 09-309-4211, rents bikes by the day, week, or month and will store or service your bicycle. The **Mountain Bike Hire Company**, 09-358-4885, delivers 21-speed Shoguns in five sizes. Both companies rent helmets (they are required), locks, water bottles, and other equipment.

# CAMPING

In the populous Auckland region, if possible, camp near the nature sites that interest you—on the west coast, north of city center on the Hauraki Gulf Coast, or on one of the Hauraki Gulf Islands. Avoid campgrounds with long commutes to nature locations. You might even consider postponing your camping experience and saving it for less populous regions. If you do book tent or RV sites at area campgrounds, ask about security precautions.

**Muriwai Beach Motor Camp,** Auckland Regional Park, Muriwai Beach, Auckland, 09-411-9262, located 40 minutes northwest of Auckland, is open year-round and has beach access. Its 100 tent sites and 66 RV sites are near black sand beaches, a gannet colony, bush walks, and a waterfall. Campers appreciate the barbecue, laundry equipment, refrigerator, take-out meals, and store.

**Piha Domain Motor Camp**, Seaview Rd., P.O. Box 52, Piha, 09-812-8815, fax 09-812-8215, is a family-run camp with 76 tent sites and 45 RV sites, and is less than an hour's drive from Auckland. Near tennis courts and a bowling ground, the camp has a children's playground, barbecue, refrigerator/freezer, microwave, and fax service.

From the beach at **Takapuna Beach Holiday Park**, 22 The Promenade, Takapuna, Auckland, you can see the sun rise over Rangitoto Island and the sailboats in Waitemata Harbour. The holiday park has 20 tent and 50 powered sites, plus cabins, on-site RV rental, and motel rooms. Guests enjoy swimming, fishing, and yachting or walking into nearby Takapuna town center. Facilities include a boat ramp, barbecue, car wash, camp store, and photocopy and fax services.

Located on a cove about 35 minutes north of Auckland, **Waiwera Holiday Park**, 37 Waiwera Pl., P.O. Box 120, Waiwera 1240, 0800-922-000 or 09-426-5270, fax 09-426-5250 www.waiwera.co.nz, has 99 RV sites, plus thermal pools, a health spa, cafés, and a restaurant. Guests can rent bikes, boats, or canoes and use a barbecue, picnic areas, and a gym. There are bush walks and good fishing spots in the area.

**Pakiri Beach Holiday Park**, Pakiri River Rd., RD 2, Wellsford, 09-422-6199, fax 09-422-6199, has 150 tent sites and 58 power sites, along with on-site RV rental, cabins, and motel rooms. Located near the Rodney/Okakari Point/Goat Island Marine Reserve, the park offers access to nine kilometers of sandy beach. Activities in the area include horseback riding, paddling kayaks (rent them here), and glass-bottom-boat tours to Kawau Island.

Located near the bird reserve, **Miranda Holiday Park**, Front Miranda Rd., Waitakaruru, RD 6, Thames, 07-867-3206, has new facilities, with 30 tent sites, 60 RV sites, and a 50-bed lodge. The park, near three golf courses and good fishing spots, adjoins a large hot mineral water pool; guests can use it at no extra charge.

**Remuera Motor Lodge Camping Ground**, 16 Minto Rd., Remuera, Auckland, 0508-244-244 or 09-524-5126, fax 09-524-5639, rml@xtra.co.nz, is a 1.5-hectare green oasis fairly close to downtown. Guests can ride city bus lines to reach downtown and the waterfront. Most campsites are powered, but 18 tent sites are also available. Facilities include a large swimming pool, barbecue area, and all-weather RV sites.

Auckland Regional Parks, Private Bag 92012, Auckland, 09-303-1530, fax 09-366-2027, has backpacking and basic camping sites at Tawharanui and Mahurangi West on the Hauraki Gulf, Anawhata on the west coast, the Karamatura Valley, Manukau Harbour, Waharau on the First of Thames, and other locations.

For more information about DOC campsites, visit the Ferry Building office, Quay Street, Auckland, 09-379-6476, fax 09-379-3609.

# LODGING

## *Auckland*

Lodging in the city center or nearby Parnell, Ponsonby, Mount Eden, Remuera, or Devonport neighborhoods is convenient for nature tour pickups or access to ferry transport to Hauraki Gulf Islands. **Novotel**, at the corner of Queen and Custom Sts., 09-377-8920, fax 09-307-3739; the **Hyatt Regency**, Waterloo Quadrant, 09-366-1234, fax 09-303-2932; **Sheraton Hotel**, 83 Symonds St., 09-379-5132, fax 09-377-9367; **Sky City Hotel**, at the corner of Victoria and Hobson Sts., 09-912-6000, fax 09-912-6031; and **Stamford Plaza**, Albert St., 09-357-9210, fax 09-303-0583, are all located close to lower Queen Street and the waterfront.

Near the Aotea Centre and upper Queen Street, the **Park Towers Hotel**, 3 Scotia Pl., P.O. Box 68199, Auckland, 0800-809-377 or 09-309-2800, fax 09-302-1964, parktowr@ihug.co.nz, has 80 rooms—either double, twin, or family units. Rooms have private baths, TVs with remotes, minibars, ironing equipment, tea and coffee service, and security systems. The hotel has a restaurant, bar, and lounge. Room service is available during restaurant hours; snacks are available 24 hours a day. Selected rooms have work desks and separate phone lines for computer modems. Prices range from NZ$120 to NZ$147.

**City Central Hotel**, corner of Wellesley and Albert Sts., P.O. Box 7564, Auckland, 0800-323-6000 or 09-307-3388, fax 09-307-0685, has rooms with adjoining baths, color TVs, phones, and coffee- and tea-making facilities. Choose from singles, doubles, twins, and family accommodations. Located near Queen Street cinemas, shopping, and the Sky Tower, City Central can also make travel arrangements for you. An in-house café serves breakfast seven days a week. A standard room costs NZ$79, larger rooms run NZ$99, with higher rates for family units.

Beyond the Auckland downtown, **Barrycourt Motor Inn**, 10-20 Gladstone Rd., Parnell, 0800-50-4466 or 09-303-3789, fax 09-377-3309, has 107 units and suites, 67 with full kitchens, many with harbor views. Refurbished suites have king- or queen-size beds. Satellite TV sets access 13 channels in several languages. The motel has a restaurant and bar on the premises. It's located 300 meters from the beach and close to shops and cafés along Parnell Road. Guests also enjoy free parking and full laundry facilities. Rates run NZ$86 to NZ$300.

**Parnell Inn**, 320 Parnell Rd., Parnell, Auckland, 09-358-0642, fax 09-367-1032, parnelin@ihug.co.nz, is a bright tidy motel with 16 units, 2 with kitchenettes. Larger units have harbor views and queen-size beds. All units have baths, TVs, phones, and tea- and coffee-making facilities. There is a guest laundry and fax service. Adjoining is a café called The Other Side, open for three meals daily. The Link and other city buses stop on the street out front. Across the street, a line of cafés runs downhill, past a complex of quaint village shops, and toward downtown. The cost is NZ$75 to NZ$110 per night for one or two people.

The very well-run **City Garden Lodge**, 25 St. George's Bay Rd., Parnell, 09-302-0880, has double, twin, and dorm rooms in a stately former home, at one time a residence for the Queen of Tonga. Located near Parnell cafés, shops, and the post office, the lodge has Swiss-born owner/managers who keep the shared kitchen, dining room, and lounge neat and tidy. Damp kitchen towels, for example, are replaced often throughout the day. A cozy wood fire burns on cool evenings. On warm days, guests may take meals outdoors to picnic tables or relax with a book in the garden. There is laundry equipment and a drying area available. Guests can get information, book tours, or send faxes here, too. Be aware that the office closes daily between noon and 3. Dorm beds and rooms range from NZ$18 to NZ$32 per night.

The roomy white-frame **Oaklands Lodge**, 5A Oaklands Rd., Mount Eden, Auckland, 09-638-6545, is in a residential area near food markets, cafés, and shops. It has a large kitchen and lounge, TV room, laundry, picnic tables, and garden. The manager and staff are unusually helpful and well-informed. The owners, who live off-premises, occasionally host barbecues for guests, who pay only NZ$3. Room rates range from NZ$17 to NZ$32 per person.

# FILM LOCATIONS:
## *THE LORD OF THE RINGS*

*In J.R.R. Tolkien's trilogy,* The Lord of the Rings, *currently being filmed in New Zealand, Frodo Baggins and his companions make an epic journey from Hobbiton through Middle Earth on a mission to destroy a magic ring. Although relentlessly pursued, they intend to throw it into the Crack of Doom—before the Dark Lord Sauron uses the ring's black magic to enslave everyone in Middle Earth.*

*"We are fortunate down here in New Zealand," says* Lord of the Rings *filmmaker Peter Jackson, "to have both the computer technology and the natural landscapes to bring the unique world of Middle Earth to life." Actors, whose images will be shrunk using computers, will play the movie's hobbits, dwarves, and elves. Computer graphics will also be used to enhance some New Zealand locations. Yet, Jackson claims, "The basis for filming truly magical, otherworldly locations already exists here." The Old Road from barrow-downs, the ferny rain forests, the mountains and plains of Mordor, the mythic, fire-spouting Mount Doom . . . the landscapes of Middle Earth exist naturally in New Zealand.*

Central Auckland homestays, offered by three different booking agencies, provide accommodations in good neighborhoods close to downtown. Options include a small historic hotel in Parnell; a small hotel in Mount Eden; a Victorian period home in Remuera; cottages in Ponsonby, Newmarket, and Mission Bay; and modern homes in wooded surroundings. Prices include breakfast. Rooms range from under NZ$80 to more than NZ$150 per night. Contact **Homestay Ltd.**, P.O. Box 146, Waimauku, Auckland, 09-411-9166, fax 09-411-9170, homestay@xtra.co.nz.

*Since New Line Cinema officially announced filming (with a budget of US$260 billion) in August 1998, speculation over possible locations for the films has ranged from Wanaka near Queenstown and central Otago on South Island to the bleak lava-filled land around Tongariro, where active volcanoes, a red crater, and emerald lakes already resemble something fantastic. Although New Line Cinema has been secretive about locations, reporters and film fans have learned about one set built in a valley near Auckland and another—apparently Hobbiton—being built in southeastern Waikato, within a triangle bounded by Karapiko, Matamata, and Okoroire. Rolling hills and trees, hot springs, and scenic reserves surround the fictional village, being constructed on a former sheep farm.*

*With a cast of around 300 and more than 15,000 extras (including members of the New Zealand armed forces), the trilogy will be filmed over an entire year. Elijah Wood has been cast as Frodo Boggins. The release date for* The Fellowship of the Ring *is summer 2001, with* The Two Towers *and* The Return of the King *scheduled to follow at perhaps six-month intervals. More than 50 million copies of Tolkien's* The Lord of the Rings *have been sold worldwide. The beloved classic has been translated into 25 different languages.*

**New Zealand Farm Holidays**, P.O. Box 256, Silverdale, Auckland, 09-307-2024, fax 09-426-8474, farm@nzaccom.co.nz, www.nzaccom. co.nz, has properties around New Zealand. **Hospitality Plus/The New Zealand Home and Farmstay Company Ltd.**, P.O. Box 56175, Auckland 3, 0800-109-175 or 09-810-9175, fax 09-810-9448, has Auckland properties, plus those farther afield. They'll work to fill your special requirements—a home-hosted dinner, for example.

YHA New Zealand has hostels in two Auckland locations. **Auckland City YHA**, at the corner of City Road and Liverpool St. near city center, P.O. Box 68-149, Auckland, 09-309-2802, fax 09-373-5083, yhaauck@yha.org.nz, has 24-hour access and staffing. Choose from singles, twin, double, triple, or dorm rooms. The Bistro, on the premises, serves breakfast and dinner. The lodge also has a sundeck, TV lounges, and safety-deposit lockers.

**Parnell YHA**, 2 Churton St., Parnell, has informative staff who can also book your transportation and tours. Choose from twin, double, or shared rooms. The property has secured storage, large shared living areas, a spacious garden, and a barbecue. Book through YHANZ, book@yha.org.nz.

## Waiheke Island

If you'd like to mix village shops, espresso bars, and good cafés with your nature experiences on scenic Waiheke, book lodging near Oneroa. For a focus on the beach and the bird reserve, stay in or near Onetangi Beach. If you want to camp on the island, go to Whakanewha Regional Park.

**Punga Lodge**, 223 Oceanview Rd., Little Oneroa, Waiheke Island, phone/fax 09-372-6675, http://nz.com/webnz/, has a quiet setting amid native bush. You can walk 150 meters to a swimming beach and also walk to Oneroa. Apartments are self-contained, with bed-and-breakfast rooms that open onto sunny verandahs. The hosts serve morning and afternoon teas. Continental breakfasts come with the room price and include fresh fruit and muffins. Prices run NZ$80 and up, with off-season discounts.

With transportation, you can easily reach Oneroa and the less-populated eastern part of Waiheke Island from the **Midway Motel**, Ostend, Waiheke Island, 09-372-8023 or 09-372-6546, fax 09-372-9669, motel@ibm.net. You can choose from small or large units. Guests get satellite TV, access to a gym, laundry facilities, and use of an indoor swimming pool.

**Onetangi Beach Apartments**, 27 The Strand, Onetangi, Waiheke Island, 0800-ONETANGI or 09-372-7051, fax 09-372-5056, bfw@ lconz.co.nz, has three one-bedroom units and three two-bedroom units. Balconies overlook long wonderful Onetangi Beach. Units are self-contained, including kitchens and laundry facilities. They are near cafés, a food shop, and the bird reserve. Kayaks can be rented on-site.

Sally McKinney

*Fossil Bay Farms offers visitors a peek at many native New Zealand plants.*

**Waiheke Visitor Information**, 2 Korora Rd. at the Artworks Complex, P.O. Box 96, Oneroa, 09-372-9999, fax 09-372-9919, waiheke@iconz.co.nz, has information about all sorts of houses, cottages, holiday apartments, and homestays near beaches or with lovely hilltop views. Some are honeymoon hideaways. Prices range from NZ$15 to more than NZ$100 a night.

## *Great Barrier*

Great Barrier Island has no electricity, unless residents generate it, and the "towns" shown on the map are tiny settlements. Savvy island residents have discouraged mass tourism. So visitor accommodation involves small lodges, some lovely B&Bs, and homestays.

**Pohutukawa Lodge**, Tryphena, Great Barrier Island, 09-429-0211, fax 09-429-0117, plodge@xtra.co.nz, is a kauri homestead with double rooms with private baths and shared rooms in a separate backpackers' lodge. You can eat at the Currach Irish Pub. Doubles cost

115

NZ$95 per night, including full breakfast. Lodge bunks are NZ$15 a night per person.

**Stray Possum Lodge**, Cape Barrier Rd., RD 1, phone/fax 09-429-0109, is set amid 25 acres of native bush. You can choose from chalets that sleep six or a separate backpacker section. Hosts will meet guests at Tryphena Harbour or Great Barrier airport.

**Medlands Beach Backpackers**, 9 Mason Rd., RD 1, 09-429-0654, is a five-minute walk from a stunning Pacific beach. The lodge has rooms with outside entrances, plus a well-equipped kitchen and lounge and shared baths. The manager has boogie boards and snorkeling equipment and can organize horseback riding trips and car or mountain bike rental.

For DOC campsites on Great Barrier, contact Hauraki Gulf Maritime Park Information Centre, Ferry Building, Quay St., Auckland, 09-379-6476, fax 09-379-3609.

## FOOD

**Angus Steak House**, on the corner of Albert and Swanson Streets in downtown Auckland, 09-379-7815, carries on the New Zealand meat-and-potato tradition, and has added a lavish salad buffet. The decor suggests a pub, but food is the main attraction, although you can have that drink, too. Begin by selecting a cut of New Zealand beef or lamb—or it could be shrimp, oysters, mussels, or smoked eels—to be grilled. Your meal will be cooked to order, or you could choose only the salad bar. Prices start at NZ$8 for the salad bar and go up from there.

The **Gallery Cafe**, First Floor, Auckland Art Gallery, on the corner of Wellesley and Kitchener Sts., 09-377-9603, is open from 10 to 4 daily. Most of the tables are located on a terrace, shaded by white market umbrellas. Overhead are the branches of great gnarled trees in adjacent Albert Park. The café serves lunch, but only until 2. Herbal teas are steeped in a pot and brought out on a tray. You could also order espresso drinks, echinacea with bee pollen, or low-alcohol beer. The inexpensive café bakes its own cakes, desserts, and muffins. While you're in the complex, visit the Auckland Art Gallery and notice how New Zealand's unique natural environment has inspired many powerful artworks.

At High Street and Freyberg Place in the Auckland city center, the **D72 Diner**, 09-379-3972, has reworked the traditional diner menu and decor to offer healthy (and sometimes high-calorie) versions of good old comfort food. This is the second restaurant of a local operation; its popularity is assured, but at peak periods there's often a wait for food. Breakfast, served anytime, might be filled egg-white omelettes, muesli and fruit, or more traditional eggs and bacon. For lunch there's a chickpea and walnut burger. Your main meal might be meat loaf or the diner's version of a TV dinner. Heart-lite selections are low in calories, fat, and sodium. A check mark inside a diamond designates a vegetarian dish.

In Mission Bay, about 10 kilometers from city center, take Tamaki Drive past Patteson Avenue and the line-up of cafés until you reach **The Positano,** 97 Tamaki Dr., 09-528-5398. What makes the difference here is a chef named Andrea from Frascati. Starters could be squid rings with lemon or a seafood medley with chili sauce. The warm seafood salad, fresh-made gnocchi, and tortellini with smoked chicken are very good. Or ask for Fish of Andrea, a whole baked fish with the chef's special sauce. The restaurant also serves beer, wine, specialty drinks, and liqueurs. Prices are moderate, and the food is very good.

Further along in St. Heliers, the expensive **Saints Waterfront Brasserie**, 425 Tamaki Dr., 09-575-9969, is another local winner—elegant without going too far. The menu features New Zealand foods given international accents. There are tua tua fritters, manuka-smoked salmon, and an artichoke risotto. Tandoori chicken and other unusual pizzas come from a wood-fired oven. The restaurant is also known for its wine cellar, with good New Zealand wines and carefully chosen imports.

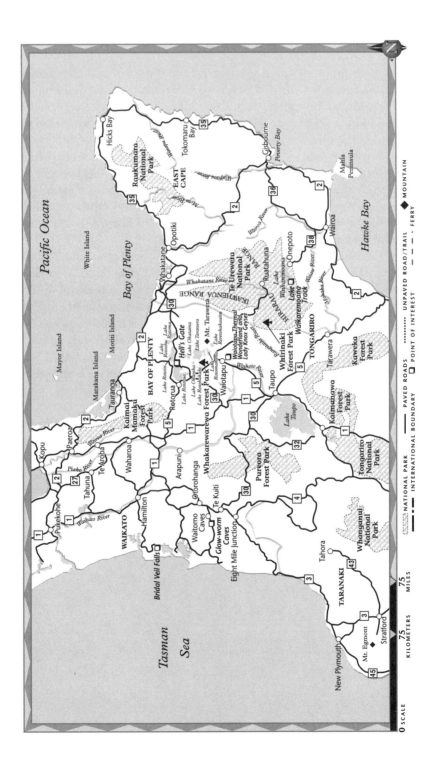

# CHAPTER 5

# The Rotorua Region

There are dozens of ways to explore Rotorua's riverine caves, spouting geysers, bubbling mud pools, hot-water streams, and other natural wonders. Imagine sitting in the open cockpit of a classic biplane, marveling at the champagne lakes below you, or standing on the deck of a small wooden boat, looking across the blue-green water at steaming cliffs. You can follow a trail that winds around a buried village, or hike through temperate rain forest, past sun-lit fern trees, and listen to bellbirds sing. More than 1.2 million people visit Rotorua each year for these and other natural and cultural experiences.

The region lies within the Taupo Volcanic Zone, a broad swath of volcanic activity reaching northeast from Tongariro National Park to the Bay of Plenty. This zone includes not only North Island's three highest mountains and Rotorua's colorful geothermal fields, but also scattered crater lakes, bush-covered hills, and actively volcanic White Island.

Enter the region from the north and you'll encounter a tiny village at Waitomo Caves, surrounded by bush-covered hills. The labyrinthine caves can be explored by water. Farther on, the larger Rotorua community, which sits on a volcanic plateau, has grown beside a large crater lake. Around it, you'll find a concentration of thermal wonders. Beyond these, scattered forests drape the hills, laced with a network of hiking trails.

Travel southeast of Rotorua, and you'll come to the Whakatane River, which flows north from rugged Te Urewera National Park into the Bay of Plenty. In the southern part of the park, the shores of Lake Waikaremoana provide a lovely setting for North Island's greatest walk.

## HISTORY, CULTURE, AND CUSTOMS

Maoris have lived in the Waitomo Caves region since 1625, using selected caves to bury their dead. Maoris were guiding tourists through the Waitomo Glowworm Cave long before the government surveyor and his party came to explore the caves in 1889. East of Waitomo Caves, history credits the Maori Ihenga with discovery of Lake Rotoiti and Lake Rotorua, claimed by Ihenga for the Arawa tribe. Later, while gathered on Mokoia Island, Arawa defenders were overwhelmed by Hongi Heke's invading force. The Arawas threw support to the government in revenge.

Before Mount Tarawera erupted on June 10, 1886, the Pink and White Terraces were ranked among the leading natural wonders of the world. During a five-hour period, the dome of the rhyolitic volcano erupted in a series of violent explosions. The devastation killed an estimated 150 people, destroyed Maori and European settlements, obliterated natural features including the famous silica terraces, and rearranged most everything else. The short-lived thermal activity created Lake Rotomahana and raised or lowered water levels in several other lakes.

As elsewhere in New Zealand, much of the native timber was cut down and hauled away; many forest-covered hills were razed for pastureland. Yet, historically, limited access to the mountainous Ureweras has protected native bush—and Maori people. In the Whakatane River Valley, the Tuhoe tribe would disappear into the remote and shadowy bush when attacked. Religious leader Te Kooti hid for a time in the Ureweras after a dramatic escape from the Chatham Islands. Today, some of the finest native bush on North Island still thrives in the Ureweras.

# NATURE AND ADVENTURE ACTIVITIES

A fledgling tourist industry grew up here in the nineteenth century focused on the region's natural wonders. Tours, hotels, and restaurants sprang up near the attractions—once operators realized their commercial value. The eruption of Mount Tarawera, which buried the Pink and White Terraces, showed people how natural features could be lost and nourished support for protecting them. Today, one in five residents of Rotorua works in tourism, and many Maoris in the region work as tour owners and operators; most Rotoruans understand the need to protect their environmental wealth.

In the Waitomo limestone country, activities center on visits to three main caves: Waitomo, Raukuri, and Aranui. There are, however, perhaps 1,500 caves in the area, and many have not been explored. *Waitomo* means "river entering a cave"; many caves have streams running through them, along with varying populations of glowworms. At least five tour companies offer boat, raft, kayak, and tube rides through caves, plus a mixture of other cave experiences: abseiling, rock climbing, walking, crawling, and gazing at glowworms. Above the ground, you might enjoy horse trekking or hiking. Follow the Raukuri Walkway in dim light and you'll see the tiny lights of glowworms in the forest.

Around Rotorua, tour companies lead visitors through active thermal fields in five main areas. Well-defined trails offer access to the various thermal phenomena. You'll even pass a small steamy public park on the way into town itself.

The Rotorua region also has many scenic day hikes; the Lake Okataina Scenic Reserve, the Waimangu Valley, the walk to Okere Falls, and Hongi's Track are among the best. Cruise boats operate on several lakes: Rotorua, Tarawera, and Rotomahana. You can also enjoy horseback riding through forest and farmland and guided one- or two-day lake kayak trips. A heli-hiking tour deposits visitors onto a trail amid native bush in Whirinaki Forest Park. Te Rehuwai Safaris, a Maori-owned company, offers guided walks and horse treks through the Ureweras. Packhorses carry heavy gear. The trek becomes a cultural exchange as hikers learn of the myriad Maori uses of plant materials.

# FLORA AND FAUNA

Various interesting creatures inhabit the moist dark caves around Waitomo, but only the glowworms put on a spectacular show. The glowworms are actually the luminous organs of the larvae of fungus gnats (*Arachnocampa luminosa*) that inhabit the caves. During the lengthy larva stage (six to nine months), these organs glow with a greenish light that attracts insects, which are trapped in sticky threads and eaten.

A mixture of podocarps—rimu, totara, rata, kahikatea, and puriri trees—is found in scattered patches of native bush near Rotorua. Many regenerated forests have been planted with California redwoods or radiata pine. Whakarewarewa Forest Park, for instance, contains towering stands of California redwoods.

In smaller patches of native bush, you might spot a tui, kaka, or red-crowned parakeet. As you walk past flowering kowhai, pohutukawa, rata, or flax in regional forests, be alert for bellbirds, the increasingly rare kokakos, and saddlebacks, birds that help pollinate a variety of species. With enough time, you can walk woodland trails and find much larger populations of birds in the forest southeast of Rotorua.

# VISITOR INFORMATION

Tourism Rotorua is located on Fenton Street between Arawa and Haupapa Streets. For more information contact Tourism Rotorua, Private Bag 3007, Rotorua, 07-348-5179, grant.delamore@rdc.govt.nz. The NZ Map & Track Shop is located within the Tourism Information Centre complex. Stock includes DOC maps for all of New Zealand, plus many specialized tramping and adventure guides. For more information phone 07-349-1845, fax 07-349-1845.

# GETTING AROUND

The Waitomo Wanderer operates daily bus service between Waitomo, Rotorua, and Taupo and does pickups and drop-offs at the area's main attractions and at accommodations. They'll transport a bicycle for an extra NZ$10.

Air New Zealand, Air New Zealand Link, and Ansett New Zealand provide domestic air service to Rotorua Airport. Call-a-Bus provides service between the airport and Rotorua hotels. Waikato Shuttle links Hamilton Airport with Rotorua.

The Geyserland Express has twice-daily rail service between Auckland and Rotorua. InterCity Coachlines, Mount Cook Landline, and Newman's Coachlines operate interurban bus services. For more information contact Rotorua Tourism, 07-348-5179, fax 07-348-6044.

Seven rental car agencies operate in the area. Taxi service is available within town and to and from nearby geothermal areas. Hikers who need transport to thermal areas or trailheads can make arrangements with Carey's Rotorua Tours, P.O. Box 402, 1108 Haupapa St., Rotorua, 07-347-1197, fax 07-347-1199, careys@careys.co.nz.

## NATURE AND ADVENTURE SIGHTS

### *Crater Lakes*

**Lake Rotorua**, roughly 10 by 12 kilometers, is one of a dozen crater lakes in the area. To find the most satisfying nature experiences, explore beyond the busy Rotorua lakefront. Some lakes, like **Blue Lake** (Tikitapu) and **Lake Okareka**, have been developed for recreation. **Lake Okataina**, surrounded by native forest and hills (actually volcanic domes), is more isolated. A road leads to Okataina Lodge on the north shore, but two roads from the south don't even reach the lakeshore.

Cradled by volcanic mountains, **Lakes Rotoma**, **Rotoehu**, and **Rotoiti** have different shapes, sizes, and water levels. Some have hot springs within them. A channel connects Rotoiti to Rotorua. Ringed by scenic reserves and Maori maraes, the lake has an irregular shoreline and a pretty little island in the middle. At **Lake Rotomahana**, where the famous Pink and White Terraces were buried, visitors can still see colorful steaming cliffs. **Lake Tarawera** borders a scenic reserve; on its shores are the Buried Village and other historic sites.

**Green Lake**, the popular name for Lake Rotokakahi, is another scenic area. At one time the lakeshore was heavily populated and the lake was known for its shellfish. About a century ago, many Maoris were massacred on Motutawa Island within the lake. Now, Green

Lake is considered *tapu* (sacred) to Maoris and off-limits to everyone. Pakehas and Maoris alike respect this status.

Kayaks offer a serene way to experience the lakes. Paddling quietly along the shore, you're close enough to see the markings on a young dabchick's head and the colors of the native fuschia and to hear the quiet hiss of steam rising through a vent in a thermal field.

Adventure Kayaking, P.O. Box 29, Rotorua, 07-348-9451, fax 07-348-9451, mobile 025-997-402, kayak@clear.net.nz, can lead you to hot-water beaches, clear springs, the tangle of green that is native bush, hidden waterfalls, and disappearing rivers. The Twilight Paddle, in which kayakers swim in hot pools, is especially popular. The company can transport you to Lake Okataina—ask about day trips. While you paddle, look for the orange mask of a welcome swallow or the white-rimmed eye of a white-faced heron.

Sunspots Go Kayaking, Okere Falls, Rotorua, 07-362-4222, fax 07-362-4324, mobile 025-872-317, offers a range of kayak tours at different skill levels, including whitewater kayaking on the Kaituna. Both companies rent kayaks and other equipment to experienced paddlers.

Boat cruises offer another way to experience the lakes. Lake Rotomahana Boat Cruises, P.O. Box 6141, Rotorua, 07-366-6137, fax 07-366-6607, katrina@voyager.co.nz, includes tours of **Waimangu Volcanic Valley**. Adult tickets cost NZ$31. Launches leave from the end of the valley and follow the route Maori guides once used to transport visitors to the Pink and White Terraces. The scenic cruises pass Patiki Island and several historic sites.

Across an isthmus is the much larger Lake Tarawera, where Tarawera Launch Cruises, P.O. Box 1969, Rotorua, 07-362-8595, fax 07-362-8883, departs from the landing. Board the classic M.V. *Reramoana* for a relaxing look at this lake flanked by scenic reserves. You'll pass Twin Streams, Hot Water Beach, and Kariri Point, sacred to the Maoris. As you cruise, the captain will tell you much about the area's natural and geologic history. Adult tickets cost NZ$22.50. Ask about family rates.

For package tours that combine lake cruises with other activities, or for transport between Rotorua and these cruises, contact Carey's Rotorua Tours, P.O. Box 402, Rotorua, 07-347-1197, fax 07-347-1199, careys@careys.co.nz, www.gisnz.co/careys.html.

*Details: Tourism Rotorua Travel and Visitor Centre, 1167 Fenton St., 07-348-5179, fax 07-346-6044, gdela@rdc.govt.nz.*

## *Lake Waikaremoana*

It's been called the most beautiful lake on North Island. Geologists believe it originated about two thousand years ago, when a natural dam blocked the headwaters of a river. The dam formed a shoreline of intricate bays and inlets. The Maoris tell another story: A water monster known as Haumapuhia became trapped here. He created the lake when he thrashed his arms and legs around while trying to reach the sea.

Lake Waikaremoana Track loops around the western part of the lake, including the Wairaumoana arm. Begin walking at Onepoto and you'll tackle the toughest climb—the ascent to **Panekiri Bluff**, 1100 meters above sea level—in the first few hours. From this vantage point you'll have spectacular views of the lake's major arms and inlets and, across the lake, the nearby Puketukutuku Range that divides them.

The track follows the Panekiri Range; you'll get great scenic view framed by richly textured branches. The walk descends along the Waipaoa Stream to the second hut (Waipaoa), and then follows the shoreline. **Kokokoro Falls**, which feeds the Wairaumoana arm of the lake, is one of many waterfalls along this route. Continue walking and you'll encounter the **Marauiti Hut** standing on a peninsula nearly surrounded by yet another bay. The **Te Puna** and **Whanganui Huts**, placed within two or three hours of one another, provide more options on the way to Hopuruahine Landing and the road.

The track is 42 kilometers long and can be hiked in three to four days from either end. You'll walk clockwise from Onepoto or counterclockwise from Hopuruahine Landing. Access to the track is via SH 38, which skirts the lake on the east. In summer, and on demand during off-season, a ferry service operates between the Waikaremoana Motor Camp and the trailheads (Onepoto or Hopuruahine) twice a day.

Because of the high altitude, summer is the best season to visit. It is also the most crowded, especially during the six-week Christmas holiday and the Easter break in early fall. Note also that your experience won't always resemble the gorgeous photographs; prepare for rain.

Consider covering some of the track by walking, other segments by paddling. Bay Kayaks, based at the Waikaremoana Motor Camp, 07-837-3818, can organize this type of tour. They also rent gear.

***Details***: *Book huts for the Lake Waikaremoana Track well in advance through the DOC, Aniwaniwa Visitor Centre, Private Bag, Wairoa, 07-837-3803. Ferry service is based at Waikaremoana Motor Camp, 07-837-3729.*

## Thermal Wonders

The story of Rotorua begins some 150,000 million years ago, when the Rotorua caldera was created by volcanic eruptions. Subsequent explosions built up Mokoia Island, within Lake Rotorua, and the Ngawha Crater in the Whakarewarewa area.

Today the Rotorua region has four main geothermal areas, each with a different assortment of hot springs, mud pools, and spouting geysers. Within the city itself, there is thermal activity in **Kuirau Park**. Walk from the Lake Plaza Rotorua Hotel along the lakefront walkway past Sulphur Bay, and you'll cross a bird sanctuary with hot springs and mud pools.

The popular and famous **Whakarewarewa** geothermal area has an amazing amount of activity concentrated in a surprisingly small area. You'll find hundreds of hot springs, boiling mud pools, and spouting geysers. The activity originates below the earth from faults with a northeasterly trend. The **Pohutu Geyser** erupts up to 20 times a day; some Pohutu eruptions reach 100 feet high. Keep to the walkways and avoid stepping onto the hot earth, which is quite thin in places. Visit "Whaka," as this thermal area is called, early in the day to avoid the crowds.

**Waiotapu**, 29 kilometers south of Rotorua on SH 5, also has hot springs and mud pools. It also has more than a dozen craters, plus silica terraces, waterfalls, and steamy lakes with borders in varying and subtle colors. The **Champagne Pool** has steamy blue-green water with a red ochre edge. The water at **Bridal Veil Falls** spills over silica terraces of several colors. You can also see the **Lady Knox Geyser**, primed to erupt each morning at 10:15.

Created by the Mount Tarawera eruption, the newer **Waimangu Volcanic Valley** has hot springs and streams, craters, and terraces in a forest setting. Walk through this scenic valley and you can see **Frying Pan Lake**, the world's largest hot spring, and the vaporous **Cathedral Rocks**. Continue walking along the stream to Lake Rotomahana and the buried **Pink and White Terraces** destroyed by the eruption of Mount Tarawera in 1886.

**Hell's Gate**, also called Tikitere, has violent boiling springs, bubbling mud holes, and smelly sulfur vents. You'll also find a hot waterfall and a forest with many birds. The "Hell by Night" show includes colorful lighting and other special effects.

Tour operators have put together various packages that mix and match visits to geothermal areas with other activities. But ask specific questions before booking a tour. How much time will you spend at each site? How long will you be on the bus? Do you want to join a tour at all or will basic transportation to and from each location suit you better?

**Details**: *Te Whakarewarewa Thermal Reserve, P.O. Box 334, Rotorua, 07-348-9047, fax 07-348-9045, reservations@maci.co.nz. Adults NZ$15.50, additional charges for concerts.*

*Waiotapu Thermal Wonderland, P.O. Box 1992, Rotorua, 07-366-6333, fax 07-366-6010, waiotapu_thermal@clear.net.nz. Adults NZ$11.*

*Waimangu Volcanic Valley, P.O. 6141, Rotorua, 07-366-6137, fax 07-366-6607, katrina@voyager.co.nz.*

*Hell's Gate, Tikitere Holdings Ltd., P.O. Box 2152, Rotorua, 07-345-3151, fax 07-345-6481. Adults NZ$10.*

## Thermal Wonders by Air

From the front seat of an open cockpit biplane at 1,000 meters, Rotorua's streets seem to be flanked by dollhouses, and lakeside parks studded with broccoli trees. Surrounded by volcanic mountains and forested hills, the region's hot steamy lakes appear to be low-lying clouds. With the wind in your face, stray locks of hair tucked in a leather helmet, and the seat belt fastened tight, there's nothing like real flying in a vintage plane.

Several air tour operators keep small planes at Rotorua Airport. They offer a range of options—from a short flight over Rotorua to a circuit of volcanic wonders including steaming lakeside cliffs to the remote active volcano at White Island off the Pacific coast. Your open cockpit biplane might be a vintage Grumman AgCat or a WWII Boeing Stearman.

Go with Volcanic Air Safaris, and you'll climb into the front seat of a converted Grumman AgCat biplane painted bright red. Two people can sit together in the front seat, strapped in behind the 450 horsepower Pratt & Whitney engine. As you fly, you can get great photos of Mount Tarawera or the nearby Blue and Green Lakes—for this plane has no windows—and no walls, for that matter! The operators will provide leather jackets, goggles, gloves, and heavier clothing if weather is cold.

Sally McKinney

*A view of Rotorua from an open-cockpit biplane*

Rotorua Air Adventure Centre offers flying experiences as well as sky dives and aerobatics. The pilot offers scenic flights in a restored silver Boeing Stearman. Its yellow wings and red tail contrast nicely with the sky. Frontair offers similar scenic flights.

*Details: To reach Rotorua Airport, take Te Ngae Road (SH 30) north-east around Lake Rotorua for about five miles. Volcanic Air Safaris, 07-348-9984, fax 07-348-4069, bastewart@extra.co.nz. Rotorua Air Adventure Centre, 0800-768-678, 07-345-7520, or 07-345-6780, fax 07-345-7850. Frontair, 07-345-4595, fax 07-345-9369.*

## The Ureweras

The same rugged terrain and remote location that helped the Tuhoe people survive the Maori Wars has saved many of the region's forests. **Whirinaki Forest Park** and the neighboring 211,062-hectare **Te Urewera National Park**, New Zealand's third largest, protect the largest continuous stretch of forest on North Island. In the remote parts of this temperate rain forest, you could encounter parakeets, silvereyes, bellbirds, tui, kaka, kokako, or native pigeons.

The Kawhenua, Hiarau, and Panekiri ranges within Te Urewera National Park are draped with forests. Streams and rivers within the park flow in different directions toward the east coast: The Whakatane River flows north into the Bay of Plenty, while the Wairoa River flows southeast into Hawke Bay. The area's intricate mixture of trees, shrubs, ferns, mosses, and fungi shifts as altitude increases. Follow a trail along the lower slopes and see meadows and rimu, rata, and tawa forests. Between about 760 and 900 meters, beech and rimu predominate. At the highest altitudes you'll find magnificent silver beech trees, draped with the textured mosses, lichen, and epiphytes in a palette of green.

Hikers have many options here. The **Whakatane River Track** begins at the unofficial Tuhoe capitol, Ruatahuna, and winds upriver through the valley. Trampers usually walk for several days, spending the night at huts along the way. The **Six Foot Track** is a historic route through forest between the Maungapohatu Road and the Waimana Valley. The **Waikaremoana Track**, which loops around the west side of the lake, is one of New Zealand's Great Walks—the only one on North Island.

Te Urewera Adventure, P.O. Box 3001, Rotorua, 07-366-3969, fax 07-366-3333, biddlemarg@clear.net.nz, was formed years ago by a group of Maori couples, before many other Maoris began launching tour companies. Known formerly as Te Rehuwai Safaris, the company organizes tramping, horse trekking, and camping for clients from overseas—Australians, Japanese, Americans, and Germans—and for other New Zealanders.

Trek with the Maoris in early spring and you might find tiny wild strawberries growing by the path. Fields of lupine raise their long violet and mauve stalks. Sporadic spring rainfall might muddy the trail, but it won't dampen your spirits, for you can take shelter under one of nature's giant umbrellas: a ponga (fern) tree. At noon, your guide will use a ponga leaf, draped on the ground, for a tablecloth. Before you reach camp, the guide will boil billy water for afternoon tea. By evening, you'll be cozy around a campfire, sedated by good food–no sleeping tablets needed. Costs for three- to seven-day guided camping/tramping trips range from NZ$400 to NZ$800. One- to five-day

Whare Biddle, operator of Te Urewera Adventures in Urewera National Park

Sally McKinney

horse trekking trips range from NZ$120 to NZ$800. A homestay costs NZ$35 per night.

Trek Whirinaki conducts two-day heli-treks into the forest that depart from and return to Rotorua. Tours include helicopter transportation, camping gear, a powhiri at a marae, and meals including a traditional Maori hangi. Your hosts trace their ancestors to the romantic union of two mythic figures: Hinepukahurangi, the Mist Maiden, and Potiki Tiketike, a mountain spirit known as the Lofty One. Although logging, possums, and browsing deer have done some damage in the Ureweras, you'll still see regal podocarps—rimu, kahikatea, matai, miro, and totara trees—that have evolved from the Jurassic era. Some trees are 65 meters high; individual specimens may be 1,000 years old. Contact Chris Birt, Whirinaki Guided Walks Limited, P.O. Box 1419, Taupo, 07-377-2363, fax 07-377-3285, for more information.

The Rotorua Connection, 07-348-5179, organizes half- and full-day guided walks in the Whirinaki National Forest, with transportation to and from Rotorua. The endangered New Zealand falcon inhabits the bush, along with the blue duck, kaka, and red- and yellow-crowned parakeet. Maori guides can point out plants and animals for you.

**Details**: For Whirinaki Forest Park, contact the DOC, Box 114, Murupara. For Te Urewera National Park, contact the DOC, Private Bag, Wairoa, 06-837-3803.

## Waitomo Caves

More than 85 kilometers of cave passageways have been surveyed, yet tourists see only a few. The **Waitomo Glowworm Cave**, with its thousands of glowworm lights; the **Raukuri Cave**, which also has glow-worms; and the **Aranui Cave**, with its distinctive limestone formations, are the three main caves.

Before rushing off with the first tour operator who wants to book you, visit the **Museum of Caves Information Centre.** Walk among the museum's displays and find out how caves form in limestone; learn more about glowworms, weta, bats, and eels; and even trace the history of cave exploration in the area. Next, study a map of the area to determine where caves are, choose the caves that interest you, and decide how to explore them. The center has a three-page chart of available tours and can book reservations for you. While there, ask about other attractions, including the Waitomo Walkway, Raukuri Natural Tunnel, Mangapohue Natural Limestone Bridge, Marokopa Falls, Opapaka Bushwalk, and Piripiri Cave.

The Waitomo Glowworm Cave has a stunning display of these fascinating larvae-lights, perhaps the best in New Zealand. Boat rides through the cave have been popular with tourists for more than a century. The most popular tour takes only 45 minutes, operates daily, and departs every half-hour. For a more personalized tour, consider the Mason's Glowworm cave tour. During the three-hour experience, a guide will escort you to two different caves and teach you much about ecology.

Beyond the basic walking or boat tours, you can have more complex experiences. You can choose to stay dry, get wet, or get really wet and dirty. You must also decide how much energy to expend, as well as how much money, for the cave tours are commercial operations. Wandering about this cave system on your own is not really an option. Despite years of experience, occasional cavers still get lost and, at times, wait in darkness for days before being found.

Four companies offer cave tubing, also known as blackwater rafting. For the tube experience, you put on a wet suit and a headlamp and climb into a floating inner tube. While observing the cave, you might also form a chain with others in the group or splash down a water slide. All the while, you're immersed in the river. Above, you'll see stalactites growing down from the ceiling and below, stalagmites growing upward ever so slowly. Some formations, like fragile cave straws, have taken 100,000 years to develop.

Depending on the tour operator, cave tubing might be combined with abseiling, rock or waterfall climbing, crossing a flying fox (a flimsy-looking rope bridge), or crawling through dark wet tunnels. Most operators provide hot showers at the end, and some give out chocolate bars. For the wet trips, wear a swimsuit (the wet suit goes over it) and bring a towel and dry clothing. For the so-called dry tours, wear sturdy clothes, long pants, and a sweater or fleece layer (caves remain cool year-round).

*Details*: *Museum of Caves Visitor Information Centre, P.O. Box 12, Waitomo Caves, 07-878-7640, fax 07-878-6184, waitomumuseum@xtra.co.nz.*

## TOUR OPERATORS

The spokesman for **Waitomo Down Under** claims Maoris have been in the tour business here for 110 years. Their tours emphasize black-water rafting, abseiling, and wild cave exploration. Adventures take two to three hours and cost NZ$50 to NZ$65. Contact Waitomo Visitor Information Centre, P.O. Box 12, Waitomo Caves, 07-878-7640, fax 07-878-6184, waitomomuseum@xtra.co.nz.

**Mason's Glowworm Cave–Easy Ecology Adventure Tour** involves two caves and includes a boat ride and glowworm display. Guides emphasize nature aspects while providing a personalized experience. Tours last three hours. The cost for adults is NZ$50; ask for family discounts. Contact the Waitomo Visitor Information Centre for more information.

**Carey's Rotorua Tours**, a large and experienced tour operator, runs nature/soft adventure tours at various sites. Knowledgeable guides—including boat captains—emphasize natural history and let you get out and see things. Experiences include thermal field walks, lake cruises, bush walks, historic tours, and four-wheel-drive trips to the top of Mount Tarawera (with two hours to explore). Carey's can also provide transport to and from various nature sites and trailheads. The company office is at 18 Haupapa St., 07-347-1199, fax 07-347-1199, careys@careys.co.nz.

**Foxwood Park**, Fairbank Rd., Rotorua, 07-345-7003, fax 07-345-7700, offers horseback riding through redwood forest, guided treks, and a Honeymoon Trek. The cost is NZ$25 for a short ride up to NZ$150 for an all-day tour with lunch.

**The Farmhouse**, Central Rd., RD 2, Rotorua, 07-332-3771, fax 07-332-3334, farmhouse@clear.co.nz, offers horseback riding, farm tours, and stays at this farm set in native bush.

**Scatcat**, 32 Kiwi St., Rotorua, 07-347-9852, based at the Rotorua Lakefront, can take you to Mokoia Island, steeped in Maori legend and history. Rental boats are another option; only boaters with permits can land on the island. The MV Ngaroto Cruise office on the lakefront handles the permits.

Through **Lakeland Queen Cruises Ltd.**, P.O. Box 1976, Rotorua, 07-348-6634, fax 07-347-1766, lakelandqueen@xtra.co.nz, you can relax in traditional style on Lake Rotorua on a replica of an early paddle steamer. The cost for adults is NZ$16 to NZ$24, including food.

## CAMPING

Located 500 meters from Waitomo Caves, **Cavelands Waitomo Holiday Park**, Main Rd., Waitomo Valley, 07-878-7639, fax 07-878-7639, has 100 tent sites and 20 powered sites, along with tourist flats and cabins. Other services include a car wash and store.

**Cosy Cottage International Holiday Park**, P.O. Box 159, 67 Whittaker Rd., Rotorua, 0800-222-424 or 07-348-3793, fax 07-347-9634, a small family park in a thermal area on Lake Rotorua's shore, is just two kilometers from city center. Guests can swim and use hot mineral water pools, a barbecue, and a natural steam oven. The lodge has heated sleeping quarters, and even the tent sites are thermally warmed.

**Rotorua Thermal Holiday Park**, South Taupo Rd., Rotorua, 0800-505-114 or 07-346-3140, fax 07-346-1324, is located southeast of the Whakawerawera geothermal park. This large park has a grassy setting with scattered shade trees. There are log cabins, self-contained tourist flats, powered RV sites, tent sites with trees and flowers, and lodge rooms. RVers can use a covered walkway to reach central park facilities. Catered meals can be ordered. Guests may use the barbecue, swim in a heated pool, and unwind in a smaller hot pool.

**Blue Lake Holiday Park & Motels**, Tarawera Rd., Blue Lake, P.O. Box 292, Rotorua, 07-362-8120, fax 07-362-8600, is set in native bush beside recreational Blue Lake. This family camp is a base for bush walks, fishing, and mountain biking. You can rent canoes, bikes, and fishing boats year-round. The park can also book activities for you. The drive to town center takes 10 minutes.

**Lake Rotoiti Lakeside Holiday Park**, Okere Rd., Okere Falls, RD 4, Rotorua, 07-362-4860, fax 07-362-4789, is a small lakeside park located 20 kilometers from Rotorua. You can walk to Okere Falls from the park. Guests also enjoy trout fishing, kayaking, and swimming, and have access to a boat ramp, store, fish smoker, and barbecue.

**Waikaremoana Motor Camp**, within Te Urewera National Park (southwest of the visitors center on SH 38), 07-837-3826, has tent sites, powered sites, cabins, chalets, and motel units in a range of prices. The camp runs a ferry service to Lake Waikaremoana trailheads, rents kayaks, and runs a small store.

You could also stage Urewera adventures from Whakatane on the Bay of Plenty. If so, **Awakeri Hot Springs Motor Camp** on the Rotorua/Whakatane Hwy., RD 2, Whakatane, 07-304-9117 or 07-304-8224, fax 07-304-9290, has tent and powered sites. Alternatively, **Riverside Motor Camp**, near Hawke Bay, 19 Marine Parade, Wairoa, 06-838-6301, fax 06-838-6341, has tent and powered campsites beside the Wairoa River.

Dozens of DOC huts are scattered throughout Te Urewera National Park. The Marauiti, Panekiri, Te Puna, Waipaoa, and Whanganui huts are on Lake Waikaremoana. The DOC also has huts in the Whirinaki forest. To book those for Te Urewera National Park, call the Aniwaniwa Visitor Centre, 07-837-3803, or the Ikawhenua Visitor Centre, 07-366-5641. For Whirinaki Forest Park, contact Te Ikawhenua Visitor Centre, Box 114, Murupara, 07-366-5641. Other DOC offices can also book huts.

# LODGING

## *Waitomo Caves Area*

The YHA-linked **Waitomo Caves Hostel**, Waitomo Caves Rd., RD 7, Otorohanga, 07-878-8204, fax 07-878-8205, has bunk rooms with adjoining lounges. Besides a location near the tourist office and museum, the hostel offers the usual kitchen, dining, and public areas; 24-hour access; and a helpful staff.

Built in 1908, the **Waitomo Caves Hotel**, RD 7, Otorohanga, 0800-7829-9484 or 07-878-8204, offers luxurious rooms in a renovated hillside building. Some rooms have verandahs that overlook the entrance to Waitomo Glowworm Cave and the not-quite-a-village of Waitomo down below. Two restaurants feature traditional New Zealand country food (meat, potatoes, vegetables); non-guest diners are welcome. Prices range from NZ$125 for a single to NZ$185 for a suite.

**Panorama Motor Inn & Restaurant**, 07-878-7640, waivin@nzhost.co.nz, a tidy motel on Waitomo Road, has 21 units with in-room facilities and an on-premises restaurant. **Glow Worm Motel** on Waitomo Caves Road close to the caves has nine units plus a large swimming pool, heated spa bath, and adjoining restaurant. Contact the motel at RD 7, Hangatiki, Otorohanga, 07-873-8214.

## *Rotorua*

**Lake Plaza Rotorua Hotel**, 6 Eruera St., P.O. Box 884, Rotorua, 07-348-1174, fax 07-346-0238, stands beside thermal park grounds, a lakeside nature trail, and a bird sanctuary. Down the road are the Polynesian Spa baths and the Government Gardens. The 250 rooms have tea- and coffee-making equipment, TVs, video channels, direct dial phones, and central heating. A restaurant and bar, heated swimming pool, and private spa baths are on the premises.

The expensive **Solitaire Lodge**, Lake Tarawera, RD 5, Rotorua, 0508-552-552 or 07-362-8208, fax 07-362-8445, solitaire@wave.co.nz, is located on a tree-studded peninsula with views of Lake Tarawera. Affiliated with the Small Luxury Hotels of the World, the place is known for personal service, good food, and wine. The contemporary guest rooms, decorated with a bold mix of patterned fabrics and bentwood furniture, have architectural interest.

**Okawa Bay Lake Resort**, SH 33, Mourea, Lake Rotoiti, Rotorua, 0800-505-900 or 07-362-4599, operates a courtesy bus and is located about 15 minutes from city center. The hotel has 44 rooms and two suites. Guests can eat in the licensed restaurant, drink in the house bar, or order 24-hour room service. The resort has a marina, boat ramp, tennis courts, and swimming pool. It is a tourism award winner for mid-range, full-service lodging.

In 1995 a flock of blue herons that hatched in a pohutukawa tree

*Thermal activity at Waiotapu Springs*

Sally McKinney

returned to their birthplace. Guests at the **Namaste Point Lakeside Retreat**, Lake Rotoiti, 07-362-4804, fax 07-362-4060, mobile 025-971-092, namaste .point@xtra.co.nz, especially enjoy watching the resident flock of blue herons, along with paddle boating, rowing, canoeing, and fishing on the lake. Owner Gillian Marks assures guests they'll receive Kiwi hospitality, seclusion, and privacy.

**Regal Geyserland Hotel**, 0800-881-882 or 07-348-2039, fax 07-348-2033, overlooks the Whakarewarewa thermal field; some windows frame the erupting Pohutu Geyser. The hotel has 60 rooms and 6 suites. It has a restaurant and bar featuring New Zealand food, beers, and wines. Guests may swim in a heated outdoor pool and use a private spa bath, sauna, and gymnasium.

**Princes Gate Hotel,** Arawa St. at the corner of Hinemaru, 07-348-1179, was brought from Waihi during the 1920s and reassembled across from the Government Gardens. Nearly a century old, the hotel has been carefully restored. Owners Brett and Vlasta Marvelly spent 12 years refurbishing the sprawling white villa; you'll appreciate the polished stairwell of native kauri. The 50 individually decorated rooms, charmingly old-fashioned, have high ceilings, fireplaces, and open verandahs. Memories Restaurant, an award winner, opens for lunch and dinner six evenings a week. Guests may take breakfast at the streetside café, drinks beside the pool, and a nightcap in the bar and lounge.

**Kiwi Paka**, 60 Tarewa Rd., P.O. Box 905, Rotorua, 07-347-0931, fax 07-346-3167, offers inexpensive lodging and also a café/brasserie, bar, hot thermal pool, and travel center.

Several motels along Lake Road have convenient locations near the lakefront and city center. These include the **Ladwich Lodge**, 12-

14 Lake Rd., 07-347-0049; **Lake Lodge Motel**, 16 Lake Rd., 07-348-5189; **South Pacific Motel**, 98 Lake Rd., 07-348-0152; and **Utuhina Lodge**, 99 Lake Rd., 07-348-5785.

Among the many Fenton Street motels, the **Wylie Court Motor Lodge**, 345 Fenton St., Rotorua, 0800-100-879 or 07-347-7879, fax 07-346-1494, has a parklike setting. It is an award-winning property with mid-range prices.

Across from the Sheraton, consider the **Aywon Motel**, 18 Trigg Ave., Rotorua, 0800-331-177 or 07-347-7659, fax 07-348-4066. Hosts Em and Beat Loosli speak English, German, and French. Choices include studios and one- and two-bedroom units. Kitchens have microwave ovens.

# FOOD

For a good inexpensive lunch with the locals, try the **Waitomo Caves Tavern Restaurant & Bar**, P.O. Box 21, Waitomo Caves, phone/fax 07-878-8448. Located near the museum/tourism office, this roomy building serves snacks, burgers, toasted sandwiches, and desserts. Add French fries and salad to anything, and it becomes a meal. The Trekking Samme (sandwich) is stacked with meat, cheese, and veggies and served with fries. Guides and bus drivers come, eat, and leave. Occasional tourists wander in, while the locals play pool and listen to a jukebox. In summer, lunch is served Monday through Saturday from noon to 2:30 and dinner from 6 to 9. Bar snacks (which are substantial) and drinks can be had when meals are not served.

**The Gazebo**, 45 Pukuatua St., Rotorua, 07-348-1911, is a moderately priced local favorite for lunch and dinner. This is a Euro-style place with smart furniture and aromatic coffees. The kitchen does interesting things with hot/cold salads and prepares New Zealand venison and lamb dishes with Asian flourishes. It is closed Sunday and Monday.

For sophisticated New Zealand food at reasonable prices, have dinner at **Poppy's Villa** in an Edwardian building at 4 Marguerita St., phone/fax 07-347-1700. The decor contrasts earthy warm colors against cool greens. The roast rack of Canterbury lamb with rosemary honey mustard and a berry sauce keeps winning awards, along with other beef and lamb dishes. Other creations include a seared ostrich salad sea-

# MAORI FEASTS

*The traditional* hangi, *a Maori feast, is a buffet made up of many kinds of food steamed slowly in an underground oven. Maoris dig a deep earthen pit to make the oven, layer hot stones in the pit, add a layer of vegetation, then add foods such as wild pig, lamb, chicken, fish, kumara, potatoes, and carrots. The food is topped with more greenery, water, and a final layer of earth and left to cook for several hours.*

*For years, large Rotorua hotels have offered guests a version of the Maori hangi, plus evening Maori concerts. These hotels include the Lake Plaza Rotorua, Quality, Millennium, Sheraton, Centra, Royal Lakeside Novotel, and Rydges.*

*A recent winner of New Zealand's Supreme Tourism Experience award, Tamaki Tours, P.O. Box 1492, Rotorua, 07-346-2823, fax 347-2913, tamaki@wave.co.nz, offers the most elaborate Maori cultural experience anywhere. Guests travel by waka, a traditional boat, to an artfully constructed village known as Te Tawa Ngahiri Pa. There, they browse among arts and crafts exhibits, enjoy a hangi feast, and watch traditional entertainment. The adult cost is NZ$55.*

*Much less dazzling, but possibly more real-world, are the hangis and concerts hosted by local Maoris, including those on the Rakeiao and Pikirangi Maraes. Rotoiti Tours will take you by bus to*

soned with chili, lime, and ginger. Mussels, fresh fish, and other seafood are given enhanced flavor with Mediterranean or Thai seasonings. Vegetarians will appreciate the tasty vegetable strudel. Prices range from NZ$20 to NZ$30. The restaurant is open for dinner daily.

**Cobb and Co. Restaurant and Bar** on the corner of Hinemoa and Fenton St. within the Grand Establishment Hotel, 07-348-2089, is part of a New Zealand chain. Although known for classic meals of sirloin steak, salad, and French fries—followed by hot apple pie—it also serves vegetarian omelettes and will make up a vegetable plate to the Rakeiao Marae for a hangi/concert. The lovely location over-looking quiet Lake Rotoiti enhances each event: the powhiri (tra-ditional welcome ceremony), feast, and entertainment. Your hosts will escort you to a pit where the buried food is steaming; the meaty, smoky aromas mingle with fresh lake air.

Served inside the carved meetinghouse, the three-course meal includes platters of tender pork, beef, chicken, and fish, plus bowls of potatoes, pumpkin (squash), and kumara cooked in the pit. These foods are complemented by crisp, chilled, or marinated sal-ads. Dessert—if you can handle it—might be a tasty cake served with whipped cream and fruit.

Talented singers and dancers perform in bright costumes in traditional patterns that set off their dusky skin tones. An action song, sung in Maori, tells a story—perhaps the legend of the Great Migration. Spears or sticks may be twirled, suggesting combat, or may mimic the movement of canoe paddles. In some dances, the poi (a ball on a string) is swung along with the other movements. In contrast to the action songs are the slower melodic love songs and the spiritual hymns that honor ancestors. The Pikirangi Hangi and Concert, P.O. Box 7049, 07-345-5459, fax 07-345-5460, mobile 025-784-419, held on Lake Rotorua, is similar. Contact Tourism Rotorua Visitor Information, 67 Fenton St., Rotorua, 07-348-5179, fax 07-348-6044, for more information.

order. Diners are served at comfortable tables, set on polished wood floors amid a decor of brown, red, and green, and accented with old-time photos of the region. Open daily for lunch and dinner.

The inexpensive and family-run **Hae Jang Kuk Chip**, 1220 Hinemaru St., 07-347-6182, has a range of Korean dishes for take-out or dining in. Patrons especially like the zippy barbecue beef or pork and the spicy squid, combined with rice and vegetable side dishes— add *kim chee*, if you like. The restaurant is open daily for lunch and dinner.

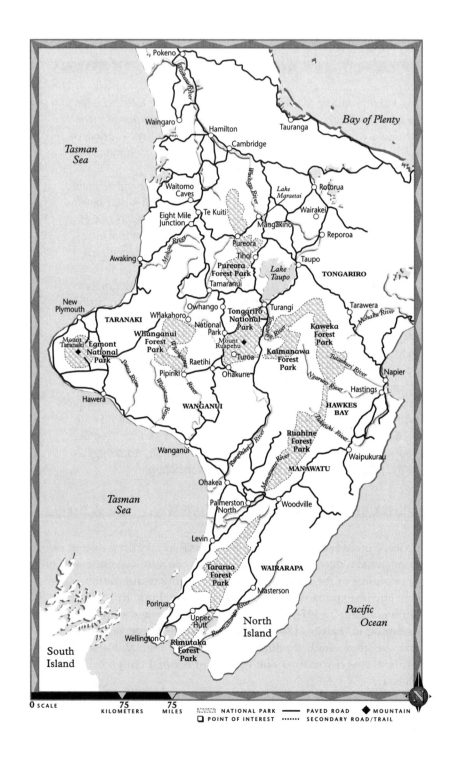

Pokeno

Waingaro

Hamilton

Cambridge

*Tasman
Sea*

*Bay of Plenty*

Tauranga

Waitomo
Caves

Te Kuiti

*Lake
Maraetai*

Rotorua

Wairakei

Eight Mile
Junction

Mangakino

Reporoa

Awaking

Pureora

Tihoi

Taupo

TONGARIRO

Pureora
Forest Park

*Lake
Taupo*

Tamaranui

New
Plymouth

TARANAKI

Whakahoro

Owhango

National
Park

Tongariro
National
Park

Turangi

Tarawera

*Mohaka River*

Kaweka
Forest
Park

Mount
Taranaki

Egmont
National
Park

Whanganui
Forest
Park

Mount
Ruapehu

Turoa

Kaimanawa
Forest
Park

Napier

Raetihi

Hastings

Pipiriki

Ohakune

Hawera

WANGANUI

HAWKES
BAY

Wanganui

Ruahine
Forest
Park

MANAWATU

Waipukurau

Ohakea

*Tasman
Sea*

Palmerston
North

Woodville

Levin

Tararua
Forest
Park

WAIRARAPA

Porirua

Masterson

*Pacific
Ocean*

Upper
Hutt

*North
Island*

Wellington

Rimutaka
Forest
Park

*South
Island*

0 SCALE        75        75
      KILOMETERS   MILES

NATIONAL PARK          PAVED ROAD        MOUNTAIN
POINT OF INTEREST      SECONDARY ROAD/TRAIL

# CHAPTER 6

# The Tongariro Region

Hike past a hot-water stream, climb the rocky saddle between volcanic mountains, catch a trout for dinner, follow a river through uninhabited bush—the diversity of the Tongariro region includes craters, lakes, mountains, deserts, and streams. North of Taupo, a town of 30,000, lies the Taupo Thermal Centre, one of three centers of geothermal activity in the Taupo Volcanic Zone. Southwest of town lies Lake Taupo, North Island's largest lake. Cliffs and woodland enhance the western bays of its irregular hilly shoreline.

Farther southwest rise the volcanic peaks of Mount Tongariro, Mount Ruapehu, and Mount Ngaurahoe. These often snow-capped peaks comprise the heart of Tongariro National Park. The Waikato, New Zealand's longest river, the Whanganui, and other rivers form on the volcanoes' upper slopes. North of the national park, which is also a UNESCO World Heritage Site, is Pureora Forest Park, home of the rare kokako. Directly east is the wild mountainous Kaimanawa Forest Park, cut by rivers and streams.

Many lake, forest, and thermal-field adventures can be staged from Taupo, which has supermarkets and outfitters for clothing and gear. At the southwest end of the lake, the small community of Turangi makes a good departure point for the Tongariro Crossing or other treks. Whakapapa Village, site of the national park

141

headquarters, and the villages of National Park and Ohakune, might also be starting points for hiking, climbing, and skiing adventures.

## HISTORY, CULTURE, AND CUSTOMS

Volcanic activity at Tongariro dates back an estimated 500,000 years. Lake Taupo, a crater lake with 616 meters of surface, was formed by a volcanic eruption about 330,000 years ago, but that wasn't the end of the action. The Lake Taupo caldera has had 28 eruptions during the last 27,000 years. Occasional and sporadic rumblings below the lake (a series was recorded in 1998) still make some homeowners nervous enough to sell. Mount Ruapehu, North Island's highest mountain at 2,797 meters, erupted as recently as 1996.

The region has been sacred to Maoris for years, and the combination of active volcanoes and other geothermal activity has inspired many Maori legends. One tells of the competition among male mountains for the favor of the lovely female mountain Pihangi. Another legend tells of Ngatoro-i-rangi, navigator of the great *Arawa* canoe, who was first to explore the region. Leaving most of his party in Taupo to fast during his absence, Ngatoro, accompanied by a female slave, began climbing the mountain. When the group back in Taupo became too hungry to continue fasting, the gods became so angry that they froze Ngatoro and his companion by sending them blizzards. Ngatoro prayed for fires that would warm them. Soon, underground fires appeared in scattered locations from Mount Tongariro to White Island. Although the Tongariro fire saved the life of Ngatoro, his companion died. He then cast her body into the Ngaurahoe crater as a sacrifice, in the hope of appeasing the gods.

European missionaries came to the region early in the nineteenth century, with other settlers arriving in 1869. Late in the nineteenth century, Tongariro's forests were targeted for development. Many were cleared, and some eventually replanted. The Maoris planned a national park, aimed at protection and preservation, and gave Tongariro to the New Zealand government. It was the country's first national park—the second in the world after Yellowstone.

It wasn't until the 1950s that Taupo took on some aspects of a holiday town. Eventually, the Huka Lodge and the area's plentiful supply of trout gained worldwide renown. Tongariro National Park acquired World Heritage status in 1991.

## NATURE AND ADVENTURE ACTIVITIES

In the past, the area's great fishing and boating, with lakeside views of distant snowcapped mountains, attracted visitors. Today you can enjoy wider variety: short day hikes along the Waikato River, through forests, or along steamy geothermal fields; mountain biking; catch-and-release fishing; horseback riding; river rafting; or a kayak ride or motor cruise past striking rock formations created by dynamic eruptions.

Less commercial than Rotorua, the town of Taupo has become the base for many soft adventure and nature tours. You'll find fishing guides, ecotours, hiking guides, cruise tours, and the equipment needed by independent explorers here. One ecotour uses swamp boats to access wetlands. Another tour offers a mountain bike descent from the upper reaches of Mount Ohakune. Southwest of Mount Tongariro, you can join a flotilla paddling down the Whanganui River through thick forests. A self-drive tour allows you to explore, at whatever pace you choose, the remote countryside west of Lake Taupo.

In winter, Taurangi and the smaller villages around Tongariro National Park overflow with skiers. In summer, fewer visitors find lower prices and a more equable climate for camping, boating, hiking, and climbing. Day hikers and campers find organized shuttles that will take them to trailheads within and around Tongariro National Park.

## FLORA AND FAUNA

Although the southwestern part of the Taupo Volcanic Zone was mostly forested when people arrived, much of the existing bush has been razed. East of Mount Tongariro, forest that once covered the slopes was destroyed by volcanic debris, creating the Rangipo Desert. Low tussock and scrub now inhabit this desolate area; near Soda

Springs you might see white ourisia, yellow buttercups, or the lavender parahebe in bloom. West of Tongariro, sheltered from the volcanic destruction, is a section of original forest.

The southern and western Tongariro forests vary. Some areas, characterized by kaikawaka and mountain beech, are home to bright parakeets and the North Island robins. Other forests, thick with ancient rimu and other giant podocarps, are favored by bellbirds, tuis, silvereyes, kakas, and kiwis. At higher altitudes on the mountains of Tongariro, snow totara, whipcord hebe, and mountain daisies flower in summer. Even higher, only the hardiest plants thrive among the chunks of lava, boulders, and melting glaciers.

The Pureora Forest Park encloses a mixed podocarp forest, some of it native, and shelters the kaka and rare kokako. Rare blue mushrooms can also be seen. Kaimanawa Forest Park has yet another mix: some parts are dominated by mountain, red, or silver beech; some feature rimu and other podocarps and giant fern trees.

## VISITOR INFORMATION

Taupo has many banks and ATMs. Farther southwest, however, consider carrying cash, hidden in a money belt, because small cafés, shuttle drivers, and tour operators in rural villages may not accept credit cards or travelers' checks.

When hiking, make sure you're prepared with extra clothing. Inclement weather can blow in on the sunniest summer day, even at low altitudes. Wear sturdy boots and carry extra socks, heavy fleece layers, hats, gloves, and waterproof jackets and pants in higher altitudes. Carry maps, sunblock, ample drinking water, and easy-to-eat high-calorie foods.

The DOC provides information about freezing temperatures at high altitudes; this information is posted in some huts. Park trails, although mostly well marked, may run through long stretches of unmarked rocky streambed or traverse ridges of loose gravel on a crater's rim. Some hikers will want a walking stick. When walking through geothermal areas, stay on the trail; a thin crust of earth beside it might give way to scalding water below. When swimming in hot-water streams or pools, be aware of shifting temperatures.

Tourism bureaus and DOC offices are open long hours in summer. These include:

- Taupo Visitor Centre, 13 Tongariro St., P.O. Box 865, Taupo, 07-378-9000, fax 07-378-9003, tuovin@nzhols.co.nz
- Whakapapa Visitor Information Centre, SH 48 Whakapapa Village, Private Bag, 07-892-3729, fax 07-892-3814
- Tongariro National Park, DOC, Whakapapa Visitor Centre, c/o Post Office, Mount Ruapehu, 07-892-3729
- Ohakune Information Centre, 54 Clyde St., P.O. Box 36, Ohakune, 06-385-8427, fax 06-385-8527
- Pureora Forest Park, DOC Pureora Field Centre, RD 7, Te Kuiti, 07-878-4773
- Kaimanawa Forest Park, DOC office, Private Bag, Turangi, 07-386-8607

# GETTING AROUND

InterCity, Newman's, and Alpine Scenic Tours operate bus service to and from Taupo, Turangi, and other villages. The Magic and Kiwi Experience networks make stops at Taupo and Turangi. Air New Zealand and Mount Cook provide service to Taupo from major North Island cities. Taupo travel agencies handle airline tickets.

In Taupo, a sightseeing bus called AdventureLink, 025-459-698, makes a circuit of nearby attractions. Among the stops in the loop are the Wairakei Geothermal Information Centre, Huka Falls, and a horse trekking center. Additional stops are made on request. One-way taxi fare to and from Huka Falls or Craters of the Moon runs NZ$13 to NZ$15; there is a taxi stand on Lake Terrace Road. Generally, nature sites west of Taupo are hard to reach. Consider getting a rental car to explore beyond Taupo.

# NATURE AND ADVENTURE SIGHTS

## *Craters of the Moon*
Four miles north of Taupo and five miles west of SH 1 lies a fascinating thermal field. On a cool morning you can take off alone on a loop track through a colorful geothermal field dating from the 1950s. You'll see

*Thermal activity at Craters of the Moon, north of Taupo*

large craters, steamy trenches, and small fissures. Roaring fumaroles and eruptions occur about four times a year.

The place steams and bubbles all day long, and you can observe without distractions—there are no crowds and no one sells tickets. There are no guides either. Follow the wooden and earthen loop track to the left. Stay on the track to prevent getting burned.

You'll learn much about the Craters of the Moon from signs along the 2,000-meter pathway. The Maori tribes who once lived in the Wairakei used the thermally heated water for cooking, bathing, and heating. Note that the field is not known for geysers, but for fumaroles. Both result when mud or shifting earth block the steam vents above super-heated water. Geysers spout in periodic bursts, fumaroles more gradually.

From the first viewing platform, notice the crater on the left and the steam that rises from its vents amid subtle colorations. This, the largest crater in the park, erupted last in 1983. Continue walking past smaller craters to reach the second viewing platform that overlooks a crater that spouts pumice and mud about four times a year. With each eruption the crater grows larger and deeper. In April 1992, eruptions covered the trail with five centimeters of mud. Although it's not likely the crater will erupt while you gaze at it from the platform, keep your camera handy—you never know!

Visitors have come to this field since the 1950s. After a series of car break-ins, the Craters of the Moon Charitable Trust organized a modest visitors center attended by helpful well-informed volunteers whose presence adds security.

*Details: Contact the Taupo Visitor Centre, 13 Tongariro St., P.O. Box 865, 07-378-9000, fax 07-378-9003, tuovin@nzhost.co.nz. Admission is free.*

## Lake Taupo

The lake is famous worldwide for trout fishing. The lake's first rainbow trout hatched from eggs shipped from California in the early 1880s. Brown trout eggs, spawned in Tasmania from fish brought from England, arrived in New Zealand even earlier than the rainbows and arrived in Lake Taupo in 1886. New Zealand hatcheries continue to supply eggs from which the trout are spawned. Today's average "double digit" (in pounds) trout weighs 1.5 kilograms; occasionally, trout from these waters can be twice as heavy.

The **Western Bays**, hugged by the Karangahape Cliffs, offer some of Lake Taupo's best fishing spots, along with the mouth of the Tongariro River. The **Waitahanui River** delta is the place for "picket fence" fishing, where avid fishermen form a fencelike line.

Taupo fishing guides, many of them with years of experience, can take you to these sites, plus wilderness rivers, spring creeks, and isolated high-country lakes. Clients include novices as well as highly skilled and experienced fishermen; fly-fishing is a specialty of area guides. Several guides access backcountry rivers in four-wheel-drive vehicles. Some arrange for helicopter adventures to remote wilderness lakes or take guests rafting on the Upper Tongariro.

Guide Ron Burgin cites 20 years of experience in central North Island. Mark Aspinal and his associates (Mark Aspinal Fly Fishing) offer several types of transport to various locations. Richie Buchanan, yet another guide, began fishing about the time he learned to walk. In 1992, he launched Buchanan Trout Guiding.

147

*Details:* Ron Burgin, phone/fax 07-378-3126, rburgin@anglers retreat.co.nz, www.anglersretreat.co.nz. Mark Aspinal Fly Fishing, P.O. Box 382, Taupo, 07-378-4453, mobile 025-904-939. Richie Buchanan, Buchanan Tackle Ltd., P.O. Box 90117, Auckland Mailing Centre, mobile 025-907-079.

## Mount Ruapehu

Mount Ruapehu, a giant heap of steaming andesite lava, rises from the southwestern end of the Taupo Volcanic Zone. A team of researchers once found themselves heading up the mountain just before it blew. Using sophisticated technology, experts continue to monitor the volcano's vibrations.

Skiers think this handsome volcanic mountain has it all: two major ski fields, a network of patrolled trails laced over 700 hectares of snowy slopes, 35 lifts, and equipment, facilities, and lessons for many levels of experience. Après-ski fun takes place in convivial restaurants and bars. What's more, skiers from the Northern Hemisphere can enjoy Down Under skiing from early June through mid-November.

On the northern side of Mount Ruapehu, is **Whakapapa**, the largest ski resort in New Zealand. It has more than 30 groomed trails, a 675-meter vertical drop, 23 lifts, and five cafeterias. You can find lodging in Whakapapa village (six kilometers below the resort) or in nearby hamlets. At Whaka, as the resort is known, parents appreciate the Wizard's Club child-care center. Beginners practice turns in Happy Valley, while more experienced skiers move swiftly up the lifts. High on the mountain, skiers choose from an array of trails. The most talented find steep chutes and couloirs for exciting off-piste thrills.

On the southwest side of the mountain, newer and smaller **Turoa** has a vertical drop of 720 meters—New Zealand's longest. The resort has a network of patrolled trails, 12 lifts including quad and triple chairs, T-bars, four-platter lifts, and rope tows: the total uphill capacity is 12,600 people an hour. You'll also find equipment rental, ski lessons, souvenir and accessory shops, and three mountain cafés. During recent seasons, snow has not fallen as hoped. Down below, however, Ohakune village is a hot spot of late-night energy.

**Tukino**, a smaller more remote ski area on the lee side of Mount Ruapehu, has a shorter season (July through October), more limited access, and fewer people. West of Ruapehu on the cape, the small **Manganui Ski Area**, on the slopes of stunning Mount Taranaki, is another North Island ski option.

*Details: Whakapapa Ski Area, Private Bag, Mount Ruapehu, 07-892-3738, fax 07-892-3732, snowphone 0900-99333, www.whakapapa.co.nz. Turoa Ski Resort, P.O. Box 46, Ohakune, 06-385-8456, snowphone 0900-99444, fax 06-384-8992. Tukino Mountain Clubs, 11 Gendon Rd., Titirangi, 09-817-8987, snowphone 06-387-6294.*

## Native Trees

About 30 kilometers northwest of Lake Taupo are groups of huge trees that survived the volcanic eruption of Mount Titiraupenga some 1,850 years ago. (Layers of ash and pumice destroyed most forests within 100 kilometers.) Some of the remaining rata and totara trees reach more than 50 meters high and measure four to five meters in diameter. Nearly a dozen people can stand inside the hollow core of one tree!

The rimu is actually a red pine that can reach a height of 50 meters. The giant rata tree begins life as an epiphyte, a twisting vine, then evolves into a great gnarled trunk. The northern rata, which can grow to 25 meters high, sports festive orange blossoms in spring. The totara, once favored by Maoris for canoes, has brown bark that hangs in stringy strips. Kahikatea, a white pine favored by native pigeons, sometimes grows taller than the red. Tawa, miro, matai, maire, and cabbage trees also grow in this area.

EcoSafaris has permission from Maori landowners to take visitors on treks past these trees. Led by guide John Paki Jr., these tours use four-wheel-drive vehicles to transport guests.

*Details: EcoSafaris, Lake Taupo, phone/fax 07-377-0127, mobile 025-787-840, fishwest@reap.org.nz, www.fishwest.co.nz.*

## Orakei Korako Geyserland and Cave

Beyond Lake Ohakuri, a lively colorful thermal area lies in a hidden valley. Cross the lake by boat and see the silica **Emerald Terrace** rising above the water in clouds of steam. Measuring 20 meters thick, the terrace extends below the lake for another 35 meters.

*Hikers trek through Tongariro National Park.*

Follow the walking track beyond the terrace and pass a sparkling geyser whose variable bursts may reach eight meters high. For your safety, stay on the track. Ahead lie three great fault scarps formed by an earthquake in about A.D. 131. You'll see the **Rainbow Terrace**, its colors created by hot-water algae, as well as small geysers and the **Hochstetter Pool**, named for a noted geologist.

From a lookout, take a closer look at the hot water flowing over the Emerald Terrace—more than 20 million liters per day. The **Golden Fleece Terrace**, known to the Maoris as Te Kapua—the cloud—is a low wide fault scarp 5 meters high and 40 meters long. Geysers occasionally erupt at its base, especially in the right-hand corner. You'll pass Elephant Rock, an old silica stump with a distinctive shape. The Artist's Palette, formed by eruptions between 15,000 and 8000 B.C., changes with variations in geothermal activity. Under certain conditions, hot water from the springs covers the silica flat, and patches of brown, green, yellow, orange, and pink algae grow around tiny clear blue pools. It is a beautiful sight.

Below the Ruatapu Cave is **Waiwhakaata**, which means Pool of Mirrors. The pool grants wishes, so it is said, guaranteed to come true if you place your hand in the water, make the wish, then keep it a total secret. The path then passes some mud pools before looping back toward the pier. Formed by heated clay, the mud pools bubble, plop, and steam. They become more active in winter and rainy weather. Pools may change locations with the migration of subterranean steam. The track through the valley ends by passing through forest, where you'll see ponga trees and get to examine a silver fern leaf, a symbol for New Zealand.

To reach the site from Taupo, follow SH 1 north to Wairakei. Head northwest when SH 1 turns toward Hamilton. After passing Palmer Mill Road, turn right on Tutukau Road. Turn left again at the sign for Orakei Korako Geyserland Resort. Total driving time is about one-half hour. You can also reach the site by floatplane from the Taupo lakefront.

**Details**: *Orakei Korako Geyserland Resort Ltd., Private Bag 3019, Rotorua, New Zealand, 07-378-3131, fax 07-378-0371, ok@reap.org.nz.*

## Tongariro Crossing

Called New Zealand's finest day hike, this fascinating route over the saddle between Mount Tongariro and Mount Ngauruhoe passes through, above, and into several volcanic craters. The **Red Crater** steams, while blue and green mountain lakes gleam as the sun's rays break through the clouds. The 15-kilometer track takes seven to eight hours to walk, claims the DOC.

The walk begins in tussock and scrub below Mangatepopo Hut; Mount Pukekaikiore rises on the right. Beyond it, you'll see magnificent Mount Ngauruhoe. The trail, which eventually accesses two of North Island's highest peaks, heads relentlessly upward through a valley. If you follow a short side track to **Soda Springs**, you'll find a moist oasis where flowers bloom in season.

Back on the track, you'll soon encounter the southwestern slope of the **Mangatepopo Saddle**. The terrain is marked by lighter older lava and is draped in places by darker newer lava flows from Mount Ngauruhoe. Mosses and lichen, followed by a succession of larger plants, cling to the rocky soil in this harsh environment. A side trail (two to three hours) leads partway up the slope of conical Mount Ngauruhoe, a 2,287-meter mountain covered with snow that tumbles over dark loose scoria.

From the main track, you can peer down into the vast empty **South Crater**. After more than a kilometer of easier flatter terrain, the track heads dramatically uphill. Loose chunks of rough volcanic rock make this a challenging climb. Wear gloves to protect your hands when the "wheels" formed by small round rocks send you rolling back downhill. You can grab a rough larger rock without scouring your hands.

The view from the top is worth all the effort. From the western rim of sulfurous **Red Crater**, the highest point on the track, you can see small lakes colored like jewels. The track then follows a loose sandy ridge toward much larger Blue Lake. To the left, a route marked with poles leads to the 1,967-meter summit of Mount Tongariro. Ahead on the left, stretches the wide **Central Crater**, spectacular in its desolation.

A walking stick will help you balance when the track descends over a narrow and treacherous sandy ridge high above the Emerald Lakes, which are colored by minerals. Ahead is Blue Lake, less often known by its long Maori name that means Rangihiroa's Mirror. (Rangihiroa explored this region in the mid-eighteenth century. One of his descendents, Te Heuheu Tukino IV, gave New Zealand the Tongariro land that became the country's first national park.)

The track skirts the slopes of **North Crater** before descending to the Ketetahi Hut in a series of switchbacks. From the upper loops you can see the hut below, although it may seem that you'll never reach it. Keep walking and you will. The hut's drinking water, toilets, and padded bunks will be very welcome.

Beyond the hut is **Ketetahi Springs**, an active thermal area that is still sacred to the Maoris who claim the waters have curative powers. There are hot pools, steam vents, and mud pools at Ketetahi, but from the track, you won't see much more than low wisps of steam. Te Heuheu did not include the thermal area in the Maori gift to New Zealand. Hikers are to keep to the track; walking about the *tapu* (sacred) Ketetahi Springs is prohibited.

The descent from Ketetahi Hut through tussock and scrub follows a rocky streambed; far below, Lake Rotoaira and Mount Pihanga form a lovely panoramic view. The descent continues for three or more kilometers. Abruptly, the track enters a lush lowland forest with streams rushing through it. In places, the forest floor is covered with tongues of hardened lava from an early flow. The steps seem endless, but keep on walking. The shuttle drivers are welcome sights in the parking lot.

Several companies provide transportation for the Tongariro Crossing and other walks. From Taupo, take Kiwi Value Tours, 07-378-9662, fax 07-378-9612 (NZ$30). From Turangi, contact the Bellbird Lodge, 07-386-8281 (NZ$18). From National Park, contact Howard's Lodge, Tongariro Crossing Transport, phone/fax 07-892-2827 (NZ$15).

A five-day Tongariro Trek summer package includes four days of hiking, transportation, lift rides, and scenic vistas—on a fine day you can see both coasts. Lodging is provided at the Grand Chateau near the Whakapapa Visitor Centre. The cost is NZ$995, with a single supplement of NZ$225. For more information contact 0800-733-944, fax 0800-733-955, grand.chateau@xtra.co.nz, www.trek.co.nz.

*Details: DOC, Tongariro/Taupo Conservancy, Private Bag, Turangi, 07-386-8607. Whakapapa Visitor Centre, Private Bag, Mount Ruapehu, 07-892-3729, fax 07-892-3814.*

## Volcanic Activity Centre

New Zealand may be the most tectonically influenced country on the planet. The Pacific Plate boundary passes under both islands, running from East Cape on North Island to Fiordland in the South. The relationship of the plates is in flux: they are being created at mid-ocean ridges and deformed or destroyed at boundaries, which are marked by mountain chains, faults, and undersea trenches.

Researchers disclose that "volcanoes are unpredictable and are not well understood." Recent eruptions are analyzed by radiocarbon dating. The dating of older eruptions—much less accurate—is done with radioactive potassium and uranium. The Taupo Volcano, below the lake, is monitored with networks of seismometers and lake-level records that measure tilt.

At the Volcanic Activity Centre north of Taupo, you can wander around hands-on exhibits that demonstrate various geological

Sally McKinney

*Mount Ngauruhoe*

phenomena. A vast three-dimensional map of the Taupo Volcanic Zone shows where various volcanoes are located in relationship to three volcanic centers: Mount Edgecumbe east of the Okataina Volcanic Centre; Mount Tauhara northeast of the Taupo Volcanic Centre; and the Tongariro Trio (Mount Tongariro, Mount Ngaurahoe, and Mount Ruapehu) within the Tongariro Volcanic Centre.

Several exhibits depict the relationship between tectonic plates; one takes the form of a jigsaw puzzle. One model shows how the movement of plates has affected New Zealand. Another exhibit shows how a geyser works; across the way is a tornado machine. A seismograph machine will help you monitor activity at Mount Ruapehu.

If you want still more information, book a tour with volcanologist Peter Otway who has had 30 years of experience, P.O. Box 1096, Taupo 2730, mobile 025-223-3524, after-hours 07-378-5901, volcanot@voyager.co.nz. A half-day cruise takes you into the western bays of Lake Taupo, where volcanic action has created spectacular cliffs and inlets. A half-day four-wheel-drive tour leads to pumice beaches formed by the Taupo Volcano. A full-day four-wheel-drive tour circles Tongariro National Park and includes a ride up the slopes of recently active Mount Ruapehu. With one more half-day you can follow the lake's eastern shore to Turangi, then see the stunning mountains of Tongariro National Park from the air. Book ahead—Otway operates only one tour at a time.

***Details****: Volcanic Activity Centre, Karetoto Rd. off Huka Falls Rd., Wairakei Park, P.O. Box 1689, Taupo, phone/fax 07-374-8375. Open daily. Staff can book Taupo Volcano Tours.*

▲  Jetboat excursion, Queenstown (©Trip/T. Bognar)

▲  Bottle-nosed dolphins (© Fiordland Travel)

▼  Stewart Island (© Tourism Northland)

▲  Kayakers on Milford Sound (© Sally McKinney)

▲ Northland children  (© Destination Northland Ltd.)

▼ Cathedral on the Octagon,
Dunedin (© Sally McKinney)

▼ Cape Reinga (© Destination
Northland Ltd.)

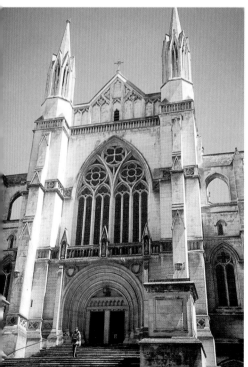

▲ Wild rose (© Jean-Paul Nacivet/Leo de Wys Inc.)

▼ Yellow-eyed penguins (© EDU-
DCC)

▼ Little spotted kiwi and eggs (© Steve
Vidler/Leo de Wys Inc.)

▲  Mt. Eden, Auckland (© Sally McKinney)

▼  Manawatu River at sunset  (© Charles Bowman/Leo de Wys Inc.)

▲  Rafting on the Tongariro River (© Trip/W Jacobs)

▼  Southern Alps (© Trip/W Jacobs)

▲  Lyttleton Harbour, Christchurch (© Paul Thompson/Photo Network)

## Western Bays Highway

The Western Bays Highway follows a wiggly course between the 80,344-hectare **Pureora Forest Park** and Lake Taupo, the island's largest lake. As you head north, you'll pass a vast stretch of native forest, rich with plant and bird life. On the right are the remote western inlets of the still-active crater lake.

You'll drive along the well-stocked Waihaha River, which flows from the forested Hauhungaroa Range into northwestern Lake Taupo. The river is known for fly fishing. During a leisurely stop enjoy food, drinks, and historic photos of the early days at the Tihoi Trading Post. Beyond Tihoi, turn left on Kakaho Road to reach the visitor center and learn more about the camping, swimming, and bush walking options in Pureora Forest Park. Continue on Kakaho Road and you'll come to a climbable tower for a great look at the forest canopy. There's a museum at the Pureora Forest Park headquarters, along with detailed maps and information. Northeast of the village of Pureora, a 30-minute walk through richly textured podocarp forest will lead you to the largest totara tree in the world.

Continue driving northeast (SH 30) to reach Mangakino and Lake Maraetai, one of a chain of lakes formed by damming the river. Beyond the lake is another vast stretch of forest. Follow SH 30 along Lake Whakamaru, then turn right onto SH 1. The road south to Taupo will take you along the Mangatutu Stream, past 897-meter Mount Manganui, and back into Taupo through the Wairakei Thermal Park.

Horse trekking, mountain biking, bird-watching, rock climbing, abseiling, and bush walks can be done in the area. Adventure Experience Outdoor provides instructors, guides, and rental equipment. Call Peter Shelton, 07-882-8136, for more information. For information about horse trekking call P&G Mist, 07-372-8009.

*Details: DOC, Pureora Field Centre, RD 7, Te Kuiti, 07-878-4773.*

## Whanganui River

The river originates on the alpine slopes of Mount Tongariro, then curves through bush and farmland before passing through the dense forests of **Whanganui National Park** and flowing into the Tasman Sea. In all, the mighty Whanganui drains 7,382 square kilometers of watershed. Maoris used the Whanganui in the early years to reach dense forested interior. Upriver you can see the remains of early European settlements.

Whanganui National Park, formed in 1987, encloses a section of the river and the second largest tract of forest on North Island. Overland tracks formerly used by Maoris and Europeans have recently been developed as hiking trails. You can take day trips on the river or longer overnight adventures. You can paddle independently or travel in a canoe or kayak flotilla with experienced guides. The most luxurious tours really are vacations, despite the remoteness, for the guides handle the work and prepare fresh delicious meals.

Some tour operators put in about 20 kilometers below the town of **Taumarunui**. If you've had no paddling experience, the guides will take time to teach you. On the first day you'll probably paddle past rural farmland and stop at historic sites. You might see waterfalls or explore little streams. Once you paddle into Whanganui National Park, you'll see mainly dense forest backed by rugged mountains 450 to 660 meters high. Along the way you can explore the **Kirikiri Steps**, the **Puraroto Caves**, and the **Bridge to Nowhere**. You'll also see several boat landings and can access two hiking trails. Several tour operators take out at Pipiriki where a road leads to **Raetihi**, a village along SH 4.

Paddlers who like to hike will enjoy the **Te Maire**, a two-hour loop walk through lovely bush. There are picnic grounds, a lookout tower, and natural pools for cool-off swims. The trailhead, upriver from Te Maire village and below Taumarunui, is accessible by boat.

The **Mangapurua Track** runs south from Whakahoro (Wade's Landing), curving away from the river before arriving at the Bridge to Nowhere/Mangapurua Landing. The walk takes three days; there are tent sites at either end. The **Matemateaonga Walkway** begins below Ramanui, downriver from the Mangapurua Track. This walk, which follows a ridge, also takes three days. You can book huts and shelters along the way. You can paddle to either trailhead or arrange transportation with a river tour operator. Well-equipped experienced paddlers and campers can organize their own downriver journeys. The upper Whanganui rapids may be class 1 or 2, described by one operator as "easy, bouncy, fun." Those with little experience will encounter fewer risks with the support of a group. In fact, tour operators will not rent gear to clients who lack adequate experience, protective clothing, and sufficient provisions.

Canoe Safaris, P.O. Box 180, Ohakune, 0800-2-PADDLE or 06-385-9237, fax 06-385-8758, canoe@voyager.co.nz, is a well-organized company with 20 years' experience. It uses roomy Canadian canoes, offers several variations of the Whanganui River adventure, and escorts groups into other areas. Ask about the Upper Mohaka Adventure (through a subalpine area with thermal hot pools) and Ngaruroro River Wilderness trips.

Also consider Yeti Tours, P.O. Box 140, Ohakune, 06-385-8197, yeti.tours@xtra.co.nz. They belong to the Whanganui River Commercial Operators Association and travel with a mountain rescue radio. They offer guided luxury and economy tours and rent equipment to qualified paddlers.

Whanganui River Jet, Wades Landing Outdoors, RD 2, Owhango, phone/fax 07-895-5995, mobile 025-797-238, also offers guided canoe trips, equipment rental, and ferry service up and down the river, including access to trails. A one-day tour includes kayak instruction, transportation into the national park, a downriver paddle on your own, and a jetboat ride to Whakahoro (Wade's Landing). The company also operates minibus shuttles and will move your car, motorbike, or camper from one location to another while you paddle.

Bridge to Nowhere Jet Boat Tours, RD 6, Pipiriki, Whanganui River, Whanganui National Park, phone/fax 06-385-4128, will take you to and from the Matemateaonga or Mangapurua Tracks by jet boat.

*Details: Whanganui National Park, Private Bag 3016, Whanganui, 06-345-2402.*

## TOUR OPERATORS

**Mountain Biking Adventures**, 07-378-7902, offers guided, north-of-Taupo tours by mountain bike to Craters of the Moon, Aratiatia Rapids, and Huka Falls on the Waikato River. They also rent 21-speed mountain bikes, helmets, water bottles, and detailed maps. (Mountain bikes are allowed on the riverside trail between Aratiatia and Huka Falls, but only hikers may use the riverside trail between the falls and the town of Taupo.)

Sally McKinney

*Below Huka Falls near Taupo*

**Lake Taupo Steamboat Cruises**, Taupo Wharf, Skipper Jack Grace, 07-378-3444 or 07-378-9000, offers one- and two-hour scenic cruises on the *Ernest Kemp*, a replica of a vintage lake steamer. Sights include Hot Water Beach, Maori rock carvings, and historic bays. During the cruise, the skipper comments on the boat, the lake, and local history. Printed commentary in French, German, Japanese, Chinese, Dutch, or Korean is available on boarding.

**Tongariro EcoTours**, the Rafting Centre on Atirau Rd., P.O. Box 281, Turangi, 0800-101-024 or 07-386-6409, fax 07-386-6445, rafting@xtra.co.nz, takes clients in a swamp boat to explore the southern wetlands of Lake Taupo. More than 40 species of birds and nine types of fish inhabit this watery marshland of raupo and flaxgrass. Using binoculars (which the guides provide) you're likely to see dabchicks, black teal, swans, and ducks. You might also sight a spotless crake, a bittern, or a banded rail.

The 17-kilometer Mount Ruapehu Downhill is organized by the **Ohakune Mountain Ride** company, 16 Miro St., P.O. Box 193, Ohakune, 06-385-8257, mobile 025-420-969. The company supplies a mountain bike that you can ride at whatever pace you choose. From the Turoa Ski Resort you'll have great views of mountains and glaciers. Along the road you'll pass alpine plants, volcanic rocks, and old lava flows. Lower you'll pass through beech forest. Toward the end you'll see podocarp forest—a mixture of rimu, matai, miro, and totara.

## CAMPING

For DOC campgrounds and huts contact Pureora Field Centre, RD 7, Te Kuiti, 07-878-4773; Whakapapa Visitor Centre, c/o Post Office,

Mount Ruapehu, 07-892-3729; and Whanganui National Park, Private Bag 3016, Whanganui, 06-345-2402.

Commercial campgrounds include **Golden Springs Holiday Park**, SH 5, Golden Springs, RD 2, Reporoa, 0800-240-403 or 07-333-8280, fax 07-333-7009. Located between Rotorua and Taupo this small campground has tent and powered sites, a restaurant, a children's playground, a seasonal swimming pool and two thermal pools, a thermal stream, and a fern glade. Two kilometers away is a boat ramp at the Waikato River. Rental boats are available.

**Taupo Motor Camp,** 15 Redoubt St., Taupo, 07-377- 3080, is a short walk from Taupo's boat harbor, yacht club, cafés, and seven-day shopping. It has 60 tent and 125 RV sites in a lakeview setting. Also in town is the **Taupo All Seasons Holiday Park**, 16 Rangatira St., P.O. Box 122, Taupo, 0800-777-272 or 07-378-4247, fax 07-378-1272, reservations@allseasons.nzl.com.

Another Taupo option, **Hilltop Caravan Park**, 39 Puriri St., Taupo, 07-378-5247, fax 07-378-5245, is a landscaped family camp. Some of its tent and RV sites have lake or mountain views. Guests enjoy a swimming pool in summer.

**Lake Taupo Holiday Park**, 28 Centennial Dr., P.O. Box 133, Taupo, 07-378-6870, fax 07-378-6870, has many large sites for tents and RVs on its 19.5 acres. The park also offers a children's playground, laundry facilities, a barbecue, and free showers.

**Turangi Cabins & Holiday Park**, Ohuanga Rd., P.O. Box 41, Turangi, 07-386-8754, fax 07-386-7162, has large private tent and RV sites in a parklike 2.8-hectare setting. You can walk from the park to town. Facilities include large drying rooms for wet clothing and gear.

**Whakapapa Holiday Park**, Tongariro National Park, Private Bag, Whakapapa Village, Mount Ruapehu, 07-892-3897, has a picturesque setting in a beech forest beside a mountain stream. The campground's 20 tent sites and 44 powered sites are near the Whakapapa Information Centre, trailheads, and the Whaka ski field.

**Taumarunui Camping Ground**, phone/fax 07-895-9345, has tent and powered campsites bordered by native bush along the Whanganui River. Besides bush walks, trout fishing, canoeing, and horseback riding in the area, there's a nearby glowworm grotto.

**Ohakune Holiday Park**, 5 Moore St., Ohakune, phone/fax 06-385-8561, stands at the gateway to Turoa ski field, Mount Ruapehu,

Sally McKinney

*Hikers make the daylong trek along the Tongariro Crossing.*

and Tongariro National Park. This quiet family camp has both powered and tent sites, a small stream, and mountain views. It's within walking distance of Ohakune town center.

The small **Garden Goodstead Holiday Park**, Oioi St., CM Box 98, Owhango 2656, phone/fax 07-895-4774, is a 30-minute drive from either Tongariro or Whanganui National Parks. It has two tent sites and five RV sites, a children's playground, and areas for outdoor games. Guests enjoy access to forest trails, mountain biking, horseback riding, fishing, canoeing, rafting, and skiing.

**Raetihi Motor Camp**, 06-385-4176, has tent and RV sites, a children's playground, and tennis courts nearby. You can also rent canoes and kayaks for outings in Whanganui River National Park.

## LODGING

You can book lodging at the Taupo Information Centre at Tongariro Street and Story Place or phone 07-378-9000, fax 07-378-9003. You can also book with the Turangi Visitor Centre, Ngawaka Pl., P.O. Box 34, Turangi, 0800-288-726 or 07-386-8999, turvin@nzhost.co.nz, www.laketaupo.tourism.co.nz/skiturangi.html.

**Lakeland of Taupo**, SH 1, Two Mile Bay, Taupo, 0800-378-389 or 07-378-3893, fax 07-378-3891, info@lakeland.co.nz, www.lakeland. co.nz, overlooks the lake with its distant scenic mountain vistas. The 64 guest rooms, restaurant, bar, outdoor pool, spa pools, and tennis court are set in landscaped grounds.

**Skotel Alpine Resort**, Whakapapa Village, Tongariro National

Park, 07-892-3719, fax 07-892-3777, set amid tussock in the upper end of the village, hosts skiers and hikers. Choices include standard or deluxe rooms or self-contained chalets. Guests enjoy a restaurant, bar, spa pool, saunas, and game room on the premises. A backpackers' wing has rooms with twin beds. The resort provides transportation up the mountain to the Whakapapa ski field. You can reach the Tongariro Crossing trailhead, horse trekking, and rock climbing sites via a 20-minute ride. Trout fishing, thermal pools, and whitewater rafting can be found about 30 minutes away at the Tongariro River.

**Pukenui Lodge**, Millar St., P.O. Box 24, National Park Village 2653, 07-892-2882, fax 07-892-2900, is a 20-minute drive to Whakapapa skiing and about 40 minutes from Turoa. In summer, guests fish for trout, walk the Tongariro Crossing route, or paddle the Whanganui River. Pukenui has a comfortable lodge with a stone fireplace. Options include singles and shared rooms. The cost of NZ$40 to NZ$60 includes breakfast and dinner or breakfast only. Expect higher rates during school holidays. Credit cards are accepted. Transportation departs daily to Tongariro hiking tracks and the Whanganui River.

**Rainbow Lodge**, 99 Titiraupenga St., Taupo, 07-378-5754, fax 07-377-1568, rainbowlodge@clear.net.nz, has comfortable backpacker lodging plus a kitchen, indoor/outdoor dining area, and lounge. Walk downhill from this well-regarded lodge and you'll be in city center, with its banks, shops, and lakefront cafés. The lodge also rents bikes.

**Powderhorn Chateau**, P.O. Box 222, Ohakune, 06-385-8888, fax 06-385-8925, is a well-furnished ski lodge with 30 rooms. Each room has a queen bed, lounge area, fridge, full bathroom, phone, TV, video channels, computer modem, and 24-hour room service. Two restaurants have indoor/outdoor dining, plus seating on two levels at the bar. There's also an indoor heated pool, ski shop, and mountain bike rental.

**Rimu Park Lodge and Chalets**, 27 Rimu St., Ohakune Junction, phone/fax 06-385-9023, near the road to the Turoa ski field, offers lodging in a 1914 villa or separate cabins. Studio units have private baths and double beds with a fold-out couch. More intriguing is the carriage studio, a restored 1934 railway car with one double and one single bed. Other chalets and carriages have assorted berths; some have potbellied stoves.

The **Ohakune YHA**, 15 Clyde St., Ohakune, 06-385-8724, fax 06-385-8725, has a view of Mount Ruapehu. Choices include family, twin, triple, and shared rooms.

**Loretta's Quality Guest House**, 135 Heu Heu St., Taupo, phone/fax 07-378-4927, is a B&B. Host Bridgette Thompson has five guest rooms and welcomes lodgers with tea and cookies. By arrangement she'll prepare additional meals. You can walk downtown and to the lakefront from the guest house.

Farm and homestays in the area give you various options. **Rural Holidays**, P.O. Box 2155, Christchurch, 0800-883-355 or 03-366-1919, fax 03-379-3087, farmstay@ruralhols.co.nz, handles reservations around the country. **New Zealand Farm Holidays**, P.O. Box 256, Silverdale, Auckland, 09-426-5430, fax 09-426-8474, farm@nzaccom.co.nz, www.nzaccom.co.nz, also covers the country and has several Taupo area listings.

## FOOD

Taupo residents who appreciate good food gather at the **Hobler Street Bar & Cafe**, 42 Tuwharetoa St., 07-378-0830. Different settings appeal to changing moods: a square wooden table for a solo lunch, cushions piled around the Table of the Long Knights for a festive dinner with friends, the Attic Bar for a tête-à-tête, and the Jungle Bar for a tribal celebration. The menu centers on chic, tasty, comfort foods: you might have hot juicy garlic sticks, a bucket of mussels, spicy potato skins, hot-and-cold salads, or a Hoblersaurus combo (rump steak, ribs, wings, and king prawns on a platter). Espresso drinks are served, but bring your own bottle of wine. Prices range from NZ$4.50 to NZ$25. The restaurant is open daily.

**Nonni's Waterfront Brasserie & Espresso Bar**, 3 Tongariro St. on the Taupo lakefront, 07-378-6894, has good espresso drinks, special breakfast dishes, and views of distant snow-capped peaks. Familiar foods like pancakes, omelettes, and French toast are given added flourishes and served in a classy yet casual open-air setting. The lunch and dinner menus emphasize Mediterranean foods. The selection of New Zealand wines includes various styles from large and boutique wineries around New Zealand.

**Cafe di Lago**, 10 Roberts St., Taupo, 07-377-1545, serves good breakfasts all day, plus an array of tasty snacks, light meals, and burgers. Your snack might be pesto bread, nachos, or chunkies (thick fried potatoes) with bacon, cheese, or sour cream or kumara fries with topping. Lunch might be a BLT with salad, vegetarian pasta, or a big hamburger with chunkies. Bruno Rossi espresso drinks go with dessert or stand alone. You'll get good value here, with prices from NZ$3.50 to NZ$12.50.

**Finch's Brasserie & Bar**, 64 Tuwharetoa St., 07-377-2425, is a casual yet upscale dining experience for all seasons. In summer, enjoy the leafy terrace. In winter, warm yourself by a glowing fire. Finch's has won awards for its beef and lamb dishes. The lunch menu features intriguing dishes centering on pasta, vegetables, beef, chicken, and salmon. The set-price lunch, which changes daily, is a good value. Dinner could be a four-course affair: soup followed by a smoked salmon plate or a mezzaluna, followed by an elaborate venison Osso Bucco, seafood bouillabaisse, or lamb shanks in puff pastry—come only when you're very hungry! Dessert might be a maple walnut cheesecake or a New Zealand cheeseboard. The restaurant bakes its own breads and smokes its meat and fish. Finch's has light and live background music on Friday and Saturday evenings.

**Valentino's**, Town Centre (above National Bank), Turangi, 07-386-8821, serves tasty dinners—New Zealand food with an Italian accent. Choose from several entrées or main courses or order a gourmet pizza. Besides classics like Spaghetti Bolognese, you might try prawns in garlic and herb butter, beef and basil ravioli in tomato sauce, or aged venison strips with sun-dried tomatoes, pine nuts, and capsicum. Main courses include salad and cooked veggies. The wine list features New Zealand and Italian wines.

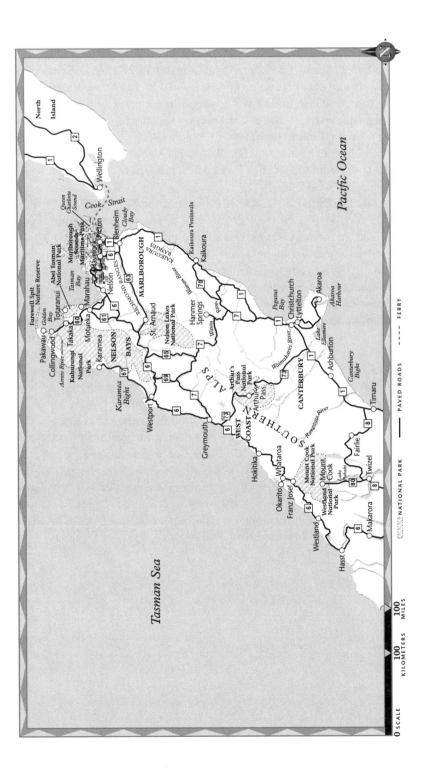

# CHAPTER 7

# Nelson and the West Coast

About 200,000 years ago South Island was joined to North Island. Cook Strait now separates New Zealand's two main islands, linking the Tasman Sea with the Pacific Ocean. View Cook Strait by air and you'll notice how the Tasman Bay dips down to Nelson, flanked on two sides by forested hills. Northwest of this city of 80,000, Cape Farewell and a lengthy sand spit shelters lovely Golden Bay. Northeast of Nelson lies the convoluted and moody seascape of Marlborough Sounds Maritime Park.

Arrive at Picton Harbour on Queen Charlotte Sound and you'll notice houses with bright tile roofs spilling down the hillsides. Follow the road west along winding river valleys and you'll see the bulky Richmond Range extending southwest and rising to 1,760 meters. Beyond tiny picturesque Havelock, the road passes log-strewn remnants of once-great forests and new-growth pines.

Nelson, with some of the best weather in New Zealand, has a harbor on Tasman Bay, a squared-off central district, and a backdrop of hillside and suburban homes. Beyond Nelson, the coast curves north to Motueka, a laid-back coastal village; the Kaiteriteri beach community; and Marahau, the southern gateway to Abel Tasman National Park. Many visitors go no farther than this lovely interplay of land and sea, where bush-clad mountains meet blue-green bays.

Cross the mountains on a valley road to reach the town of Takaka and scenic Golden Bay with its fine sand beach backed by mountains. Some nature enthusiasts stage their adventures from Takaka or from the tiny historic village of Collingwood. The windswept Farewell Spit, which extends into the bay, has become a bird sanctuary. The Heaphy Track and even more rugged trails run through mountainous Kahurangi National Park, a vast complex of forested slopes and stream-laced valleys.

The wild, fabulous, and often rainy west coast of South Island can be accessed from Karamea southwest to Haast Pass via a coastal road that links isolated towns bordered by snow-covered mountains. Glacial meltwater and rainwater feed the rocky icy rivers that rush toward the Tasman Sea. You can see striking rock formations, seal colonies, native rain forest, old mining towns, and bird sanctuaries along this coast, set against the stunning Southern Alps.

## HISTORY, CULTURE, AND CUSTOMS

Maori tribes were living along South Island's northeast coast by the sixteenth century. They explored the west coast as well, in a quest for pounamu, the greenstone jade. The Dutch explorer Abel Tasman visited the north coast of what is now South Island in 1642; Captain James Cook explored the region in the eighteenth century. It was Cook who noted the strait that connected the Tasman Sea and the Pacific Ocean. By the time mid-nineteenth-century whaling and mission stations were established, many Maoris had been killed in intertribal wars.

Settlers at Nelson had a difficult history. They lost 22 leaders in the Wairau Rebellion, then scrambled to survive when the New Zealand Company—the source of most jobs—went bankrupt in 1842. Once perceived as a backwater, Nelson now flourishes as a commercial center. It is a popular holiday destination (visitors can access three national parks) and retirement community. Artists and craftspeople flourish along this coast, residents enjoy an outdoor lifestyle that combines beaches and mountains, and residents and visitors alike appreciate fresh regional food, microbrews, and wines from Nelson and Marlborough.

# NATURE AND ADVENTURE ACTIVITIES

Whether you explore either coast or venture farther inland, the region has an amazing variety of appealing nature areas and an unusual number of choices. In the complex Marlborough Sounds Maritime Park, you can take a mail boat cruise into remote inlets where just one house is located. Your captain delivers the residents' letters, packages, and supplies. From French Pass you can explore rugged D'Urville Island by mountain bike or hiking trails or paddle a sea kayak to nearby island sanctuaries.

You can stay overnight at B&Bs along the Queen Charlotte Walkway. Nelson itself has garden parks, a riverside trail, and hiking tracks from the city into the surrounding hills. Bicycling is easy around Nelson's flat central district. Near Nelson you'll find lovely beaches and riverside parks. You can go horse trekking on a farm or sail on Tasman Bay.

Popular Abel Tasman National Park, busiest during New Zealand's summer holidays, is a year-round playground for paddlers,

*Yellow kayaks on Okarito Lagoon*

hikers, and beachcombers. There are distinctive granite formations in the park and sinkholes and caves nearby.

Development of Golden Bay has been slowed by limited access—to the delight of many. Highway 60, which cuts through the mountains, is the main road in. There are few organized tours here, so the area appeals to the self-entertaining. You can stage overnight adventures into Kahurangi National Park from Collingwood or book overnight lodging along Golden Bay and enjoy a variety of day hikes. You'll also find four-wheel-drive tours of the bird sanctuary on sandy Farewell Spit, a lonely windswept place to which only two tour operators have access. You'll encounter seals and migratory birds there in season.

Many of the mountains of Kahurangi National Park to the southwest reach more than 1,600 meters high. The vast forested interior of the park, cut by rivers and streams, has no roads, but several hiking trails run through it. Here you'll encounter beech forests, nikau palms, fields of tussock, and dense coastal rain forest. Keep in mind that the best access to Nelson Lakes National Park is from Highway 6 to Westport.

On the remote west coast, you can stroll along beaches, pan for gold, hike up river valleys, and visit bird reserves and a seal colony. High in the alpine lakes, you can go canoeing or paddle a raft down a rocky river.

## FLORA AND FAUNA

As in the rest of New Zealand, you'll encounter intriguing creatures away from more populous areas. This region of South Island, with its irregular shoreline, offshore islands, forested mountains, and isolated west coast, has several important wildlife habitats.

The outer islands of Marlborough Sounds, buffeted by powerful Cook Strait winds and currents and isolated from the mainland, have retained their wild character. On D'Urville Island, which stretches for 27 kilometers from Sauvage Point to Cape Stephens, there are wind-bent forests of mahoe, kohekohe, and ngaio. Dolphins swim offshore, and you can also see colonies of seals. Gulls, shearwaters, petrels, gannets, and terns are commonly seen; the king shag, giant petrel, and mollymawk less often. The tuatara, a creature whose ancestors coexisted with dinosaurs, lives on Stephens Island, a wildlife sanctuary. Unique to Stephens is a frog with dark bulging eyes. Fairy prions, also called dove petrels, make the island their home.

Near Golden Bay you'll see species of flora and fauna whose ancestors crossed the land bridge from North Island or migrated from the south during one of several ice ages. You'll also encounter nikau palm trees, New Zealand's only native species of palm. You might also happen upon a large carnivorous bush snail, another unusual native species. On Farewell Spit, a curved elongated arm of sand, more than 100 species of birds—many of them migratory—visit at some time during the year. You'll probably find flocks of oyster-catchers or bar-tailed godwits feeding along the shore. Here and there, you're also likely to find a seal or two napping on the sand or lumbering off toward the water.

## VISITOR INFORMATION

A huge amount of travel information is available, especially in Nelson where tours around the area are heavily promoted. Rather than try to cover the whole region, choose a few appealing areas, then decide how best to explore.

Destination Marlborough, 03-577-5520, fax 03-577-5530, dest. marlborough@xtra.co.nz, www.destination.co.nz/marlborough, has information on this area of islands, peninsulas, inlets, and bays. Ask about the Queen Charlotte Track and tours of the Marlborough wine region. Tourism Nelson, 03-546-6228, fax 03-546-9008, info@tourism nelson.co.nz, www.nelson.net.nz, can help you match the region's natural areas with suitable activities. Tourism West Coast, First Floor Regent Theatre Building, Greymouth, West Coast, 03-768-6633, fax 03-768-7680, tourismwc@minidata.co.nz, can also help you locate what you're after in this rainy, isolated, and very beautiful region.

Several DOC offices can provide maps, trail descriptions, book-ings at DOC huts, and information on getting to and from remote parks and trails. Contact the Picton Field Centre, DOC, Nelson Conservancy, 03-573-7582, for information on Marlborough Sounds. (Note that the D'Urville Valley Track is in Nelson Lakes National Park, not on D'Urville Island in Marlborough Sounds.) The Havelock

Field Centre, DOC, Nelson Conservancy, 03-574-2019, is near several walking tracks that suit various fitness levels. Contact the Motueka Field Centre, DOC, Nelson Conservancy, 03-528-9117, for information about Abel Tasman and Kahurangi National Parks. The Takaka Field Centre on Golden Bay, DOC, Nelson Conservancy, 03-525-8026, is another source of information.

## GETTING AROUND

Walking, bicycling, and local bus service will get you around Nelson. Suburban Bus Lines, 03-548-3290, covers the area from its Lower Bridge Street terminal. InterCity, 03-548-1539, and Mount Cook Landline, 03-548-2304, provide connections to Greymouth, Picton, and Christchurch. Abel Tasman National Park Enterprises, 03-548-7801, is a large operator with service to Motueka, Takaka, and the park, plus boat transport to Awaroa Lodge and other park locations.

## NATURE AND ADVENTURE SIGHTS

### Abel Tasman National Park

If you have just one day to explore Abel Tasman National Park, you might travel by water taxi to Anchorage Bay, explore the Torrent River delta by kayak, and perhaps go into the bays beyond. With two or three days, you can explore some of the 15 bays, coves, and inlets in the park between Totaranui and Marahau.

The main entrance to the park is at **Marahau**. Several sea kayak tour operators and outfitters are based here. If you choose the sheltered aquamarine water between Coquille Bay and Watering Cove, you can polish your paddling technique. You'll pass Fisherman Island and the larger Adele Island. Here and there you might paddle along with seals, catch sight of a dolphin, or pass little penguin nests—depending on the season.

At **Torrent Bay**, across from the lovely Anchorage, you can follow a track upriver to Cleopatra's Pool or follow another route to Pitt Head and Te Pukatea Bay, where you'll find signs of early Maori habitation. Depending on your mood, and the tides, you might remain in the estuary watching wading birds feed in the mudflats as they return to their roosts.

Beyond Torrent Bay lie more watery coastal indentations: Frenchman's Bay, used for boat-building in the nineteenth century; Sandfly Bay, fed by the Falls River; Falls River Lagoon; and Bark Bay, which has nearby waterfalls.

The marine reserve begins beyond Bark Bay, enclosing the area beyond **Tonga Island** and reaching to Awaroa Head. A colony of New Zealand fur seals inhabits Tonga Island. If you're tired from paddling, you can beach your craft at **Onetahuti** (Tonga Bay) and walk to **Awaroa Lodge**. Note that this hike may be a one- to three-hour journey, depending on the tides in the Awaroa estuary.

The Awaroa Lodge complex has an appealing restaurant with good fresh food. Walking trails fan out from the lodge in several directions. Some hikers take their meal breaks here, and others relax with coffee in a French press pot, while birds stand poised waiting to dive for crumbs.

Beyond Awaroa Bay the coast is more regular, yet is still bordered by sandy beach. Few paddlers come this far from Marahau. If you reach Totaranui Beach, consider following the hiking track up Gibbs Hill for a view of **Farewell Spit**.

Several companies offer guided trips and rent equipment. Abel Tasman Kayaks Limited, Marahau Beach, RD 2, Motueka, 03-527-8022, fax 03-527-8032, atk@kayaktours.co.nz, www.kayaktours.co.nz, has years of experience, plus concern for the environment and your safety. Their three-day, remote, guided, nature tour involves camping on the beach, kayaking with seals, walking through the bush past scenic rock formations, visiting the shag colony, and exploring the marine reserve. The company provides camping and cooking gear; you bring your own food. The cost is NZ$295. Their four-day kayak and walk tour, fully catered, involves camping plus last-night accommodation at Awaroa Lodge.

Abel Tasman National Park Enterprises, 265 High St., Motueka, Nelson, 03-528-7801, fax 03-528-6087, info@abeltasman.co.nz, www.abeltasman.co.nz, operates sea kayak tours, along with water taxis and an array of park package options.

Ocean River Adventure Company, Marahau Beach, RD 2 Motueka, 03-527-8266, fax 03-527-8006, ocean.river@xtra.co.nz, http://webnz.

com/ocean_river, is a solid family-run operation. Southern Exposure Sea Kayaking, 71B Tahunanui Dr., Nelson, 03-546-4038, fax 03-546-4048, mobile 025-374-037, a.rynn@southexp-seakayak.co.nz, www.nzkayak. co.nz, also operates in Marlborough Sounds.

Anyone on a boat cruising past **Tonga Island** is likely to spot a few seals basking on rocks. They rest and dry their fur in the sun, then dive back into the water to feed. You might want to swim with them. Under the terms of the Marine Mammal License, no one is allowed to touch or feed the seals or to coax them from the rocks into the water. Yet seals are curious and playful and just might plunge in when they see you swimming. It's amazing how the seals, which lumber about on the rocks, become so graceful in water.

Albie Clapshaw and Paula Armstrong, based in Marahau, run the Abel Tasman Seal Swim, which has morning departures (afternoons on request). The swim can be linked with other park experiences like hiking or sea kayaking. For instance, after a seal swim, you might walk the coastal track back to Marahau (this could take two to four hours). Before you go swimming with the seals, you'll need to put on your swimsuit. The tour company provides full wetsuits, snorkels, masks, and fins. You might also see dolphins around, but there's no guarantee. The eight-meter boat has covered and open seating. On a scenic tour you'll learn about the area's history and more about marine mammals.

For more information contact Abel Tasman Seal Swim and Water Taxi, Marahau Valley Rd., RD 2, Motueka, 0800-527-8136, phone/fax 03-527-8136. Seal swims range from NZ$65 to NZ$83.

*Details*: DOC, Abel Tasman National Park, P.O. Box 97, Motueka, 03-528-9117.

## Abel Tasman Coastal Track

One of New Zealand's Great Walks, this trail leads past aquamarine bays with borders of golden sand. On the route between Totaranui and Marahau, you'll cross forested peninsulas, see granite rock formations, and skirt tidal estuaries. Weather in the area is generally favorable, and the track is open year-round. High forested mountains rise on one side; you often have a splendid scenic view on the other.

Many walkers begin with a cruise from Kaiteriteri to Totaranui, along a scenic stretch of coast. Check the tide tables at Totaranui

*Tonga Island Marine Reserve off the coast of Abel Tasman National Park*

before you start. If the tides are right you can walk from the beach along Goat Bay to the **Awaroa estuary**, the largest in Abel Tasman National Park, where many shorebirds feed. Follow the track across the inlet at low tide to reach the peninsula at Awaroa Bay. Several tracks around the lodge lead back to the estuary or through native bush.

The coastal track continues over the Tonga saddle and passes an abandoned stone quarry and granite archways washed by the sea. Along the coast you'll see regenerating forest in various stages of succession. Fantails, tuis, and wood pigeons inhabit the forests. Clearwater creeks run through bush, then empty into small bays bordered by sheltered beaches. Picnics are fun—but first, spread on insect repellent to ward off sand flies.

You might see paddlers exploring **Torrent Bay**, fed by a mountain river. Some visitors walk inland through native forests to see the waterfalls. Park forests are mixtures of species, including southern rata, manuka, kowhai, and rewa rewa; visitors experience diverse habitats that extend from the seacoast upriver to the hills. The last

173

segment of the coastal trail leads to Marahau; you'll see trees framing more estuaries, crystalline coves, and offshore islands.

Despite the natural setting, hikers are not isolated. Some do only day walks; others combine walking with sea kayak experiences. Expensive catered and guided trips are popular, but many hikers find it satisfying to hike on their own. DOC huts are found along the way, plus lodging and a good restaurant at **Awaroa Bay**. Trampers can arrange for water-taxi arrivals and departures, with pickup points at designated beaches.

The high season for guided walks is mid-October through mid-April. On a guided walk you will carry only lunch and your daypack items. Other luggage will be taken ahead to the lodge. The tour company handles meals, lodging, and transportation.

Abel Tasman National Park Enterprises, Ltd., P.O. Box 351, Motueka, Nelson, 0800-221-888 or 03-528-7801, fax 03-528-6087, info@abeltasman.co.nz, www.abeltasman.co.nz, organizes three- and five-day guided walks and three- and five-day kayaking-trekking tours. Rates run from NZ$580 to NZ$1,100 and include daypacks and 30-liter luggage bags, plus bus transport to and from Motueka or Nelson. Trampers will need proper footgear and outdoor clothing, warm fleece layers, and waterproof rain gear.

Abel Tasman Seafaris, Marahau, RD 2, Motueka, 03-527-8083, fax 03-527-8282, mobile 025-397-990, offers water-taxi service, scenic cruises, and day walks.

Abel Tasman Coachlines, departing from 27 Bridge St., Nelson, 03-548-0285 or 03-528-8850, offers service to Kaiteriteri, Totaranui, Marahau, and other area destinations.

The Kahurangi Bus, East Takaka Rd., Takaka, 03-525-9434, http://nelson.net.nz/kahurangi, has daily service to more than a dozen locations between Nelson and Collingwood, including Kaiteriteri Beach, the Marahau Park Cafe, and the Totaranui Information Centre/Beach.

*Details*: *Abel Tasman National Park, P.O. Box 97, Motueka, 03-528-9117.*

## Farewell Spit

At the end of Cape Farewell, there's a broad expanse of smooth mounded sand, topped by blowing wisps. The marine blue Tasman

Sea rolls in from the left. On the right are sand dunes—a few capped by grasses, others blown bare. Beyond this low landscape of muted colors you can catch an occasional glimpse of steel blue mountains beyond Golden Bay. On a clear day, you might even see elegant snow-capped **Mount Taranaki**.

The Original Farewell Spit Safari, one of two tours that will take you onto this spit, begins at **Collingwood**, a village on **Golden Bay**. Established in 1946, the tour blends education and entertainment. You'll board a vintage R. L. Bedford, a sturdy, trucklike vehicle, for the 55-kilometer ride. Beyond the village you'll see Golden Bay on the right and bush-clad mountains on the left. Ponga trees thrive in the forest; black swans glide on a pond feeding on eelgrass, snails, and small fish. Wading birds stand in shallow tidal waters.

The inner beach along Golden Bay has a covering of cockleshells. The outer beach, along the Tasman Coast, has a border of shifting sand with marram and other grasses sometimes topping the dunes. Pinago, which also grows on the sand, is a native sedge; Maoris have traditionally used it for weaving. Along the shore you might see white-fronted terns, black oystercatchers with red bills, or "white" oyster-catchers, actually patterned in white and black.

On the bayside beach beyond Pakawau, whales sometimes beach themselves. More whales soon join them, and these great beached mammals draw crowds who watch or help with the rescue.

Beyond the beach lies the **Farewell Spit Nature Reserve**, a wet-land of international importance. This wildlife sanctuary is 27 kilo-meters long, and more than 100 species of birds feed or make nests in its bleak windswept environment. Some have migrated from Siberia, others from elsewhere in New Zealand. A walking track leads into the reserve along the bayshore. However, only licensed tour operators in four-wheel-drive vehicles are permitted to visit the lighthouse and the gannet colony nearby. Depending on the wind, weather, tides, and time of day, you'll see a varying number of birds on the sand spit.

About 2,000 turnstones inhabit the spit; you might also see god-wits, curlews, banded dotterels, black shags, white herons, gannets, or spoonbills. Both the white herons and the spoonbills, now referred to as Australasian, migrated to New Zealand from Australia. In sum-mer you might see the Caspian tern with its wingspan of 1.5 meters, a species that migrates to and from Siberia.

At the end of the spit lives one of four gannet colonies in New Zealand. Adults have wingspans of two meters. The sand spit—the end is the most northerly point on New Zealand's South Island—was noted by Captain Cook during his visit.

The family-run Original Farewell Spit Safari, Tasman St., P.O. Box 15, Collingwood, Golden Bay, 0800-808-257 or 03-524-8257, fax 03-524-8939, offers a variety of tours. The Farewell Spit Nature Tour, P.O. Box 61, Collingwood, 0800-250-500 or 03-524-8188, fax 030-524-8091, offers a similar tour in more modern vehicles.

*Details: DOC, Private Bag, Nelson, 03-546-9335.*

## Franz Josef Glacier

This famous glacier in **Westland National Park** is a vast river of ice, 11 kilometers long, that's shifting slowly toward the Tasman Sea. You can take Glacier Road to the parking lot near the end, do the 15-minute **Sentinel Rock Walk**, and view the glacier's terminal face from a wooden gallery. Park farther down Glacier Road, at the Alex Knob parking lot, and you can hike the **Roberts Point Track** to another overlook above the valley. Other trails between Franz Josef village and the glacier follow riverbed gravel, explore lateral and terminal glacial moraines, pass old water tunnels, cross rivers on swinging bridges, and lead to kettle lakes.

The glacier itself has been formed by a natural cyclic process: rain and snow brought by winds from the Tasman Sea splash onto alpine slopes and form a moving ice river that sends meltwater into the Waiho River, which flows into the Tasman Sea. The Franz Josef has variable terrain. From the lower face to the top, sinkholes, crevasses, ice pinnacles, blue ice, and névé snow can be found in different areas. An awesome reminder of the powerful forces that rearranged landscapes during former ice ages, the glacier ends just 19 kilometers from the sea.

Bill Hayward, Graham Place, Franz Josef village, 03-752-0793, offers guided walks (one or two hours long) to view the glacier and the terminal face. Other options include a Waiho Valley tour, a visit to Okarito and the lagoon, and a tour of Fox Valley.

*Details: Franz Josef Area Office and Visitor Centre, DOC, P.O. Box 14, Franz Josef Glacier, 03-752-0796, fax 03-752-0797. A brochure titled "The*

*Glacier Region" has maps and details about hiking in the area.*

## French Pass

From the deck of a ferry crossing Cook Strait you'll get an unexpected introduction to Marlborough Sounds, with its intricate pattern of rugged peninsulas, bush-draped islands, and tranquil blue-water bays. The area is rich in history and nature experiences. Some homes here are remote and surrounded by dense bush, without access by road. Instead, supplies and mail are delivered by boat, and children attend school via correspondence courses.

*Franz Joseph Glacier in Westland National Park*

French Pass Road follows a peninsula along Admiralty Bay. The road ends at a narrow strait across from **D'Urville Island**, a large nature reserve surrounded by marine reserves and wildlife sanctuary islands. The French explorer Dumont D'Urville, for whom the island was named, visited the area in 1827.

You'll board a small boat on a French Pass Sea Safari and follow a personalized itinerary that includes D'Urville Island's intricate coastline and offshore islands. A narrow strait, French Pass, separates D'Urville from the peninsula. According to Maori legend, a cormorant formed the waterway.

As you cruise, you might see an occasional fishing boat or a dinghy moored in a sheltered cove. At Catherine Cove, you'll find a resort at which guests arrive and depart by boat. You'll pass the Trio Islands, a wildlife sanctuary, and a monument to Captain Cook, an early visitor. On forested D'Urville you'll find a mountain bike track and walking trails, but no roads. **Stephens Island**, northeast and offshore from D'Urville, has become a wildlife sanctuary. The island has a lighthouse and supports the tuatara, Stephens Island frog, and other species.

Ornithologist Rob Schuckard, an expert on the king shag (cormorant), one of several rare species in the area, leads the Sea Safari Outer Sounds Bird Trip. The marine environment is rich in nutrients, and bird life abounds. On this small boat cruise you're likely to see shearwaters, gannets, petrels, terns, and little blue penguins, along with the shags. On some tours you might also sight a giant petrel, mollymawk, or cape pigeon. In addition to the birds, bottlenosed dolphins, orca whales, blue sharks, and fur seals can sometimes be seen. Late spring and summer are perhaps the best times to go.

French Pass Sea Safari also offers water-taxi transport to walking tracks and mountain bike trails, guided sea kayak tours, dinghy or kayak equipment rental, sport-fishing trips, and snorkeling excursions.

*Details: French Pass Motel & Sea Safaris, RD 3 Rai Valley, Marlborough Sounds, New Zealand, phone/fax 03-576-5204. Hotel accommodations run NZ$68 to NZ$88 per unit. Nature tours begin at NZ$40 per person. One-day guided sea kayak trips cost NZ$85 per person, with a minimum of two people.*

*The DOC has huts on D'Urville Island; call Picton Field Centre, 03-573-7582, for information.*

## Heaphy Track

A network of walking tracks leads into the interior of New Zealand's second largest—and newest—national park, **Kahurangi National Park**. There are no roads in the park. It contains 50 percent of all New Zealand plant species and 80 percent of the country's alpine species. Mount Gouland rises to 1,468 meters.

Named for Charles Heaphy, an explorer who followed a coastal route from Golden Bay to Westland, the 77-kilometer Heaphy Track heads upward into the **Aorere River Valley**, crosses the Perry Saddle and Gouland Downs, then descends along the Heaphy River. You'll walk a historic route through beech forest, past red tussock, unusual glacial karst (limestone) formations, and coastal podocarp, before reaching the Tasman coast.

A special feature of the track is the visit to **Gouland Downs**, some 30 kilometers long, the habitat for more than 400 species of native plants. Dominated by red tussock and cut by a rocky stream, the Downs has an array of herbs, orchids, and lilies blooming in season.

October to April is the season for this walk; allow four or five days. Some hikers travel with a companion. Some hire hiking guides to organize transportation, supply food, provide trail information, and share knowledge of Kahurangi National Park—its geology, history, flora, and fauna. Along the trail, you might see kea (the alpine parrot), kaka, blue ducks, or yellow-crowned parakeets.

Other possible hikes involve the **Wangapeka Track**, known for its scenic beauty, and the lengthy **Leslie/Karamea Track**, which runs through awesome backcountry and might require six to seven days to complete.

Bush & Beyond, Orinoco, RD 1, Motueka, New Zealand, 03-528-9054 or 03-526-8856 (both are residence numbers), fax 03-526-6093, works toward conservation and preservation of this unique area. The company offers tours of varying lengths, suitable for people of different fitness levels. They can also organize trips around special interests: photography, birds, rare plants, etc.

Kahurangi Guided Walks, Dodson Rd., RD 1, Golden Bay, phone/fax 03-525-7177, croxfords@xtra.co.nz, takes small groups along tracks in the Kahurangi wilderness. These could be short walks through forests, meadows, along beaches, or into gold-mining areas; special interests can be accommodated. The operators also run a homestay near Takaka.

Trek Express, 03-540-2042, offers four-wheel-drive service for selected Kahurangi National Park tracks. Transport to and from Wangapeka, Mount Arthur, and the Cobb Valley runs NZ$59 to NZ$69.

*Details: DOC, Kahurangi National Park, Private Bag, Nelson, 03-546-9335.*

## Okarito Lagoon

Okarito Lagoon, fed by freshwater lakes, is New Zealand's largest unmodified wetland. More than 70 species of birds have been identified here. With its 3,240 hectares of shallow water, the lagoon is the main feeding ground for white herons that nest in the **Waitangiroto Nature Reserve**.

Okarito Nature Tours, Private Bag 777, Hokitika, phone/fax 03-753-4014, operates small-boat tours and rents kayaks. Paddlers can explore the Okarito Lagoon, tidal flats, narrow channels, and remote inlets of the estuary.

White Heron Sanctuary Tours, P.O. Box 19, Whataroa, West Coast, 0800-523-456 or 03-753-4120, fax 03-753-4087, guides visitors into the sanctuary beside the Waitangi Taona River, where white herons nest between November and February among little shags, royal spoonbills, and other species. You'll be guided along a 500-meter boardwalk through native rain forest.

Explore the Okarito Lagoon and, depending on tides, you might find black-billed gulls or oystercatchers near the mud flats in the late afternoon. The seawater nearest the outlet for the lagoon gives way to freshwater further in. Beyond a peninsula, coastal forest—southern rata, kahikatea, rimu, ponga, and cabbage trees—casts reflections onto still dark water. An eel might be seen just below the surface. You might also find a tui feeding on nectar from a kowhai tree or photograph a native pigeon high on a branch.

Beyond the lagoon is coastal forest—lush rain forest in a tangle of textured greens. Beyond that the forested slopes lead to melting glaciers and rocky blue-water rivers. Even farther beyond you'll see the jagged peaks of the Southern Alps, majestic mountains capped with snow.

**Details**: *Franz Josef Glacier Visitor Centre, P.O. Box 14, Franz Josef, 03-752-0796.*

## TOUR OPERATORS

Small, family-run **Dolphin Watch Marlborough**, P.O. Box 197, Picton, South Island, 03-573-8040, fax 03-573-7906, offers guided bus and boat tours into Queen Charlotte Sound, home to three species of dolphins at different times of the year, seals in winter, and, occasionally, orca whales. The company's four-hour Motuara Island-Ship Cove Tour involves a cruise plus a walk through a bird sanctuary. The cost per adult is NZ$55. The Birdwatcher's Special, also four hours, takes you through the Motuara Sanctuary and includes visits to a fluttering shearwater nesting site and the roosting place of rare king shags. The cost per adult is NZ$65.

**NZ Explorer Cruise**, P.O. Box 40, Picton, 0800-272-452 or 03-573-5225, fax 03-573-5255, mobile 025-484-197, offers three-day cruises on the 38-meter *New Zealand Explorer*. Cabins, on either A or C deck, have private facilities. Guests enjoy the dining area and a licensed bar. You'll

Sally McKinney

*Children wait for a boat in remote Marlborough Sounds.*

cruise past Marlborough's watery landscapes or visit nature sites in the ship's tender. The cost is NZ$425 to NZ$530 per person for shared cabins; NZ$775 to NZ$895 for single cabins. The price includes meals.

The **M.V.** *Mavis*, a classic launch made of New Zealand kauri, 65A Main Rd., Havelock Outdoors Centre, Havelock, phone/fax 03-574-2114, mobile 025-774-871, is a 40-foot boat that's been used for whaling, fishing, delivering mail, and work at a mussel farm. Day cruises involve bush walks, picnics, swimming, and visits to a mussel farm.

**Stonehurst Farm Horse Treks**, Haycock Rd., RD 1, Nelson, 030-542-4121, fax 030-542-3823, offers tours that vary in length, from the one-hour scenic Rambler Tour to a four-hour Cattle Muster. After a ride through rivers and past fossil beds, you can relax over tea in the historic Stonehurst stables.

**Sail Tasman,** 13A Palm Ave., Stoke, Nelson, 03-547-2754, sail-tasman@xtra.co.nz, http://webnz.co.nz/sailtasman, is run by a well-qualified South Pacific skipper who'll take you on day sails or overnight adventures on the yacht *Quadriga*. The itinerary is personalized; the yacht accommodates up to eight people on day sails and five on longer trips. The cost runs NZ$35 to NZ$40 for short trips and NZ$295 per person for a two-day sail.

**Aorere Adventure Tramps and Walks**, Pakawau, Collingwood, Golden Bay, 03-524-8040, is run by Jonathan and Katie Hearn, who also operate the Inn-let (see Lodging). They offer guided one- to four-day walks into the Aorere Goldfields, through rain forest, over the Kaituna Trail, and along an underground river. The cost is NZ$55 for shorter walks, NZ$140 for an overnight with camping and food.

**Norwest Adventures**, Westport, 0800-116-686 or 03-789-6686, fax 03-789-8922, offers caving adventures that might involve a walk through a cave system, tubing, abseiling, crawling through narrow passages, a visit to a glowworm display, or a walk through native bush.

# CAMPING

**Parklands Marina Holiday Park**, 10 Beach Rd., Waikawa Marina, Picton, phone/fax 03-573-6343, parklands@powerglobe.de, operates a spacious campground on seven acres of greenery, including stands of native bush. There are tent and powered sites plus on-site caravans, cabins, and flats. Guests can use the kitchen and fridge, a dining room, and laundry facilities. You can phone for a free pickup from the ferry or town. The staff also speaks German, French, and Italian.

Located 15 kilometers west of Havelock village, **Pinedale Motor Camp**, Wakamarina Valley, RD 1, Canvastown, Havelock, 03-574-2349, has 28 tent sites and 22 powered sites plus other lodging set in a peaceful forest. Guests have use of kitchen and locker fridges, a dining room, laundry and shower facilities, and entertainment areas. Children will enjoy the playground and farmyard with small animals.

Nelson Valley Motor Camps has two campgrounds in native bush settings. **Brook Valley Motor Camp**, 4.5 kilometers from city center, P.O. Box 294, Nelson, 03-548-0399, fax 03-548-7582, has tent and powered sites, 24 lodging units, and a swimming pool. **Maitai Valley Motor Camp**, six kilometers from city center, P.O. Box 294, Nelson, 03-548-7729, open summer only, has tent and powered sites plus five lodging units and river swimming.

**Marahau Beach Camp**, RD 2, Motueka, 03-527-8176, fax 03-527-

8176, at the southern entrance to Abel Tasman National Park, has RV sites, a few tent sites, and a small lodge. Kayak hire and water-taxi service can be organized at the camp.

The large **Pohara Beach Holiday Park**, Abel Tasman Dr., RD 1, Takaka, 03-525-9500, fax 03-525-8689, has 99 tent sites and 136 powered sites plus cabins and motel units. The beachfront property, located on Golden Bay, has five hectares of campsites. Facilities include a children's playground, boat ramp, and barbecue. The owners reside on the property, and the staff speaks several languages. A restaurant across from the camp is open seven days.

**Pakawau Beach Park**, Collingwood-Puponga Rd., SH 60, Pakawau, Golden Bay, 03-524-8327, fax 03-524-8509, sits by the beach 15 kilometers from the village of Collingwood. The campground has a range of facilities plus a children's playground, boat ramp, and general store. A café sits across the road. Guests can enjoy horse trekking, kayaking (available on-site), windsurfing, nearby walking tracks, and a safari to Farewell Spit.

**Franz Josef Holiday Park & Waiho Motel**, Main Rd., P.O. Box 27, Franz Josef, 03-752-0766, fax 03-752-0066, lies 500 meters from town near the Glacier Access Road. Set in 7.2 acres of forest with a backdrop of mountains, the campground has 60 tent sites and 34 powered sites plus cottages, flats, and motel units that sleep several people. Facilities are modern and include microwave kitchens, a laundry room, lounge, and game room. Hosts can book activities.

The DOC runs a number of campgrounds and huts. For the Queen Charlotte Walkway, call Picton Field Centre, 03-573-7582. For the Abel Tasman Tracks (coastal and inland), call the Motueka Field Centre, 03-528-9117, or the Takaka Field Centre, 03-525-8026. For the Heaphy Track, Wangapeka Track, or Leslie/Karamea Track, call Takaka Field Centre, 03-525-8026, or Karamea Field Centre, 03-782-6852. For the Franz Josef and the glacier region, call Franz Josef Waiau Area Office, 03-752-0796.

# LODGING

The **Rutherford Hotel**, Trafalgar Square, Nelson, 0800-822-888 or 03-548-2299, fax 03-546-3003, escape@rutherfordhotel.co.nz, is

# NEW ZEALAND WINES
# AND WINE REGIONS

*New Zealand has about 250 wine-making enterprises. Most restaurants provide a wine list, including domestic wines, with their menus. The history of the New Zealand wine industry dates to 1825, when James Busby, a British official and an avid gardener, published a book on viticulture. Since the mid-twentieth century, immigrant wine makers from Europe have made important contributions to the industry. New Zealand white table wines like Cloudy Bay are known overseas, and Cabernet Sauvignons and other reds are increasingly respectable. The wine industry now ranges from big producers like Montana and Corbans to boutique enterprises like Mudbrick and Stonyridge.*

*Wine aficionados can learn much by keeping a guidebook handy throughout their travels. In The Penguin Good New Zealand Wine Guide, updated annually, Vic Williams describes and rates the country's wines. He even suggests pairings with foods.*

*Travel around New Zealand and you'll find several wine-making regions on North Island: they include Auckland, Hawke's*

located in the city center. Pleasant rooms have private baths, TVs, and tea- and coffee- making equipment. The large lobby has ample seating and adjoins Rutherford Cafe and Bar. You can enjoy good coffees, pastries, and meals here or dine in the Cathedral Restaurant. Rates from NZ$95.

**Trailways Motor Inn**, 66 Trafalgar St., Nelson, 03-548-7049, fax 03-546-8495, trailway@ts.co.nz, has 41 rooms beside the Matai River and is close to city center. Rooms are well equipped. You'll also enjoy a riverside restaurant and bar. Prices are moderate.

**South Street Cottages**, 1 and 12 South St., Nelson, phone/fax

Bay/Gisborne, and Martinborough. On South Island you'll find the Blenheim/Marlborough region, as well as wineries in Nelson, Canterbury, and Central Otago.

Well, then, what styles might you enjoy? Chardonnay is the white you'll most often hear people ordering. Some New Zealand Chards are aged in barrels; some are softened through malolactic fermentation. New Zealand has a cool climate, an advantage in making Sauvignon Blanc; some interesting blends are made with Semillon. Consider also the spicy Gewürztraminer, the popular (and inexpensive) Muller-Thurgau, Pinot Gris, or Riesling. Among the reds, Cabernet Sauvignon can be enjoyed alone or blended with Merlot, a variety that matures more acceptably in New Zealand's maritime climate. Consider also a Pinot Noir.

New Zealand also produces sparkling wines, labeled Methode Champenoise or Method Traditionelle—no one dares call them champagne. A cautionary note: be leery when ordering wine by the glass. Too many restaurants will open the wine bottle, then keep it too long between servings, letting it "go off" before you taste it. If you must order by the glass, order a Chardonnay or whatever seems popular.

03-540-2769, mobile 025-363-858, are small charming 1860's homes transformed into memorable—and expensive—accommodations. The cottages are fully serviced and have laundry and kitchen equipment. Wood fires provide heat. A simple self-service breakfast is provided.

**Cathedral Inn**, 369 Trafalgar St. S., Nelson, 03-548-7369, cathedral.inn@clear.net.nz, www.friars.co.nz/hosts/cathedral.html, has seven bedrooms, all with private baths, in a renovated manor house. Guest rooms and public areas are decorated with rich colors, polished wood period furnishings, and patterned fabrics. Guests can mingle in a plush comfortable living room, relax in the drawing room, or sit on a sheltered verandah. Rates are expensive.

**Cambria House**, 7 Cambria St., Nelson, 03-548-4681, fax 03-546-6649, cambria@clear.net.nz, www.friars.co.nz/hosts/cambria.html, has upscale B&B rooms in a renovated 130-year-old homestead. Each well-appointed room has a private bath; there are some luxury suites. The building has heat in winter; guests also get electric blankets. A guest lounge with a fireplace opens to a private courtyard and garden.

**Bronte Lodge**, Bronte Rd. E. off SH 60, RD1, Upper Moutere, Nelson, 03-540-2422, fax 03-540-2637, margaret@brontelodge.co.nz, is located a half-hour's drive from Nelson, near Kahurangi National Park, and about an hour from Abel Tasman National Park. The Bronte has rooms, suites, and villas. Breakfast is served on the deck or in a formal dining room. Guests have views of the Waimea estuary and forests beyond and can use a canoe, dinghy, or Windsurfer. A lavish garden blooms amid green lawns. Prices are high.

**Sans Souci Inn**, Richmond Rd., RD 1, Pohara, Takaka, phone/fax 03-525-8663, has rooms at NZ$65 for two people and NZ$45 for one person. Family rooms can accommodate several people. Guests have a choice of breakfasts; dinner and dessert menus are fixed. The inn is close to Pohara Beach on Golden Bay, Pupu Springs, Farewell Spit, and Abel Tasman National Park.

**Ocean View Chalets,** Marahau, RD 2, Motueka, 03-527-8232, fax 03-527-8211, o.v.ch@xtra.co.nz, http://abel.tasman.chalets.webnz.co.nz/, is located in a farmland setting near Abel Tasman National Park. Guests have views of Tasman Bay. One- and two-bedroom chalets have baths, kitchens, and living areas. Studio units have baths and tea-making facilities. All units have a radio, TV, phone, and private balcony. Breakfast is served buffet style in the dining room. Guided walking tours, sea kayaking, boat cruises, horse trekking, and swimming with the seals can be done nearby.

**The Barn**, Backpacker Accommodation and Camping, Harvey Rd., Marahau, RD 2, Motueka, 03-527-8043, has an excellent location near the Abel Tasman National Park entrance, Park Cafe, bus stop, and Tasman Bay. Lodging is in a dormitory, double or twin rooms, or tent sites. Other sleeping options include an outdoor hammock, house truck, or tepee. Guests can use the kitchen, laundry room, and barbecue and can buy supplies at the shop.

# FOOD

You can eat very well along the coast between Golden Bay and Marlborough Sounds—a wine-making region that also grows food. If you stop at Havelock on the way to Nelson, try the local green-lipped mussels. In Nelson you'll find creative luncheon dishes served at sunny cafés, good pub food, lots of seafood dishes, sophisticated vegetarian food, regional wines, and microbrews. Beyond Nelson you can eat at the **Park Cafe**, 03-527-8270, Marahau, located at the entrance to Abel Tasman National Park, and at **Awaroa Lodge and Cafe**, 03-528-8758, surrounded by Abel Tasman National Park and located on Awaroa River estuary.

In Nelson at **Zippy's Espresso and Juice Bar**, 276 Hardy St., 03-546-6348, manager Zanna Bird oversees an all-vegan kitchen, which turns out interesting and freshly made food. Guests gather at high round tables and climb onto high scissor chairs. Music might be Manu Dibango or Roni Size, while decor involves eclectic artworks and brightly colored paint spread over most surfaces. A few loyal patrons come for the excellent espresso drinks or to display elaborate body jewelry and layered vintage costumes. One noontime regular, dressed in a suit, helped save Zippy's during a rough period when rent had gone unpaid for much too long. Most locals come to eat the creative vegan dishes built around lasagna, calzone, or Panini bread. That doesn't mean you'll eat Italian, though. You might choose a zucchini, blue cheese, herb, and rice cake or a tortilla stack, the flat circles layered with zesty chilis, tomato, spinach, sour cream, and cheese. The place is BYO licensed, so bring wine if you like. Before you leave, check the blackboard gig guide and the message board. After you've eaten, stop in at Small Planet Recycling next door.

**Faces Café Bar**, 136 Hardy St., 03-548-8755, decorated with masks, serves light tasty New Zealand food with flair. The restaurant has been declared a "fry-free zone." One of the owners of this family-run business comes up with great ideas, which work their way onto the blackboard menu. Fettucine with asparagus, bacon, and walnuts works well for lunch. Dinner might be a medallion of beef with a sherry cream sauce and crisp salad. Or you might be satisfied with pork, topped with a mixed berry compote and some scalloped potatoes. Delicious hot tea is served in a pot; you can also order espresso

*Le Chef Restaurant in Nelson*

drinks. The wine list emphasizes New Zealand regions; a few wines are French. Prices range from NZ$12 to NZ$20. The restaurant is open Monday to Saturday for lunch and dinner; Sunday dinner only.

**Le Chef Cottage Restaurant**, 20 Harley St. between Hardy and Bridge Sts., 030-548-7200, fax 03-548-7206, lechef@xtra.co.nz, is located in a quaint historic house. The restaurant has won awards for service and its creative use of New Zealand beef and lamb. Stefan and Marifé run the place, with a little help from Phantom the cat. Fresh-baked bread comes with garlic and olive oil or just plain butter. Soup du jour might be followed with tiger prawns made with herbs and a Chardonnay cream sauce or baked green-lipped mussels with tomato salsa and Parmesan cheese. The main course might be fresh fish or venison short loin with asparagus tips, spiced sweet potato cake, and an apple-pear sauce. Other dishes feature salmon or chicken. The menu at times even features medallions of wild goat, kangaroo loin, or lamb sausage. Vegetarians could have the *mille-feuille* served with a spicy green sweet pepper sauce and tender potatoes. Desserts include flan, a homemade liqueur ice cream, and the chef's special: a creamy licorice parfait with orange lemon sauce. Prices range from NZ$6.50 for soup to main courses from NZ$20 to NZ$26. Open for dinner.

The **Victorian Rose Pub 'n' Cafe**, 281 Trafalgar St., Nelson, phone/fax 03-548-7631, run by Kevin and Carolynn Hannah, serves snacks, light meals, burgers, and pasta dishes, plus main meals—seafood platter, roast chicken, rib eye steak—that come with salad and fries. Historic decoration and lots of wood surfaces make an inviting setting. The full bar has a range of New Zealand wines and beers, spirits, and mixed drinks. Check the schedule: there's often live music in the evening. Snacks and starter portions run from NZ$2 for a curry roll and NZ$6.50 for scallop bites and fries to NZ$21 for the Victorian Rose Challenge. Open for lunch and dinner seven days a week.

**Little Rock Cafe and Bar**, 165 Bridge St., Nelson, phone/fax 03-546-8800, specializes in "stonegrill" dining: steaks, seafood, chicken, and other meats are grilled and served on stones for best temperature and flavor. Meats are trimmed of fat, and no fats are used in cooking. Accompanying roasted potatoes and vegetables are spread around a platter. For more information about this method, call Stonegrill International Pty. Ltd., Australia, 018-335-337. The angled stone bar is the main decorative feature of the restaurant, which also serves snacks like sushi nori made with manuka-smoked salmon and fish and crab cakes with chili dipping sauce. Pastas include lamb and sun-dried tomato fettucine. Pizzas include the Good Earth, with an array of colorful vegetables, feta cheese, and olives. A typical main course is a baked fresh salmon steak, served with a corn and potato cake and seasonal greens. Dessert might be Banoffi pie. Most wines come from New Zealand's Nelson, Marlborough, and Hawkes Bay regions; a few come from Australia. Espresso and liqueur drinks are also served. Prices range from NZ$3 to NZ$7 for snacks, NZ$9 to NZ$11 for smaller servings, and NZ$16 to NZ$23 for full meals. Open seven days.

**Nelson City Super Value Plus**, on the corner of Bridge Street and Collingwood, is a well-stocked supermarket with a variety of fresh and preserved New Zealand and imported foods, plus a very helpful staff.

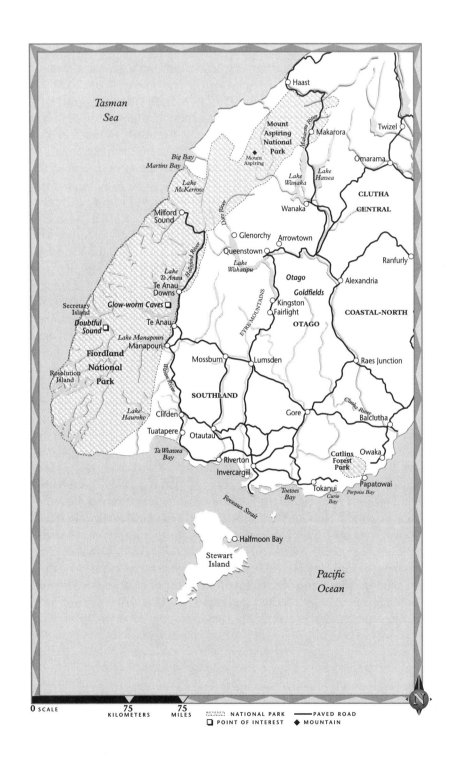

Tasman
Sea

Haast

Mount
Aspiring
National
Park

Twizel

Makarora

Makarora River

Big Bay
Martins Bay

Mount
Aspiring

Omarama

Lake
Wanaka

Lake
Hawea

CLUTHA
CENTRAL

Lake
McKerrow

Dart River

Milford
Sound

Wanaka

Hollyford River

Glenorchy

Arrowtown

Queenstown

Ranfurly

Lake
Wakatipu

Lake
Te Anau

Te Anau
Downs

Otago

Goldfields

Alexandria

Secretary
Island

Glow-worm Caves

EYRE MOUNTAINS

Kingston
Fairlight

COASTAL-NORTH

OTAGO

Doubtful
Sound

Te Anau

Lake Manapouri

Manapouri

Fiordland
National
Park

Waiau River

Mossburn

Lumsden

Raes Junction

Resolution
Island

SOUTHLAND

Lake
Hauroko

Clifden

Gore

Clutha River

Balclutha

Tuatapere

Otautau

Catlins
Forest
Park

Owaka

Ta Weawea
Bay

Riverton

Invercargill

Tokanui

Papatowai

Porpoise Bay

Toetoes
Bay

Curio
Bay

Foveaux Strait

Halfmoon Bay

Stewart
Island

Pacific
Ocean

0 SCALE          75              75
              KILOMETERS      MILES

▨ NATIONAL PARK    ── PAVED ROAD
▢ POINT OF INTEREST  ◆ MOUNTAIN

N

# CHAPTER 8

# Fiordland

Fiordland and the southwestern region are known for alpine mountains, deep lakes, high plateaus, and intricate fjords accessed mainly by water. Fiordland has vast dense forests without roads.

Traveling inland from the west coast, you'll follow a rocky river road below mountains, you'll cross Haast Pass, then enter southern lake country, a highland region of deep elongated lakes and mountains that reach 2,000 meters. The small towns of Makarora and Wanaka can be staging areas for mountain and ranch adventures or activities geared to rivers and lakes. West of Wanaka, beyond the lake of the same name, is stunning 3,027-meter Mount Aspiring.

Several parks in the region are inside the Fiordland UNESCO World Heritage Site, known in the Maori language as Te Wahi Pounamu. In addition to the vast Fiordland National Park, you can explore the little-known Pyke and Snowdon Forests, the Dean and Rowallan Forests, Mavora Lakes Park, and the Waitutu Forest. The entire World Heritage land area is 1,210,000 hectares.

Queenstown, a town of perhaps 30,000 permanent residents, climbs the hills above lovely Lake Wakatipu, offering views of the Remarkables, often covered with snow. Touted as an adrenaline capital for thrill seekers, Queenstown also offers soft and nature adventures. For example, you can follow narrow twisting roads into historic

*Southland residents enjoy an outdoor lifestyle.*

Tourism Southland

valleys in a four-wheel-drive vehicle, paddle down swift mountain rivers, take a guided overnight horse trek combined with camping, or hike over a mountain saddle into lush coastal rain forest.

This small town, somewhat reminiscent of Vancouver—without the couple million people—has a wonderful lakefront town center with appealing restaurants, cafés, and nightclubs. A large park borders downtown, and ducks swim near the lakeshore. At the upper end of Lake Wakatipu, small-town Glenorchy and Paradise Valley, nourished by braided rivers, could also be bases for high-country adventures.

Southwest of Queenstown—you must travel around the Eyre Mountains to get there—is Fiordland National Park; Te Anau is its most practical gateway. Scenic flights and tour buses to Milford Sound also leave from Queenstown. But except for the (wonderful) two-hour cruise, the lengthy bus ride eats up most of a day.

Smaller, fast-growing Te Anau, with about 3,000 people, sits beside a vast lake that reaches between the mountains. The summer population rises to about 10,000. The town has shops, cafés, and various lodgings, although it lacks Queenstown's luxurious upscale spin. Highway 94 to Milford Sound, the only Fiordland sound accessible by road, runs through Te Anau; the distance to Milford Sound from Te Anau is 121 kilometers. Claiming to be "the Walking Capital of the World," Te Anau has transport to major walking tracks in the area. Farther down the road at Te Anau Downs, launches depart for glowworm caves and the Milford Track trailhead. Manapouri, a small settlement farther south, is the departure point for Manapouri lake cruises and the brief van ride to Doubtful Sound.

# HISTORY, CULTURE, AND CUSTOMS

According to Maori myth, the demigod Tuterakiwhanoa carved the intricate Fiordland coastline. Maori groups explored the southwest in their quest for greenstone; they lived in the region seasonally and did not grow crops. Europeans established a whaling station at Preservation Inlet in southwest Fiordland in 1829, but the cold, rain, and remote location discouraged permanent settlement.

Europeans visited Lake Manapouri in 1852 and explored some of central Otago the following year, aided by Maori guides. A block of Otago land, purchased from the Maoris before the 1860s gold rush, encouraged more settlers. Guided treks to Milford Sound, over what has become the Milford Track, were first offered to visitors in 1889.

Modern residents of this region live an outdoor lifestyle throughout four seasons. The high country north of Queenstown, with its ranches, orchards, lakes, and forests, still has the feel of a frontier. Even so, lodging, cafés, and well-organized tours can be found in key towns. Vast stretches of Fiordland National Park, typically accessed by water, have no settlements at all, however.

# NATURE AND ADVENTURE ACTIVITIES

In the high country around Queenstown, you might enjoy paddling adventures on mountain rivers, horse trekking on bridle trails through scenic areas, mountain biking, hiking, or a jet-boat ride along a swift, rocky, mountain river. In summer you can hike the alpine environment of Mount Aspiring.

The tourism and DOC offices in Te Anau, along with the lodge operators, offer a wealth of information about tramping—you can access 500 kilometers of hiking trails in the area. Guided or independent day hikes are possible; the area also has several longer Great Walks tracks. The lovely Hollyford route, which crosses no alpine passes, can be hiked year-round.

When planning a visit to Fiordland, plan to take in sweeping views (and panoramic photographs) of the fjords, which are 30 to 40 kilometers long. Move in closer to observe the waterfalls and plant life on the fjords' steep rock walls. Then try to get even closer to see Fiordland's unusual plants and animals. If time and budget allow, you may want to view the area's fascinating marine life forms as well.

Fiordland National Park is usually explored by some combination of bus, launch, and shuttle transport—and that's just to reach the fjord. After you arrive, a motor cruise excursion is one travel option for it combines lodging, meals, and transportation. These overnight trips are adventure cruises, not luxury cruises—even though they're expensive. They usually give you time for snorkeling, paddling a kayak, and bush walking through magical coastal forests. Longer cruises last several nights and explore several fjords. One cruise goes past all the fjords to reach Stewart Island.

Note that you may not experience the mild temperatures and sunny skies shown on tourist brochures here. Even in spring, snow can fall at high altitudes. A cruise vessel's heated lounge, hot shower, and warm food will be extremely welcome after a cold wet outing.

## FLORA AND FAUNA

Getting into the forests of the southwest is fairly easy, if you follow one of the many hiking trails. The richly textured beech forests, with their complex and dependent species of plant life, have a mystical beauty. Viewing wildlife and marine life in this area is more difficult, yet can be done with the help of tour operators and outfitters.

On and around the Southern Lakes north of Queenstown, you might see brown teal, blue ducks, or the southern crested grebe. You might see a chukor, the New Zealand falcon—it feeds on pipits and other small animals. In the high country, deer and feral goats have overgrazed some areas. These animals are held in check by hunting.

Eglinton Valley, Snowdon Forest, and Mavora Lakes Park are known for their rich bird life. You might see grey warblers or bellbirds (at least you'll hear them), fantails, tomtits, yellowheads, South Island robins, kaka, or perhaps a long-tailed bat. The Murchison and Stewart Mountains have small colonies of takahe, but visits are restricted. South Island saddlebacks have been reintroduced on Breaksea Island.

Despite the area's watery expanse of coastal and inland fjords, it has only two marine reserves, at Milford and Doubtful Sounds.

Sally McKinney

*Yellow lupine at Lake Hawea*

Without going below the water, you could well see bottle-nosed dolphins and seals in either Milford or Doubtful Sound. Because of heavy rainfall, the seawater inlets in the sounds are covered with a freshwater layer. Thus, marine life varies with temperature, salinity, and natural light at different levels, down to 40 meters. Along with sponges, corals, and various kinds of fish, there are large groups of black coral trees in the Fiordland sounds.

## VISITOR INFORMATION

About 3,500 people live in and around the town of Wanaka. Typically sunny, it may receive about 62 centimeters of rain a year. Contact the Wanaka Promotion Association, Inc., P.O. Box 147, Wanaka, 03-443-1233, fax 03-443-9238, wpa@wanaka.co.nz, www.wanaka.co.nz.

The Queenstown area, including the smaller Arrowtown, Glenorchy, and Wakatipu basin communities, has a permanent population of 14,285. During summer and winter high seasons, visitors can outnumber locals three to one. The hot dry summer days may reach 18 to 30 degrees Celsius. The clear crisp winter days have temperatures of 5 to 10 degrees Celsius, with cold nights. The area has been cited as a "Best," "Good Value," and "Most Friendly" destination by various travel magazines. Contact Destination Queenstown, P.O. Box 353, Queenstown, 0800-478-336 or 03-442-7440, fax 03-442-7441, queenstown@xtra.co.nz, www.queenstown-nz.co.nz.

The gateway to Fiordland, Te Anau (the self-proclaimed Walking Capital of the World), has an excellent network of transport options to the trailheads—so you don't have to walk to get there! The population varies from a winter low of 3,000 year-rounders to a summer high of 10,000. The average daytime Te Anau temperature in mid-summer is in the low 20s Celsius. On a winter day, say June or July, the average could be 5 to 8 degrees Celsius, with early morning frosts. Contact Fiordland Promotion Association, P.O. Box 155, Te Anau, 03-249-7959, fpai@xtra.co.nz, www.fiordland.org.nz or www.milfordsound.co.nz. Fiordland Travel Ltd. runs an information center at the waterfront, 03-249-8900, fax 03-249-7022. The DOC office, also on the waterfront, can be reached by phoning 03-249-7921 or faxing 03-249-7613.

## GETTING AROUND

You can fly into Queensland or smaller regional airports or travel overland. Visitors traveling overland often come via Highway 6 from the west coast or Highway 1 and the loop Highway 8 from the east. Allow a half-day or more for these journeys. Keep in mind that Queenstown receives 450,000 international and 200,000 domestic visitors a year. Peak seasons are December to mid-February (Christmas holidays) and summer (ski season), so book well ahead.

Air New Zealand and Ansett New Zealand offer daily service to Queenstown from Auckland, Christchurch, and other cities. Air New Zealand also offers weekly direct flights from Sydney and flights from Brisbane during ski season, when Qantas also adds flights. Cars can be rented in Queenstown, which also offers taxi service.

From Queenstown, the main overland route to Te Anau and Milford Sound is Highway 6 along Lake Wakatipu, then Highway 94 west to Lake Te Anau, then north. Mount Cook, Ansett, Air Fiordland

Ltd., and Waterwings, Ltd. offer air service to Te Anau and Fiordland. Aircraft include Boeing 737s and ATR 72s. Hertz and Budget rental cars, along with lake boats and kayaks, can also be hired in Te Anau.

## NATURE AND ADVENTURE SIGHTS

### Dart River

The region was a moa-hunting ground for early Maori tribes. Later, European adventurers explored the Dart River Valley and made several assaults on Mount Earnslaw. Guide Harry Birley finally climbed the 2,819-meter East Peak toward the end of the nineteenth century. Eventually, the Mount Earnslaw climb became a favorite of the New Zealand Alpine Club. The Rees-Dart Tracks, which follow the high country valleys that flank Mount Earnslaw, were cut during the 1930s. The walks became popular after World War II.

You can explore the river on a safari that includes a van ride through **Glenorchy** farm country, a guided walk through beech

Dart River Jet Safari

*Jet boat safari on the Dart River*

197

*Milford Sound, home to bottle-nosed dolphins*

forest, and two Dart River segments. The Dart River portions are done on jet boats—invented by New Zealanders who needed access to farms through shallow water.

You'll leave from Queenstown and travel in a small van along Lake Wakatipu to Glenorchy. Along the 45-kilometer route, the driver will provide information and make photo stops. On **Lake Wakatipu**, fed by the Dart and Rees Rivers, the water rises and falls a few inches every day; a Maori legend claims this action is caused by the heavy breathing of a giant who sleeps in the lake.

At Glenorchy, you'll try on some spray gear. You can wear it if it's raining or stuff it into a daypack for the boat. You'll then travel through **Paradise Valley**. Near noon, before the walk, you'll break for juice and biscuits (provided on the tour).

The walk through beech forest is marvelous. Mosses, ferns, and lichens cling to rocks and trees. You might see a native pigeon; a rock wren; or the kea, the native alpine parrot.

Clad in your spray suit, you'll then climb aboard a jet boat. It cruises past **Chinaman Flat** and the **Unknown Lake**. The beech forests around you shift as you ascend the Dart River. The mountain and red beech found below 800 meters give way to a dominant silver beech forest. Trout and other fish swim in the river, which is fed by snow, rain, and melting ice from nearby mountains.

The jet boat takes you to **Sandy Bluff** before turning around and descending rapidly. The guide will let the group decide the level of thrills on the descent. Some of the guide's favorite maneuvers involve skirting huge boulders and throwing riders around during swirling turns (hence the spray jackets). For a slower descent, ask about making your way down by Funyak (inflatable kayak). Before returning to Glenorchy, the guide will order lunch over the mobile phone on the jet boat—you'll eat soon after you arrive.

On the full-day Dart River Jet Safari and Funyaks tour, you'll paddle inflatable canoes downriver during part of the tour. On the Great Outdoor Adventure tour, you'll take a scenic flight to Milford Sound, cruise the sound, then fly back for the jet boat safari. The optional ending for this trip is an outdoor barbecue. A Rees-Dart Track Package combines three or four days of tramping with a day of river paddling in Funyaks and transport to and from the track. For all trips, wear or bring warm clothing and carry rain gear, sunscreen, insect repellent, and drinking water.

*Details: Dart River Jet Safari, P.O. Box 76, Queenstown, 03-442-9992, fax 03-442-6728, mobile 025-332-123, http://nz.com/Queenstown/. You can also book through the Queenstown Information Centre, Shotover and Camp Sts., Queenstown, 03-442-7318, fax 03-442-6749.*

## Doubtful Sound

In Doubtful Sound, you'll hear—and perhaps see—tuis, wood pigeons, and bellbirds in the coastal rain forest. You'll see amazing varieties of ferns: crown, grass skirt, carrot, and even peppertree. Dolphins, fur seals, and yellow-crested penguins swim on the surface of the water. Wrasse spotties, spiny crayfish, and sea perch can be found below. The freshwater layer over the saltier seawater layer acts as a sun filter, enabling rare black coral trees to grow at shallower depths.

You can explore the fjords by kayak—combined with sorties into the forest on foot—with the hope of sighting the Fiordland yellow-crested penguin. The scenery is spectacular, and rain alters the quality of the light, making the fjord walls and waterfalls seem wondrous. Fiordland Wilderness Experiences offers many kayaking and tramping excursions in the region—from 1 to 56 days. They also rent sea kayaks—no solo rentals—and can advise you on exploring this remote, rainy, and very challenging region of lakes, fjords, mountains, cliffs, rain forest, ocean, and sky. Contact Fiordland Wilderness Experiences at 03-249-7700, fax 03-249-7768, fiordland.sea.kayak @clear.net.nz. Adventure Charters, P.O. Box 24, Manapouri, 03-249-6923, information@fiordlandadventure.co.nz, www.fiordlandadventure.co.nz, also offers sea and lake kayaking. A full-day kayak and cruise on Doubtful costs NZ$159 per person. Other tours are available, along with equipment rental.

**Details**: *Fiordland National Park Visitor Centre, P.O. Box 29, Te Anau, 03-249-7921.*

## Great Walks

Fiordland's Great Walks range from two- to five-day adventures. You'll need to plan early and book DOC huts along the way. (When the Great Walks are all booked, it's still possible to take a satisfying one-day guided walk. You'll carry only a daypack.)

The 39-kilometer **Routeburn Track** takes you between Glenorchy and the Milford Road through an alpine environment with dramatic scenery. There are four huts along the way, but some hikers complete this Great Walk with only two overnight stays. The season runs late October to late April. In winter, the track may be impassable.

The newer 67-kilometer **Kepler Track** loops out from Lake Te Anau and returns to it. There are three DOC huts along the way, although some hikers complete this walk in three days, not four. The best time for the walk is late October to mid-April. The alpine section of the track may be impassable in winter or spring. The annual Kepler Challenge Run takes place here in early December.

The 56-kilometer **Hollyford Valley Walk**, connecting Hollyford River and the coast, is a lower altitude route. It is of moderate difficulty except for the rocky Demon Trail. On this four- to five-day walk, you'll pass through beech and podocarp forest and see waterfalls, distant mountain peaks, glacial valleys, and coastal Lake McKerrow. There are six huts along the way, equipped with bunks, mattresses, water, toilets, and wood-burning stoves. Mountains surround the bush-filled valley, yet the walk has no alpine crossing, so it can be done year-round. There's a seal colony at **Martins Bay**, where you might also see crested penguins. Some hikers fly to Martins Bay, then walk the trail in reverse.

The 54-kilometer **Milford Track** follows the historic route to Milford Sound—before a tunnel and road were built. The trailhead, on the western shore of Lake Te Anau, is accessible only by boat, so you'll begin "hiking" with a launch cruise from Te Anau or Te Anau Downs. The route cuts through lush dense areas of rain forest and crosses alpine MacKinnon Pass with a steep rocky descent on the other side. In the life of every hiker some rain must fall, and it could well happen on the Milford. There are three DOC huts along the way, available from late October to mid-April. You'll need to book in early July for the following (austral) summer. The booking system limits trekkers to a maximum of 40 per day. In winter, snow, avalanches, or damage from storms can make the track impassable.

Many guided Great Walks are available. Trips and Tramps, P.O. Box 69, Te Anau, 03-249-7081, fax 03-249-7089, offers one-day guided excursions. Tours are in small groups, with an emphasis on natural history. Richard Bryant's Guided Nature Walks, P.O. Box 347, Queenstown, 03-442-7126, fax 03-442-7128, walk@inq.co.nz, can organize a tour from your Queenstown location.

On the Hollyford Valley Guided Walk, P.O. Box 360, Queenstown, 0800-832-226 or 03-442-3760, fax 03-442-3761, hvwalk@voyager.co.nz, you'll get a full briefing and transport to the trailhead. Hikers carry only day gear. Meals are prepared by lodge cooks and sometimes feature local venison, trout, or whitebait. You'll sleep in two- to four-person rooms on bunks outfitted with sheets and duvets. The trip includes a scenic flight and launch cruise on Milford Sound (dolphins might be frolicking near the entrance to the sound).

*Details: For Great Walks bookings, contact the DOC, P.O. Box 29, Te Anau, 03-249-8514, fax 03-249-8515. For maps, trail, and transportation information, phone 03-249-7924. Fiordland Promotion Association, Inc., P.O. Box 155, Te Anau, 03-249-7959, fax 03-249-7949, mobile 025-343-952, fpai@teanau.co.nz, www.fiordland.org.nz, offers additional information on the tracks. For transportation contact Fiordland Track Transport, P.O. Box 81, Te Anau, 03-249-7777, fax 03-247-7536, teanau@xtra.co.nz.*

## High Country

The high country around Queenstown, surrounded by snowcapped ranges mirrored in lakes, contains farms and ranches. You'll also find great locations for horseback riding here.

From Queenstown you can easily reach the Wanaka area, at the south end of Lake Wanaka, backed by the Crown Range. Two area companies offer horseback experiences. Backcountry Saddle Expeditions, RD 1, Cardrona Valley, Wanaka, 03-443-8151, fax 03-443-1712, has two-hour, half-day, full-day, and longer treks. When you mount an Appaloosa and head into the scenic surroundings, you'll understand why film companies occasionally make commercials and Westerns here. Rates start at NZ$45 for a two-hour ride and NZ$130 for an overnight. Mount Iron Saddle Adventures Ltd., Anderson Rd., Wanaka, 03-443-7777, horsetrek@wanaka.gen.nz, offers a two-hour guided horse trek through native kanuka forest. You'll see ranches and merino sheep, along with lake and mountain views. Another more challenging option involves riding across rolling open fields to the **Clutha River**. Again, the scenery is spectacular.

If you're staying in Te Anau, you can easily reach Glenorchy and Paradise Valley, where the Dart and Rees Rivers flow into upper Lake Te Anau. Here, along the braided river channels, High Country Horse Treks, 03-442-9915, organizes guided horse treks and rents horses to qualified riders. The company also supplies helmets and transportation. Beginners can start with riding lessons. Especially appealing is a guided twilight ride that includes transportation from Queenstown. The staff can also guide you partway for an unguided ride through the **Greenstone Valley** or set up an all-day unguided ride to a remote mountain valley. Dart Stables, P.O. Box 47, Glenorchy, 03-442-5688, riding@glenorchy.co.nz, www.glenorchy.co.nz, has a more personalized approach. They offer a range of experiences, from short rides for beginners to overnight treks.

**Details**: *Queenstown Travel and Visitor Centre, P.O. Box 253, Queenstown, 03-442-4100, qvc@xtra.co.nz.*

## Milford Sound

In early evening, the day-cruise boats have been silenced; the water slaps gently against them as they float moored to the dock. By then, the *Milford Wanderer* has already departed for a twilight cruise through the fjord to the open sea. The ship navigates alone on the silver water, passing the steep darkening rock walls that rise to peaks on either side. Dinner is served, but you'll be glad to be interrupted when the message ripples through the crowd: dolphins are swimming outside.

A visit to Milford Sound could very well be the highlight of your trip to New Zealand. This world-class destination deserves to be seen at twilight—and at dawn. Both the early morning and late-day light will enhance your photographs.

From Queenstown (you can also join the tour at Te Anau), you'll start with a cruise across Lake Wakatipu, then board a van for a trip through the **Von Valley**. The high-country road is also the ranchers' road through one stock gate after another. You'll visit an early musterer's hut and drink morning tea boiled on the traditional billy.

Once you reach the Milford Road, the scene changes to a stunning landscape of snow-topped mountain peaks, cliff faces that descend to the road, scattered snow piles, and tracks that follow rushing streams through lush beech forest.

Ahead, the scenery opens to a Miter Peak calendar scene, familiar from photographs, yet more dramatic when you're really there. You'll board the *Milford Wanderer*, stow your luggage under a bunk, and relax over herbed tomato soup and chunks of warm bread. As the boat heads through the channel, stand on the open deck and you can appreciate the waterfalls and watch the seals. Soon you'll get to paddle a sea kayak from the boat.

Dinner is a relaxing affair in the large comfortable dining salon—until someone sights dolphins. Cameras in hand, diners

*View of Mitre Peak from Milford Sound*

scurry to the open decks for this sound and light show—and it's real! After the sunset, sleep comes easily in the warm, cozy cabins. The moored boat rocks gently, and you can dream of awaking at dawn in Milford Sound.

The *Milford Wanderer* Overnight from Milford costs NZ$125, with an additional charge for the Backroad Adventure tour. Also consider the smaller *Friendship* Overnight Cruise, which involves more nature activities. The *Friendship* sleeps 12. The cost is NZ$125.

**Details**: *Fiordland Travel, P.O. Box 94, Queenstown, 03-442-7500, fax 03-442-7504, infor@fiordlandtravel.co.nz, www.fiordlandtravel.co.nz.*

## Te Ana-au Glowworm Caves

Maoris living in the area in the late eighteenth century named these riverine caves "the Caves of Rushing Waters." The caves, located in Fiordland National Park and across Lake Te Anau, are also known for a lovely glowworm grotto. Above the lakeside caves, a rare colony of takahe lives on the slopes of Mount Murchison.

The cave tour begins with a shuttle ride from Te Anau to Te Anau Downs, where you will board a motor launch. You'll cruise past the beautiful southern arm of Lake Te Anau; 344 kilometers in area, it is the second largest lake in New Zealand. At the base of the mountains, you'll disembark at a long ramshackle jetty. You'll cross a stream called Tunnel Burn and reach a visitors center with displays that explain what you're about to see.

The caves are perhaps 15,000 years old, and they're still being formed—eroded by the water that flows through them. Te Ana-au, as the caves are known, are linked to the older Aurora Cave system, which existed before the last glaciation. Tunnel Burn was once a surface stream that cut its way into glacial moraine—so now it flows through the cave system. Over the years, the stream's level has shifted with changes in the water level of Lake Te Anau.

When you visit Te Ana-au, you'll hear the roaring water before you see it. You'll walk past a whirlpool and waterfalls, visit several caves in the system, explore lower and upper river segments by small boat, and view other sections on walkways. Along the way, you'll notice a few glowworms in scattered locations; the largest display is in the glowworm grotto. The koaro, a native trout, also inhabits the cave.

*Visitors explore glowworm caves.*

Classified as *Arachnocampa luminosa* and known as the fungus gnat, glowworms develop through four stages: egg (three weeks), larva (nine months), pupa (three weeks), and adult fly (76 hours). Tiny insects in the larva stage form the main glowworm display, which can be viewed from a boat in the dark grotto. The hungrier the larvae become, the brighter they glow—as a way to attract prey. The larvae also spin dozens of silky threads, used to entrap the flying insects on which they feed. The glow also attracts mates.

**Details**: *For cave tours contact Fiordland Travel Information Center, P.O. Box 1, Te Anau, 03-249-7419, fax 03-249-7022. Tours afternoon and evening year-round, with additional departures during summer.*

## TOUR OPERATORS

**Fiordland Ecology Holidays**, 1 Home St., Manapouri, Southland, phone/fax 03-249-6600, mobile 0800-249-660, eco@xtra.co.nz, www.

fiordland.gen.nz, offers 3- to 10-day adventure cruises on the M.S.V. *Breaksea Girl,* a 25-meter steel ketch, centrally heated and equipped for travel as far south as New Zealand's subantarctic islands. Tours visit Milford and other sounds, including Doubtful, Breaksea, Dusky, and Chalky, along with Preservation Inlet. The operators don't accept charters involving any type of extraction from the environment (as in fishing). They offer tours year-round and offset the cost of environmental research by selling tourists (might this be you?) spare berths on scientific charters.

Skipper Lance Shaw spent 12 years on a research vessel operated by New Zealand's DOC. His partner, Ruth Dalley, holds a commercial launchmaster's ticket and has had 20 years of marine experience. Their cruises focus on natural history and combine hiking and non-extractive snorkeling and diving with penguin and marine mammal observation and environmental education. Your hosts have a Marine Mammal Watching Permit from the DOC, so guests can swim with seals or dolphins. (Doubtful Sound apparently has a resident pod of dolphins.) On a particular trip you can expect to see dusky, bottlenosed, or common dolphins, as well as fur seals, albatrosses, and Fiordland crested penguins. The forests are a mixture of beech, rimu, totara, southern rata, and other species. Below the water, there are corals, anemones, sponges, and unique species of fish.

The *Breaksea Girl* sleeps 12 people in bunks. Meals are healthy and tasty; special diets and people with disabilities can be accommodated. A dinghy provides access to shore. Bring boat shoes or rubber boots, hiking boots or walking shoes for visits to shore, rain jackets and pants, warm fleece layers, a warm hat and gloves, swimsuits, a camera, and lots of film. Rates range from NZ$590 for three days on Doubtful Sound to NZ$1,250 for a seven-day research trip.

**Fiordland Travel**, P.O. Box 27, Manapouri, 0800-656-502 or 03-249-6602, fax 03-249-6603, info@fiordlandtravel.co.nz, www.fiordlandtravel.co.nz, also offers tours to southwest Fiordland and Stewart Island. Their modern vessel holds up to 38 passengers. Activities include shore visits, kayaking, and viewing historic sites. Rates range from NZ$330 for a three-day Doubtful Sound Cruise to NZ$1,250 for a seven-day cruise that includes Preservation Inlet.

The **Kingston Flyer,** 03-248-8848, fax 03-248-8881, operating between Kingston and Fairlight with connections from Queenstown via Alpine Taxis, 03-442-6666, operates twice daily October through April. The vintage locomotives date to 1925, and the oldest of the seven wooden carriages dates to 1898. The excursion involves a 14-kilometer ride and takes less than an hour. Drinks and snacks can be purchased on board. Adult return fare from Queenstown, including taxi service, is NZ$50. Adult fare for Kingston to Fairlight and return is NZ$20.

**Alpine River Guides,** The Adventure Centre, 99 Ardmore St., Wanaka, 0800-684-468 or 03-443-8174, fax 03-443-9023, organizes one-day kayak adventures for beginning and intermediate paddlers on the Upper Clutha River in the Matukituki Valley or on the Hawea River. More experienced kayakers can arrange for transport and guide service on the Makarora and Kawarau Rivers. In its concern for your safety and fun, the company will match you with the appropriate river run.

**Funyaks**, P.O. Box 1241, Queenstown, 03-442-7374, fax 03-442-6536, funyaks@inc.co.nz, www.funyaks.com, offers a Dart River tour combining transportation from Queenstown, a jet-boat ride upriver, a bush walk, and a downriver paddle in an inflatable three-seat canoe. Among other things, the company supplies river clothing and footwear, plus dry bags for cameras. Ask about hike/canoe options.

The **TSS** *Earnslaw* first took passengers on Lake Wakatipu in 1912. Built in Dunedin, the boat was brought to the lake by train, then reassembled. The 168-foot twin-screw steamer has carried cargo, livestock, and passengers in its long and varied history. Using the original engine, it cruises at a speed of 13 knots. The cruise visits a tourist farm and restaurant at the site of the original Walter Peak Station. (At the height of its success, the station included 170,000 acres of land with 40,000 sheep.) The cruise may be booked at Fiordland Travel, Queenstown Steamer Wharf, P.O. Box 94, Queenstown, 0800-656-503 or 03-442-7500, fax 03-442-7504, info@fiordlandtravel.co.nz. The cost is NZ$25 for the cruise only, NZ$67 for the evening cruise and dinner.

**Skippers Canyon Queenstown Heritage Tours**, P.O. Box 219, Queenstown, 03-442-5949, fax 03-441-8989, qtown.heritage.tours @clear.net.nz, will take you in a four-wheel-drive vehicle along the Coronet Peak Road—a narrow winding road once used by fortune hunters during the gold rush—into Skippers Canyon. Guide Bill

Sally McKinney

*Visitors search the canopy of trees for birds near Mavora Lake.*

Forsyth's grandparents were among the early settlers here. You'll visit the site of the frontier town and enjoy regional delicacies like smoked salmon rolls and tea or wine on a terrace overlooking the Shotover River. The cost is NZ$55. The Nevis Valley tour visits spectacular farm and ranch country and features a riverside gourmet picnic.

**Adventure Biking,** Infomation and Track Centre, Shotover St., Queenstown, 03-442-9708, offers a nine-kilometer Moke Creek Valley ride that crosses the river and visits several early gold mining sites. The cost of NZ$55 includes transportation, bikes, and snacks.

**Aspiring Images** in Wanaka, 03-443-8358, has developed a personalized tour, designed to improve your photography skills, using a four-wheel-drive vehicle. You'll shoot landscapes and lifestyle photos in the Wanaka area and enjoy a picnic lunch. Camera equipment and film are available if you need them.

Via **Arrowtown Express**, you can use daily bus service between Queenstown and historic Arrowtown and tour at your own pace. Five departures a day begin at 9:30 a.m.; the last departure from Arrowtown leaves at 4:30 p.m. Buses leave from the Frankton Bus Stop and other locations. The trip costs NZ$5 one way, takes 25 minutes, and includes a commentary.

## CAMPING

**Lake Hawea Holiday Park**, SH 6, P.O. Box 46, Lake Hawea, Otago, phone/fax 03-443-1767, set among trees and on the lakeshore, has 130 tent sites and 82 powered sites. Guests enjoy boating, fishing, swimming, windsurfing, and hiking. Besides a playground, guests can also use the fridge, microwave oven, laundry equipment, and barbecue.

**Wanaka Pleasant Lodge Holiday Park**, Glendhu Bay Rd., P.O. Box 125, Wanaka, 03-443-7360, fax 03-443-7354, has lake and mountain views, an adventure playground for children, and a swimming pool with a three-lane slide. The park offers 60 tent and 70 powered sites. Guests appreciate the store, cooking facilities, clothes dryer, barbecue, and photocopy/fax service.

**Queenstown Motor Park**, Main St., P.O. Box 59, Queenstown, 03-443-7252, fax 03-442-7253, kiwi@inq.co.nz, overlooks Lake Wakatipu. You can also walk to the center of town in a few minutes. The park has 180 tent sites and 220 RV sites—try to remember where you're camping! Or you can stay in the 72-bed lodge. Guest can use a cooler, fridge, and dryers and can shop at the camp store.

**Glenorchy Holiday Park**, 2 Oban St., P.O. Box 4, Glenorchy, Otago, 03-442-9939, fax 03-442-9940, has 60 tent sites and 23 RV sites in a lovely mountain setting near Lake Wakatipu. Located beside the tourist information center, the park offers good access to several walking tracks, horse trekking, and activities on the Dart River. Guests can use kitchen, laundry, and various other facilities and rent boats here.

**Manapouri Lakeview Motels & Motor Park**, Manapouri-Te Anau Rd., P.O. Box 3, Manapouri, 03-249-6624, fax 03-249-6699, has 110 tent sites and 35 RV sites, as well as cabins, some of them overlooking Lake Manapouri. Children will enjoy the playground and game room. An array of facilities includes a store and take-out meals. This location is the departure point for Lake Manapouri launch cruises—the access to Doubtful Sound.

To book DOC huts on the Milford, Routeburn, and Kepler Great Walks, contact **Great Walks Booking Desk**, DOC, P.O. Box 29, Te Anau, 03-249-8514, fax 03-249-8515, greatwalksbooking@doc.govt.nz. Between October 27 and April 21, visit the DOC Information Centre, 37 Shotover St., Queenstown; DOC Visitor Centre, Oban and Mull Sts., Glenorchy; or the DOC Visitor Centre, Lake Front Dr., Te Anau. The Wanaka Field Centre, 03-443-7660; Te Anau Field Centre, 03-249-7921; and Glenorchy Field Centre, 03-442-9937, can also help with hiking, lodging, and transportation questions.

# LODGING

## *Queenstown*

**The Lodges**, 8 Lake Esplanade, P.O. Box 244, Queenstown, 03-442-7552, fax 03-442-6493, the.lodges@xtra.co.nz, has 13 pleasant apartments with views of the lake and mountains. A short walk from town center, the apartments offer private balconies, continental breakfast on request, and lockers for bulky equipment. The sizes and numbers of beds vary, but all apartments have full kitchens, TVs, radios, laundry facilities, and private showers and toilets. Some have baths or spa baths. Rates are moderate.

The more expensive **Lakeland Hotel**, 35–54 Lake Esplanade, P.O. Box 454, Queenstown, 03-442-7600, fax 03-442-9653, lakeland@inq.co.nz, is also quite close to town center and on the lake. The hotel has 275 rooms and three suites. Rooms are well furnished and well equipped, as is the complex, with a swimming pool, spa, sauna, 24-hour room service, travel desk, à la carte restaurant, and fireside bar.

**Quality Resort Terraces**, 88 Frankton Rd., P.O. Box 155, Queenstown, 03-442-7950, on the main route into and near city center, has 85 rooms of various sizes. Rooms have balconies or private courtyards and are well equipped. There's a restaurant and café/bar on the premises. Prices are moderate.

**Queenstown YHA**, 80 Lake Esplanade, Queenstown, 03-442-8413, fax 03-442-6561, yhaqutn@yha.org.nz, is a sprawling lakefront facility with twin, double, family, and shared rooms. Guests have 24-hour access and laundry and shared kitchen facilities. The staff has information on nearby activities and transportation and can book YHA lodging ahead. Rates are low.

## *Glenorchy*

**Glenorchy Hotel**, P.O. Box 30, Glenorchy, 0800-453-667, fax 03-442-9912, glenorchy.hotel@xtra.co.nz, is a classic country hotel at the head of Lake Wakatipu. Owners James and Lynn Campbell are genial New Zealand hosts. Most of the pleasant rooms have private baths; all have scenic views. The rustic restaurant and full bar, open all day, features à la carte meals and stone-grill dinners.

## Te Anau

The more expensive **Fiordland Hotel**, P.O. Box 63, Te Anau, 03-249-7511, fax 03-249-8944, has 80 refurbished rooms, all with private baths, and a licensed restaurant. Set in four acres of gardens and parks, it overlooks the lake. Manager Owen Johnston promises Kiwi hospitality and good service. Rooms have coffee and tea-making equipment, phones, and refrigerators. The hotel has an enclosed swimming pool and spa pools, plus a barbecue and bar.

*The Fishbone Bar and Grill in Queenstown*

Sally McKinney

The moderate **Te Anau Travelodge**, Lakefront Dr., Te Anau, 03-249-7411, fax 03-249-7947,travelodge.teanau@xtra.co.nz, has 112 guest rooms including villa rooms and suites. It has two spa pools, a sauna, and a restaurant.

The higher-end **Luxmore Hotel**, Town Centre, Te Anau, 03-249-7526, fax 03-249-7272, has 148 rooms, from standard to suites. Accommodations are tastefully decorated and well equipped. A popular restaurant on the premises serves regional food. The hotel is located two blocks from the information center and the lake.

**Grumpy's Backpackers**, SH 94, Te Anau–Milford Sound Hwy., P.O. Box 19, Te Anau, 03-249-8133, fax 03-249-7753, Grumpys @xtra.co.nz, is a highly rated backpackers' lodge with many facilities and services, including free luggage storage and free car parking for guests walking long tracks. "Grumpy" (a.k.a. Dave Moss) also runs a restaurant and bar, plus assorted other lodging. Standard rooms are NZ$40. A bunk in a shared room starts at NZ$10.

The moderate **Te Anau Downs Motor Inn**, also run by Dave Moss (same contact information as above), has modern motel units of various sizes that sleep from one to six. Beds have electric blankets. Equipment includes extra cots and highchairs. Launch departure for the Milford Track leaves from the lakeshore at Te Anau Downs, which also has the closest acceptable accommodation to Milford Sound.

# FOOD

## *Wanaka*

**Relishes Cafe**, 1/99 Ardmore St., Wanaka, 03-443-9018, operates with a blackboard menu and comfortable country decor. You can enjoy fresh-air seating in summer, fireside tables in winter. Baked goods are made fresh daily. Snacks, lunches, and meals can be had with espresso drinks, tea, New Zealand wines, or beer. Prices range from NZ$4.50 to NZ$20. Open for breakfast, lunch, and dinner.

## *Queenstown*

**Gourmet Express**, Bay Centre, Shotover St., Queenstown, 03-442-9619, similar to a California coffee shop, has swift service and tasty meals from 6:30 a.m. until evening. Drinks are refilled free with any meal. Breakfasts include the Kiwi Grill, Miner's Breakfast, and blackberry pancakes. Prices range from NZ$4.95 to NZ$21.95—for a steak and breaded-shrimp meal. A senior lunch or dinner costs NZ$10.95.

**Vudu's**, 23 Beach St., Queenstown, 03-442-5357, www.vudu.co.nz, has great espresso drinks and awesome muffins, intriguing lunch dishes in a vibrant atmosphere with refreshing decor, and pulsing music. Prices are moderate.

The **Wholefood Cafe**, Plaza Arcade, Beach St., Queenstown, 03-442-8991, offers mostly healthy and vegetarian food. The café is tucked away from the street. Walk up the beach, away from the lake, and down a passageway between Beach and Shotover Streets. Breakfasts are served until 10:30 a.m. The lunch crowd comes for gourmet sandwiches (you choose what goes in), feta and olive pizza, salads, muffins, and more (try the devil's food cake). Prices run NZ$3 to NZ$10. Open daily.

Frequented by locals, the **Fishbone Grill,** 7 Beach St., Queenstown, 03-442-6768, offers an array of good fish dishes. You could have a fish-filet burger, crayfish (the New Zealand rock lobster), Akaroa sea run salmon, green-lipped mussels, or other seafood. Chicken and steak are also available. Dinner is served with salad and fries, potatoes, or rice. You can order beer or wine or bring your own. Open October to April for lunch and dinner. Dinners run NZ$16.50 to NZ$24.

The **Moa Bar and Cafe**, upstairs and downstairs at number 5 on the mall, 030-442-8372, serves breakfast, lunch, and dinner. You can sit near the fireplace in winter; a window wall opens to fresh air in summer. You'll choose from many lovely dishes. The chocolate cake is memorable.

## *Te Anau*

**The Moose**, Lake Front Dr., Te Anau, 03-249-7100, teanau.moose@ xtra.co.nz, is a large place with a wide outdoor terrace—much classier than the name suggests. You can have gourmet pizzas whenever the bar is open or an NZ$8 meal of hamburger, fries, and beer. Plates are piled high; the choices include vegetarian nachos, venison burgers, and a warm seafood salad. The Tramper's All-Day Breakfast has eggs, pancakes, bacon, sausages, tomato, and hash browns—how will you have room for the toast? Main dinners might be Steak Diane, chicken schnitzel, or mint and apricot chicken. Side orders start at NZ$2.95, lunch dishes run around NZ$15, main meals are closer to NZ$20.

**Bailiez Cafe Bar** at the corner of Mokonui St. and Town Centre in Te Anau adjoins the Luxmore Hotel. Chef Paul Austin serves breakfast all day and prepares stuffed baked potatoes, steaks, and lots of fish and game dishes. Some examples include a cranberry venison and red wine hot pot, and mussels steamed in white wine seasoned with lemon, dill, and cream. There is also a Trampers Billy Soup served with house bread. The price range is NZ$5 to NZ$25.

**Redcliff Cafe and Bar**, located just off the main thoroughfare, 03-249-7431, has strong local support—for socializing around the bar and for celebratory dining. The fireplace, bar, and dining areas in this renovated house have the winning coziness of a ski lodge; antique furnishings could have come from a settlers' cottage. Chef/owner Peter Taia creates "simple, healthy, modern" food using fresh regional ingredients.

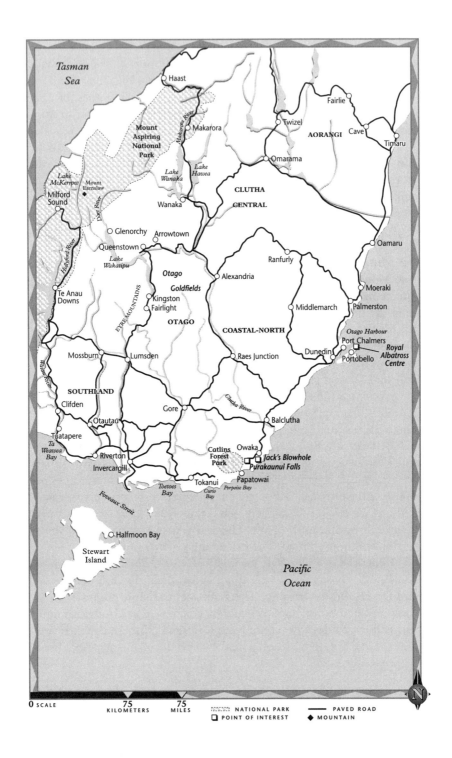

Tasman
Sea

Haast

Fairlie

Makarora

Twizel

Cave

Mount
Aspiring
National
Park

AORANGI

Timaru

Omarama

Lake
Wanaka

Lake
Hawea

Lake
McKerrow

Mount
Earnslaw

CLUTHA

Milford
Sound

Wanaka

CENTRAL

Oamaru

Glenorchy

Arrowtown

Queenstown

Ranfurly

Lake
Wakatipu

Otago

Alexandria

Moeraki

Goldfields

Te Anau
Downs

EYRE MOUNTAINS

Kingston
Fairlight

OTAGO

Middlemarch

Palmerston

COASTAL-NORTH

Otago Harbour

Port Chalmers

Mossburn

Lumsden

Raes Junction

Dunedin

Royal
Albatross
Centre

Portobello

SOUTHLAND

Clifden

Gore

Clutha River

Balclutha

Otautau

Catlins
Forest
Park

Owaka

Jack's Blowhole

Tuatapere

Purakaunui Falls

Ta
Weavea
Bay

Riverton

Invercargill

Tokanui

Papatowai

Toetoes
Bay

Curio
Bay

Porpoise Bay

Foveaux Strait

Halfmoon Bay

Stewart
Island

Pacific
Ocean

0 SCALE

75
KILOMETERS

75
MILES

NATIONAL PARK

PAVED ROAD

POINT OF INTEREST

MOUNTAIN

N

# CHAPTER 9

# Dunedin and the South

South Island's southern lakes and alpine streams nourish a watershed of rocky rivers that course through canyons and wind across plateaus toward the eastern and southern coasts. Study a detailed map of this region and you'll see more blue-veined rivers than brown roads that link communities.

The first Europeans to arrive found a few Maori settlements on the coast. The gold rush drew some settlers inland, while other pioneers built communities beside coastal ports. Modern residents make their living in agriculture, transportation, and tourism. The region's largest city, Dunedin (New Zealand's sixth largest city), is a manufacturing, commercial, and educational center with about 110,000 residents. Invercargill, involved in farming, timber, and mining, has about 50,000 people. Other towns and villages are much smaller.

Drive down from the north, via Highway 1, and you'll discover a loose chain of small communities along the road and cross rivers fed by high-country lakes and streams. Along the Pacific coast you'll see rocky headlands, sandy beaches, and tiny offshore islets. Seals sun themselves on rocky promontories, seabirds build nests, and wading birds with pointed bills and stiltlike legs feed in the tidal estuaries. Inland is a higher and somewhat drier region of tussock and grassland, sheep farms, and orchards.

The Otago Peninsula, 25 kilometers long, juts northeast of Dunedin and shelters Otago Harbour and Port Chalmers, the deep-water port. Protected colonies of albatross and yellow-eyed penguins live along the irregular peninsula.

The southern third of the region contains small and scattered forest parks; the largest is Catlins Forest Park, where hills rise to 700 meters. Farther south at Balclutha, the mighty Clutha River—New Zealand's biggest in terms of volume entering the Pacific—flows into the sea after a long journey from its Lake Wanaka source.

To reach Stewart Island off the southern coast, you can fly or take a ferry from the town of Bluff across Foveaux Strait. The island's main settlement is at Half Moon Bay. Stewart is a forested island, with an uneven coastline and scattered smaller offshore islands. Transport is mainly by boat or walking track; a 19-kilometer segment of coastal road runs northwest of Half Moon Bay.

You can visit New Zealand's subantarctic islands on seafaring vessels from the region's ports. The Auckland Islands, southwest of Stewart Island, have a total of 575 kilometers of land. The smaller Campbell Islands lie southeast of the Aucklands, while Bounty Island and the Antipodes lie east of South Island's coast in the remote Pacific. The Chatham Islands, east of Christchurch, are best accessed from its port of Lyttelton (see Chapter 10).

## HISTORY, CULTURE, AND CUSTOMS

Groups of Maori hunted in the central Otago region, the hilly and river-laced plateau between Queenstown and Dunedin, around A.D. 1000. In an effort to entrap the moa, the Maoris burned forests and scrubland. Here and there on the Pacific coast, the Maoris built settlements, but left no evidence of agriculture.

Early Europeans constructed coastal stations and wharves here. The area now known as the Catlins was settled in the early nineteenth century by sealers, followed by whalers and farmers. In 1848, several hundred settlers arrived by ship from Scotland and settled on the Otago Peninsula, naming their community Dun Edin, the Celtic name for Edinburgh.

After an Australian discovered gold near what is now Queenstown in 1861, prospectors followed the Clutha River upstream on their way to the goldfields. For a time, Clyde became a boomtown and coastal ports thrived—the economy focused on overland transporting, ware-housing, and shipping of gold, timber, and other commodities. Prospectors searched much of central Otago in an effort to find more gold. Drawing on their Scottish heritage, early residents constructed many buildings of regional stone.

The marshy Waihopai River estuary, near Invercargill, was termed unfit for settlement in the early years, delaying development of the area. Near Dunedin, Port Chalmers eventually took over most of the region's shipping business. In 1871, Otago University became the first university in New Zealand. By 1882, enterprising South Islanders were ready to ship the first refrigerated meat on a sailing vessel, called *Dunedin*, to be sold in England.

The legendary race horse Phar Lap (which means "lightning flash" in Sinhalese) was bred near Timaru, a center for farming and sheep ranching. Sold to an Australian in 1928, Phar Lap became famous as a Melbourne Cup winner, then raced in North America.

Today, dry parts of central Otago are being irrigated, allowing cultivation of orchards and farms. Tourism has been growing throughout the region, and you'll find historic sites, natural areas, and facilities for visitors. Many interesting natural areas remain undeveloped.

## NATURE AND ADVENTURE ACTIVITIES

You'll find fewer organized tours in this region than in the others, but that doesn't mean there's little to see or do. In the interior, you can paddle inflatable canoes or kayaks on lakes and rivers, ride a bicycle over an old rail trail, travel on horseback, or visit ramshackle ghost towns. You can take a four-wheel-drive ride over rough mountain roads, visit unusual rock formations and country hamlets, travel by rail through a scenic gorge, or spend four days on a fascinating historic journey by stagecoach.

The eastern coast, with its beaches, headlands, and rocky islets washed by the Pacific Ocean, offers additional activities. In scattered locations you'll find early Maori archaeological sites: middens and pas. On the coast, you can see geological formations like the Moeraki Boulders or walk onto rugged promontories with seal colonies, picturesque lighthouses, and rich bird life. You can watch a colony of little blue penguins at Oamaru from viewing stands built by residents who also protect the colony from human intrusion.

The city of Dunedin has a network of walking tracks that extend onto the Otago Peninsula. On a boat cruise offshore, you could perhaps see marine mammals—seals, dolphins, and whales. On the peninsula itself, you can visit a nesting colony of royal albatross at Taiaroa Head and a museum that studies and protects them. Nearby, an array of seabirds and assorted blue penguins make their nests. On the southeast side of the peninsula, you can hike over hills and through a sheep pasture to view yellow-eyed penguins. Wading birds feed in the peninsula's tidal estuaries.

Farther south, in the Catlins region, you can visit Maori archaeological sites, search for fossils, watch various types of birds in their natural habitat, explore broad rocky beaches at low tide, paddle down a river, and hike through forests with giant native trees.

Along the Southern Scenic Route, you can walk to waterfalls, hike through native forests, watch for dolphins from rocky headlands, explore beaches at low tide, and hunt for yellow-eyed penguins with your camera. One of the Waitutu Tracks follows the coastline and crosses Maori land. The other more rugged trail crosses a ridge on the way to an inland lake in the southern corner of Fiordland National Park.

## FLORA AND FAUNA

Early human settlements in this region were bases for intrusive human activities: hunting of moas by Maoris, hunting of seals and whales by Europeans, mining of gold, and cutting of forests by anyone who could wield a saw. Central Otago has been especially changed by human activity, as have the coastal towns. In the 1840s, the area had vast expanses of grassland and some beech forests. There were podocarp (native pine) and hardwood forests along the coast. Today, you'll find scattered forest reserves in the interior, in the Catlins, and on most of Stewart Island.

# INTERESTING NATIVE FAUNA

*New Zealand's early separation from other land masses allowed flightless birds, such as the moa, to develop without the threat of predators—until Homo sapiens arrived to hunt them down. The islands also separated from other land masses before snakes evolved, so don't expect to find one slithering around your grassy campground. However, tropical sea snakes do sometimes visit the country's warmer waters.*

*New Zealand does not lack for other creepie crawlers, however. The bite of the katipo spider is poisonous. Look under rocks or leaves and you might find a centipede or a millipede. The peripatus, a grayish-green creature with tiny legs, serves as a link between worms and arthropods. Wetas, insects related to grasshoppers, include the giant weta, with a body up to 100 meters long; the cave weta; and the common tree weta.*

*New Zealand also has a reptile called the tuatara, the only survivor of similar creatures that wandered about 60 million years ago. The tuatara has stubby legs, a long pointed tail, and a serrated jawbone instead of teeth. The tuatara can grow up to 600 meters long and live more than one hundred years.*

*Some of the country's most interesting species inhabit the ocean or reside along the shore. Mussels, cockles, tua tuas, toheroas, and pipis all sport distinctive shells. Several kinds of sharks swim offshore, including the white shark, although the smaller school sharks and other species are more common. The elephant fish, found off Sumner Beach and in other locations on South Island, has a trunklike snout and deposits eggs inside a brown horny case.*

Keas, hawks, and the chukor, a falcon that feeds on pipits, live in the mountainous southern lakes country. These lakes are noted for fishing and are stocked with brown and rainbow trout. In the region's remaining forests, there are populations of goats and introduced deer. Their numbers are held in check by hunting.

The slopes of the lower mountain ranges in central Otago contain fields of tussock and patches of beech forest. Names like wild Irishmen (matagouri trees) and Spaniard (a plant with a spiked flower) hint at early rivalries among settlers from different backgrounds. The Clutha River runs through this landscape, nourishing green oases of poplars, willows, and matagouri.

Considering its proximity to an urban center, the Otago Peninsula has unusual concentrations of wildlife. It is the northern boundary for the albatross and the yellow-eyed penguin. In addition to royal albatross, Hooker's sea lions, yellow-eyed and blue penguins, and New Zealand fur seals, your peninsular nature tour guide can also point out bar-tailed godwits, grey teal, mallards, paradise shelducks, pied oystercatchers, spur-winged plovers—and a whole lot more. The Australasian harrier, a raptor, can be seen during the breeding season hunting young birds. On the peninsula and elsewhere down the coast, you might also see Caspian terns, both little and spotted shags, and white-fronted terns.

Beech forest, mixed with rimu and kamahi, cloaks the high ridges of the Catlins, where there are bellbirds, tuis, and native pigeons. Red deer and wild pigs are hunted in the back country. Trout and eels swim in the rivers, and wetas and glowworms can be seen in caves. The Catlins hold still-impressive patches of native coastal forest, the luxurious coastal bush that once formed a long border along this coast. Rare fern birds and yellowheads can sometimes be seen. Underwater and offshore are vast kelp fields, while seals, dolphins, and whales swim in the cool seawater.

Stewart Island is mostly back country, with hills from 600 to 900 meters high and a perimeter of granite rocks, marshes, peninsulas and headlands, untouched bays, estuaries, and beaches. Podocarps and kamahi dominate the island's forests, and the red southern rata blooms in season. Native orchids and assorted ferns and fern trees thrive, and there are red- and yellow-crowned parakeets, tuis, bellbirds, wood pigeons, oystercatchers, godwits, and dotterels. A group

Sally McKinney

*Royal albatross at the colony on Otago Peninsula*

of offshore islands just southwest of Stewart Island are named for muttonbirds.

New Zealand's remote and bleak subantarctic islands—some forested, others desolate chunks of rock—have important areas of vegetation untouched by humans, along with remnants of early human habitation. Thousands of seabirds and penguins breed on the islands, and marine mammals inhabit the sea.

## VISITOR INFORMATION

The communities of Oamaru, Alexandra, Dunedin, Balclutha, Gore, Invercargill, Half Moon Bay, Te Anau, and Queenstown have Visitor Information Centres. The staff can answer your questions and help you plan your activities. Visitor centers near the nature areas described in this chapter are at:
* 1 Thames St., Oamaru, 03-434-1656, fax 03-434-1657
* 48 The Octagon, Dunedin, 03-474-3300, fax 03-474-3311

- Clyde St., Balclutha, 03-418-0388, fax 03-318-1877
- Queens Park, Invercargill, 03-214-6243, fax 03-218-9753

In most places, DOC offices also offer information on nature areas and transportation options. DOC track maps, which cost NZ$1, are excellent, with directions and detailed information on the trails' geology, history, flora, and fauna. Contact the following offices:

- Dunedin DOC, 77 Lower Stuart St., 03-477-0677
- Invercargill DOC, Don St., 03-214-4589
- Te Anau DOC, Lakefront Dr., Te Anau, 03-249-7924
- Tuatapere DOC, Main Rd., 03-226-6607

# GETTING AROUND

Christchurch has an international airport. There are other airports at Timaru, Dunedin, Invercargill, Half Moon Bay, Te Anau, and Queenstown.

InterCity, 03-379-9020, info@intercitycoach.co.nz, operates a network of buses in the area. Southern Link Shuttles, 03-358-8355, has daily service between Christchurch, Picton, Dunedin, Queenstown, Wanaka, and Invercargill. Buchanan Motors, 03-218-3308, provides transportation between Dunedin or Invercargill and Balclutha. The Bottom Bus travels in a loop that encircles the area, with a side trip to Milford Sound. Overnight stops include Te Anau, Queenstown, Dunedin, and Riverton west of Invercargill. Buses run in both directions, visit nature sites, and depart daily from mid-November through the end of March. The loop takes three days, but passengers can get off when they wish, explore an area, then catch another bus the next day or days later. Passengers book their own lodging; the cost is NZ$238. For more information phone 03-442-9708.

# NATURE AND ADVENTURE SIGHTS

## Moeraki Boulders

Near the village of Moeraki, only three kilometers from SH 1, the beach is strewn with spherical boulders. Uplifted from the seabed some 15 million years ago, they were formed much earlier from bubbles in sediment on the sea floor. In a complex process, the sediment was replaced by calcite. Geologists estimate that the largest of the Moeraki Beach boulders took 4 million years to grow. The Maoris have a different story: the spherical rocks were water containers washed ashore from the wreckage of *Arai-te-uru*, a great canoe used in the Maori migration.

Southeast of Moeraki Beach, the **Lighthouse Road** winds past an intricate coastline of headlands, points, and islets on its way to Katiki Point. Stock graze along this rough coastal road to a lighthouse built in 1878. In 1943, the coal- and oil-burning beacon was converted to electricity. In 1975 the lighthouse became automated.

Moeraki and the nearby **Katiki Pa** were two of about 20 Maori villages on the Otago coast. By the mid-nineteenth-century gold rush, Moeraki, the site of an earlier whaling station, had become a thriving port. Eventually, Oamaru flourished, while Moeraki did not.

*Details: DOC Dunedin Field Centre, P.O. Box 5244, Moray Place, 77 Stuart St., Dunedin, 03-477-0677, fax 03-477-8626. For transportation, lodging, and restaurant information, contact Oamaru Visitor Centre, Severn St., Private Bag 50058, Oamaru, 03-434-5643, fax 03-434-8442.*

## *Oamaru Blue Penguin Colony*

This rare colony of little blue penguins is monitored and protected by the residents of a small town on the shores of Friendly Bay. Penguins live in burrows, but the growing colony had begun making nests in various manmade structures, underneath buildings, and in machinery. So residents built nesting boxes, set in earth mounds in the penguins' traditional nesting area. They landscaped the surroundings with native trees and provided a viewing area so that people can observe the penguins without disturbing their activities.

During the day, penguins forage for food, traveling up to 20 kilometers out to sea. They feed on small fish and later regurgitate the food for any chicks in the nest. After dark, the penguins cross the beach between the wharf and a lighthouse.

Viewing takes place each night after dark. You can hear the penguins calling as they gather in small groups, separate into pairs, and pass the viewing stand on the way to the nesting area. Visitors are not

*Visitors cross a sheep pasture to reach the penguin colony on Otago Peninsula.*

allowed to use flashlights or flashbulbs. High-speed film is recommended for photographs. Viewers must also keep quiet and remain at the view stands. The town of Oamaru, between Dunedin and Timaru on SH 1, also has vintage buildings along Tyne Street. The town is known for the **Oamaru Gardens**—among the top ten in New Zealand—and for Oamaru stone, used in building.

*Details: Oamaru Visitor Centre, Severn St., Private Bag 50058, Oamaru, 03-434-5643, fax 03-434-8442.*

## *Otago Central Rail Trail*

The Otago Central Rail Trail runs from Middlemarch to Daisybank (also called Carey's Crossing). You can guide yourself over the 37-kilometer route by bicycle. There are camping facilities at Middlemarch and beyond the end of the trail at Ranfurly.

Note that the Taieri Gorge Railway excursion (see page 228) could be your transport from Dunedin to Middlemarch; you can take your bike on the train. There is also a mountain bike track in the area called Chain Hills Road. You can pick up a "Mountain Bike Rides in Dunedin" brochure at the Dunedin Visitor Centre.

*Details: Dunedin Visitor Centre, 48 the Octagon, Dunedine, 03-474-3300, visitor.centre@dcc.govt.nz.*


## Southern Scenic Route

The Southern Scenic Route is a self-drive tour between Balclutha and Te Anau. Impressive arrays of natural and historic sites line the route. Some do the tour in a rental car or camper. The segment from Balclutha to Invercargill can be done using Catlins Coastal Link, which combines transportation with driver/guides who stop at natural and historic sites along the way.

Southwest of Balclutha you'll enter a region of forested mountains and rivers that feed the bays of rugged, irregular coastline. In the **Awakiki Bush Scenic Reserve**, near the highway, you can see a remnant of totara forest near the Clutha River floodplain.

The town of Owaka could be a base for exploration of the **Catlin Forest Park**. South of Owaka near the coast, **Jack's Blowhole**—on cliffs about 200 meters from the sea—is a 30-minute walk from the road. Farther along, **Purakaunui Falls** is a 10-minute walk through the forest from a roadside picnic area.

Continue to Tahakopa Bay and you'll find coastal podocarp forest beside the sandy inlet. Here you can walk (40 minutes both ways) along the Old Coach Road to visit an early Maori moa-hunting camp near the mouth of the river. Beyond Papatowai, the Tautuku Estuary Boardwalk takes you to view fernbirds. From Rewcastle Road, a track to **McLean Falls** is under construction. Travel farther and you might see Hector's dolphins in **Porpoise Bay**. Even farther, you can visit a lighthouse on a side trip to **Waipapa Point**.

In Invercargill, you'll find many natural and maritime history exhibits in the modern **Southland Museum**. Ferries to Stewart Island depart from the port of Bluff, south of the city. The fishing port of Riverton has short forest and coastal walks. Continue to **Cosy Nook**, and you'll find a sheltered cove only five kilometers from the highway. An early Maori settlement here was known as Pahi's village. Travel on to **McCracken's Rest** for an overlook of Waewae Bay, where you can see Solander Island and possibly Hector's dolphins.

Here the road heads north to Te Anau, skirting a series of inland lakes at the edge of Fiordland. **Tuatapere** is a small center with shops and accommodations. At Clifden you can see a suspension bridge built in 1898. Follow the side road west for 30 kilometers and you'll reach **Lake Hauroko**, the deepest in New Zealand. The Waitutu Hump Ridge Track runs south of the lake to **Bluecliffs Beach**, and the Waitutu Coastal Track runs west of the beach (see Waitutu Tracks).

Continue north and you'll pass through the Waiau River Valley, where the walls of the limestone caves have been deco-

*McLean Falls in Catlins*

rated with Maori rock art. At **Manapouri**, departure point for the lake crossing to Doubtful Sound, several walking tracks can be reached by boat.

DOC and tourism offices can provide excellent color brochure/maps of the route, which can be driven in either direction. A total of 315 kilometers, the drive could be done in one day, but it's better—if time allows—to take two days or more, stopping at special sites along the way.

*Details*: *Clutha Information Centre, 4 Clyde St., Balclutha, 03-418-0388, fax 03-418-1877. Invercargill Visitor Centre, Southland Museum and Art Gallery, Victoria Ave., Invercargill, 03-214-6243, fax 03-218-9753. Te Anau Visitor Information Network, Lakefront Dr., Te Anau, 03-249-8900, fax 03-249-7022. Tourism Southland, P.O. Box 903, Invercargill, 03-214-9733, fax 03-218-9460.*

## Subantarctic Islands

New Zealand's subantarctic islands in the Southern Ocean have recently been named a UNESCO World Heritage Site. One hundred and twenty-six species of birds have been noted in these islands, including five species that breed nowhere else.

Board the seagoing vessel operated by Heritage Expeditions (NZ) Ltd. and you could be heading for any of several subantarctic destinations. Voyage 1691 explores the remote **Auckland Islands**, and Voyage 1692, titled Birding Down Under, visits several subantarctic islands. Voyage 1693 visits Golden Bay, and Voyage 1694 visits the **Chatham Islands**. Other expeditions explore the Ross Sea region and various sites explored by Scott and Shackleton.

The Subantarctic Aucklands Voyage visits **Erebus Cove**, site of the 1849 arrival of colonists on the *Samuel Enderby*. The settlers could not farm the poor land. The fledgling colony was buffeted by storms, and many died. Nearby Enderby Island has a colony of rare Hooker's sea lions on Sandy Bay Beach. In the evening, visitors can see yellow-eyed penguins that nest in the forest. Bellbirds, red-crowned parakeets, and tomtits can also be heard and seen. Beyond the forest is a colony of royal albatross. Dotterels are endemic to these islands.

Tours begin in Invercargill with a visit to the Southland Museum. The expedition vessel *Akademik Shokalskiy* carries 38 passengers and departs from the nearby port of Bluff. While cruising, guests can view seabirds, dolphins, and whales from the bridge; hear lectures about marine life and the Auckland Islands; and learn more about navigation from the ship's officers.

The 72-meter ship, built in 1983, has various levels of accommodation on three decks. Powered by two 1,156-horsepower diesel engines, the ship can travel at up to 12 knots. The vessel is fully ice-strengthened and fitted with stabilizers. Chefs prepare outstanding meals. The ship has a dining hall, bar, library, and lounge.

*Details: Heritage Expeditions (NZ) Ltd., P.O. Box 6282, Christchurch, 03-338-9944, toll free within New Zealand 0800-262-8873, toll free within Australia 800-143-585, fax 03-338-3311, hertexp@ibm.net.*


## *Taiaroa Heads*

Taiaroa Heads is the site of the only royal albatross breeding colony on the mainland. Start your tour at the **Albatross Gallery** and the **Royal Albatross Centre**. The center is built downhill from the headland, which screens the nesting albatross colony from view and protects it from human disturbance. From behind the center, adult birds can at times be seen soaring above the headland. Visitors can also view the birds on closed-circuit television monitors in the Albatross Gallery.

For a closer look, you can take one of three tours offered by the center (the numbers of viewers are strictly controlled). All three tours include colony viewing from Richdale Observatory. The **Fort Taiaroa** guided tour examines early Maori and European occupation of the headland.

The birds, which also inhabit New Zealand's remote offshore islands, have been systematically studied, counted, and banded. The first royal albatrosses arrived at Taiaroa Head between 1914 and 1919; the first egg was discovered in 1920. During the 1930s, an ornithologist and other locals worked to protect the growing colony from human interference. There are now about 100 birds at Taiaroa Head. Adults arrive in September. They court and mate during October. Eggs are laid in November and incubated in December. During summer, the chicks hatch, to be fed by the parents until August. In September, the chicks fly away.

*Details*: *Royal Albatross Centre, Taiaroa Head, P.O. Box 492, Dunedin, 03-478-0499, fax 03-478-0575, albatros@es.co.nz. Tours range from NZ$12 to NZ$27. Proceeds support the work of the center.*

## *Taieri Gorge*

On a railway journey from Dunedin to Pukerangi or Middlemarch, you'll pass through the scenic Taieri Gorge and learn how people and nature have shaped the heritage of the area. While seated comfortably in a passenger car, you can discover a variety of plant and animal life amid unique schist rock formations, note the stonework on bridges and tunnels, see grand viaducts built to span deep ravines, and disembark to see interesting sites like the historic **Reefs Hotel**. At the end of the line, in Middlemarch, you'll have several options. You can continue by bus to Queenstown. You can continue by bicycle over the Rail Trail. Or you can take an Otago Goldfields Stage Coach Tour.

The Taieri Gorge Railway tour operates all year. The tour begins in Dunedin, where the train departs from the vintage Edwardian railroad station. On the outward journey, you'll hear informative commentary. The modern carriages have air-conditioning, seating around tables, and wide windows for panoramic views. Other carriages are traditional wooden cars with sash windows, single or couple seating, and rollover seats. Snacks, tea, coffee, wines, and ales are sold onboard.

The Otago Goldfields Stagecoach Tour operates between Middlemarch and Wanaka over old trails. Most trips last from three to six days. However, the trip can be custom designed, taking into account your interests, budget, and time. The tour takes you through rugged mountain passes. You'll stand on tussock hills for sweeping views of mountain scenery. You'll wander through ghost towns and see interesting goldfield relics.

*Details: Taieri Gorge Railway, Dunedin Railway Station, Anzac Ave., P.O. Box 140, Dunedin, 03-477-4449, fax 03-477-4953,reserve@taieri.co.nz. The railway also has information about rail/bus service between Dunedin and Queenstown. Otago Goldfields Stage Coach Tours, P.O. Box 28, Middlemarch, Otago, phone/fax 03-464-3815.*

## Waitutu Tracks

There are two Waitutu Tracks. The **South Coast Track** goes west from Bluecliffs Beach to Big River. The **Hump Route** begins on the coast, crosses a ridge, then follows Lake Hauroko before ending at the Hauroko parking lot. Either track can be walked independently. A guided walk combines the two routes and takes you up the Wairaurahiri River to Lake Hauroko.

The South Coast Track begins at Bluecliffs Beach, which you can walk at low tide. Ahead, rivers and creeks flow from the upper slopes of the Hump Range, which rises to 1,067 meters, into the southern Pacific Ocean. Fiordland crested penguins, New Zealand fur seals, and Hector dolphins inhabit this coastal area. In the coastal forests, you'll see ancient rimu and totara trees. At Port Craig, an early schoolhouse has been converted to a tramper's hut.

The Hump Route also begins at Bluecliffs Beach and, with permission of the owners, crosses Maori land. After following a road, the track enters the bush and mature forest. After crossing the Hump Ridge, the trail descends to the shore of Lake Hauroko.

Kiwi Wilderness Walks, Riverton Rock, 136 Palmerston St.,

Riverton, 03-234-8886, fax 03-234-8816, kiwiwalks@riverton.co.nz, www.riverton.co.nz, offers guided hiking tours on the Waitutu Tracks and Stewart Island. Before and after the tour, you can opt for lodging in the Riverton Rock Guesthouse, a restored historic hotel. During the trek, hikers stay in bush huts or tents. The guides and staff handle meals, transport (over land or water), and all the camping and cooking equipment. The four-day Waitutu Track trip costs NZ$650 per person from Riverton or Invercargill.

**Details**: *Contact DOC offices in Tuatapere, 03-226-6607; Te Anau, 03-249-7924; or Invercargill, 03-214-4589.*

## TOUR OPERATORS

**Catlins Tours**, operated by Nancy and David Hamill, 025-224-1649 or 03-230-4576, departs from Invercargill and takes you to the Waipapa Lighthouse, fossil forests in Curio Bay, Cathedral Caves at low tide, and Purakaunui Falls. Trips include tea and a light lunch. Farm stays are available. The cost is NZ$58 per person.

**Dunedin Shark and Wildlife Encounters**, 7 Henderson St., Mornington, Dunedin, 03-453-6614, fax 03-453-6679, mobile 021-617-699, gavin@encounters.co.nz, www.encounters.co.nz, offers a tour focused on shark and wildlife viewing. A portion of the tour involves locating and tagging sharks as part of a NIWA program on shark ecology and conservation. You might encounter blue, mako, or great white sharks. If no sharks are sighted, you'll get a partial refund. The four-hour tour, which leaves from the visitor center on the Octagon, includes a visit to the New Zealand Marine Studies Centre, an aquarium tour, background on shark ecology, and a visit to Taiaroa Head. Tours operate daily except Sunday in summer; other seasons or Sundays on request. Book ahead. The cost is NZ$89 per person with a NZ$30 refund if no sharks are seen.

**Wings of Kotuku**, 6A Elliffe Place, P.O. Box 8058, Dunedin, 03-454-5169, wingsok@es.co.nz, specializes in small group natural history tours (up to eight people) to see native trees, plants, and birds in their habitats. A morning tour visits the yellow-eyed penguin colony at sunrise, when the birds make their way from the nesting area across the beach and into the ocean. The tour includes a homestay at Nisbet

Cottage, which overlooks Otago Harbour. Artfully furnished double and twin rooms have private baths and various amenities. Breakfast is included.

**Bravo Adventure Cruises,** Phillip and Diane Smith, P.O. Box 104, Stewart Island, 03-219-1144, fax 03-219-1144, operates twilight cruises on the 48-foot M.V. *Volantis* to visit the habitat of nocturnal brown kiwis. The Stewart Island brown kiwi (*Apteryx australis lawryi*) is a subspecies of the bird that lives on New Zealand's two largest islands. The Stewart Island version has larger legs and a longer beak; females are larger than males. To reach the kiwis, common over most of the island, take a short walk through native bush to a beach. There you'll watch the birds forage for sandhoppers under washed-up kelp. Guides ask that you have a good level of fitness and bring a flashlight. Tours operate on alternate nights and depend on favorable weather conditions. Tours are not appropriate for children under 10.

**Catlins Wildlife Trackers,** RD 2, Owaka, South Otago, New

*A lush lagoon on Stewart Island*

Tourism Southland

231

Zealand, 0800-CATLINS, phone/fax 03-415-8613, catlinw@es.co.nz, based in Papatowai on South Island's southeast coast, take small groups (up to eight) on personalized ecotours into a variety of natural areas. You might walk through native forests, wander about beaches or headlands, or observe tidal estuaries. Owner/guides Mary and Fergus Sutherland emphasize conservation. The Sutherlands' coastal Papatowai home overlooks native forest, the river estuary, a beach, and the southern Pacific Ocean. Behind it is the vast Catlins Forest Park, where rivers flow between tablelands and rolling hills. Clients/guests typically combine two or four days of touring with a stay in the large home or in a separate self-catered lodge.

The Sutherlands coordinate these tours with your travel to and from Balclutha. They will help design your tour, selecting from a menu of 24 possibilities that might fit your time frame. Options include viewing large native trees or visiting wildlife—sea lions and fur seals, penguins, seabirds, wading birds, and forest birds—in its natural environment. You can learn about spiders, wetas, or glowworms; study the southern sky; hunt for fossils; kayak downriver; snorkel through kelp forests; or study in the Sutherlands' natural history library. The well-educated couple, trained as teachers, now serves as honorary DOC rangers. They are dedicated to a code of sustainable environmental practice and work on various conservation projects.

**Elm Wildlife Tours,** 74 Elm Row, Dunedin, 03-474-1872, fax 03-477-8808, elm_wildlife_tour@compuserve.com, http://ourworld. compuserve.com:80/homepage/elm_wildlife_tour, will show you around Taiaroa Head and other nature sites on Otago Peninsula. After a visit to the Albatross Gallery, the tour continues with a short walk to watch seabirds nesting on cliffs and a longer hike to watch yellow-eyed penguins arrive at a remote beach at dusk. Continuing by van, you'll see Hooker's sea lions and New Zealand fur seals, little blue penguin nests, and the habitat of pukekos and shags. The driver will provide background as you ride. During frequent stops in peninsular habitats, you can photograph blue herons, black-backed gulls, pied stilts, and oystercatchers. Here and there, black swans swim on rippling silver water. You'll pass Otakou village, site of an early Maori community. The tour costs NZ$55.

# CAMPING

At **Oamaru Gardens Holiday Park**, Chelmer St., Oamaru, 03-434-7666, fax 03-434-7662, you'll camp next to the lovely Oamaru Gardens, ranked among the top 10 in the country. The park has 40 tent sites and 50 powered sites, plus tourist cabins and bathing pools during summer. Next to a children's playground, the park is a one-kilometer walk from town center and a few minutes' drive from blue and yellow-eyed penguin colonies.

**Moeraki Motor Camp**, Moeraki, RD 2, Palmerston, 03-439-4759, 40 kilometers south of Oamaru, has 30 powered sites and some tent sites, plus motel rooms, tourist flats, and cabins. The array of facilities includes a gas station, store, and a boat launch.

At the end of the Taieri Gorge rail excursion and the beginning of the Rail Trail, **Blind Billy's Holiday Camp**, Mold St., Middlemarch, 03-464-3355, fax 03-464-3322, btheyers@rnzfb.org.nz, has tent and powered sites, along with motel rooms, cabins, on-site caravans, and backpackers lodging. You can ride horses at nearby Salt Lake. Rates range from NZ$8 to NZ$65.

**Portobello Village Tourist Park**, 27 Hereweka St., Portobello, Dunedin, 03-478-0359, fax 03-478-0359, one of the area's smaller campgrounds, has 16 tent sites and 16 powered sites. The park is near Otago Peninsula wildlife reserves—about a 20-minute drive—and close to Dunedin's network of scenic walks onto the peninsula.

**Naish Park Motor Camp**, 56 Charlotte St., Balclutha, 03-418-0088, fax 03-418-0767, is located just off SH 1. It has 40 tent sites and 17 powered sites, plus modern cabins. Guests can use a refrigerator, clothes dryer, and microwave oven. The park is located next to a playground and near the town center and swimming pool.

**Kaka Point Camping Ground,** 39 Tarata St., Kaka Point, South Otago, 03-412-8818, fax 03-412-8800, 22 kilometers from Balclutha, has bush walks and a golden sand beach nearby. There are 16 tent sites, 26 powered sites, and two cabins that sleep four people each. You can use the clothes dryer, refrigerator, and freezer. The park sells take-out meals and is located near a restaurant, store, and other commercial enterprises.

Located inland and near the Mataura River, **Gore Motor Camp**, 35 Broughton St., Gore, 03-208-4919, fax 03-208-4919, has 40 tent sites and 54 RV sites, plus other lodging. Kitchen and laundry facilities are available.

**Beach Road Motor Camp & Tourist Flats**, Oreti Beach, RD 9, Invercargill, 03-213-0400, is set on a 13-acre site in Sandy Point Domain. The campground, managed by the owners, offers 25 RV sites, 25 cabins, and some tent sites. You can use a communal kitchen and laundry room. A swimming beach is one kilometer away. Children will enjoy the play area with its swings, slide, and trampoline. Rates range from tent sites at NZ$6 to a tourist flat at NZ$27. For DOC huts along the Waitutu Coastal Track and the Hump Route, contact the Tuatapere Field Centre, 03-226-6607. For huts on Stewart Island's Rakiura Track (Great Walk) or Northwest Circuit, contact the Stewart Island Field Centre, 03-219-1130.

# LODGING

The region has some appealing accommodations in vintage buildings at a range of levels. The traditional renovated **Southern Cross Hotel**, 118 High St., Dunedin, 03-477-0752, fax 03-477-5776, is centrally located near the Octagon. Dating from 1883, it has 134 smartly decorated rooms and eight suites. All rooms have TVs, 24-hour video, irons and hair dryers, phones with computer lines, tea- and coffee-making services, and mini-bars. The hotel has a bar and three restaurants—for formal, brasserie, or café-style dining.

Several motels can be found on Cumberland Street near the university in Dunedin. Consider the **Cable Court Motel/Apartments**, 833 Cumberland St., 03-477-3525, fax 03-474-0382, which has studios and one-, two-, and three-bedroom units. The **Commodore Luxury Motel**, 932 Cumberland St., 03-477-7766, fax 03-477-7750, has motel units and apartments to accommodate from one to nine people. A restaurant, spa, swimming pool, and sauna are in the complex. The **Cumberland Motel**, 821 Cumberland St., 03-477-1321, fax 03-477-1320, has large units that sleep up to five people. Guest accommodations have kitchen facilities and microwave ovens, electric blankets, and direct-dial phones.

Other Dunedin motels can be found on George Street. They include the **Allan Court Motel**, 590 George St., 03-477-7526; **Best**

**Western Tourist Court Motels**, 842 George St., 03-477-4270; and **Garden Motel**, 958 George St., phone/fax 03-477-8251.

The hillside **Elm Lodge**, 74 Elm Row, Dunedin, 03-474-1872, has budget accommodations in single, double, and shared rooms in what was once a large family residence. Owners, who are associated with the Elm Wildlife Tours, provide a sheltered garden with a barbecue, plus the usual shared kitchen and laundry facilities. The comfortable rooms have space heaters; rates begin at NZ$13 per person.

At the **Albatross Inn**, a bed-and-breakfast at 770 George St., phone/fax 03-477-2727, your breakfast will be a lavish buffet. Located just a few blocks from the Octagon, the former Edwardian home has been charmingly decorated; the dining room has a floor of polished native rimu. All bedrooms are heated, with private bathrooms, tea- and coffee-making equipment, and chairs or couches. Large beds have warm duvets and electric blankets. Some bedrooms also have kitchenettes. A midday checkout can be arranged at no extra charge.

In the Catlins area, June and Murray Stratford rent a bush cabin near Cathedral Caves and Curio Bay, where dolphins swim offshore. The owners' homestead is two kilometers away. Set in forest, your cabin will be surrounded by 1,000 acres of farmland, with sheep, deer, and cattle. You can see the coastline from the top of a hill. If you like, you can help the Stratfords with farmwork or join them in community activities. On request, they'll provide home-cooked meals. Contact the Stratfords at Progress Valley, RD 1, Tokanui, ;03-246-8863.

**Homestead Villa Motel**, on the corner of Dee and Avenal Sts., Invercargill, 03-214-0408, fax 03-214-0478, villa@ilt.co.nz, is about a 10-minute drive from downtown Invercargill and across from a Cobb and Co. Restaurant. The Southland Museum is about five minutes away on foot. The motel has 25 luxury units, each with full kitchens. Rates are NZ$88 for a studio, NZ$98 for a one-bedroom unit, NZ$103 for a two-bedroom unit, and more for suites.

**Western Southland Farm Hosting**, P.O. Box 52, phone/fax 03-225-8485, Otautau, lists 20 homestays between Te Anau and Invercargill—many along the Waiau or Aparima Rivers. Guest rooms are warm and comfortable. This is an important sheep-producing region where you'll see distant vistas of snow-dusted peaks beyond the grazing livestock. Guests can fish in the area rivers and streams, enjoy other outdoor activities, and sometimes help with farmwork. On request, your hosts will prepare home-cooked meals.

# FOOD

With its Scottish heritage, it's not surprising that Dunedin has a Scottish restaurant in a building that looks like a castle. The **Clan Restaurant and Bar**, 131 High St., 03-474-9674, fax 03-474-0354, offers traditional dishes for each course. Along with a bowl of Scotch Broth, a hearty lamb and vegetable soup, you might also start the meal by tasting haggis, the Scottish sausage, served on potatoes. Your main course might be Gaelic Steak with a scotch whiskey and red currant jelly, chicken with potatoes, onions, and an apricot sauce, or Rumbledethumps, a vegetarian dish of chopped vegetables and grated cheese served with tomato bread. Dessert might be a whisky gateau or a dish called Cranachan, which has layers of berries, toasted oatmeal, whisky, and a honey-cream. Open Tuesday through Saturday for dinner.

Named for the Egyptian sun god, **Ra Street Bar and Cafe**, 21 the Octagon, Dunedin, phone/fax 03-477-6080, Ra.bar@xtra.co.nz, has sidewalk seating for nice days and a bright, warm interior for cold or rainy ones. The menu lists familiar combinations, done with a flourish. Brunch might be eggs Benedict. You'll find New Zealand favorites like curried sausages and mash, fresh seafood, and South Pacific dishes made with vegetables, curry seasoning, coconut, and bananas. You can also order crumbed calamari rings with tartar sauce, a beef burger with gourmet cheese, or a snack of potato wedges with fancy toppings. Prices range from NZ$2.50 to NZ$19. The bar has New Zealand beer and wine, plus espresso drinks.

**Bennu Cafe and Bar**, Savoy Building, 12 Moray Pl., Dunedin, 03-474-5055, is run by the same people as Ra. It features Mexican dishes and gourmet pizzas and pastas. The place is more upscale than Ra; you'll notice more customers wearing suits.

**Bacchus Wine Bar & Restaurant**, 12 the Octagon (upstairs), Dunedin, 03-474-0824, does interesting things to fresh New Zealand ingredients. The local deer appears as a venison fajita, served on pimento rice and garnished with coriander salsa. You'll find an eggs

Sally McKinney

*Outdoor cafés line this historic street in Dunedin.*

Benedict on a toasted sesame bagel with local smoked salmon and hollandaise sauce. Another winner is an Italian vegetable torte. The extensive wine list includes New Zealand and imported wines. Smoking is not allowed. Prices range from NZ$9 to NZ$20.

**Passion**, 153 Lower Stuart St. between the Octagon and the DOC center, 03-477-7084, will get your attention with its color scheme of purple, violet, and red and its mosaic bar. Owner Liane Farry has expressed a "passion for life" by creating a vivid haven with the focus on "good, simple, fresh food." Even when rushed, the waitstaff is charming. A scotch filet comes with roasted vegetables and a mushroom sauce. You might try the breadless burger—a lamb patty between potato cakes—or a cold vegetable salad prepared Lebanese-style. Drinks include herbal teas, coffees, Phoenix mineral waters, fresh juices, and smoothies. Passion is open Tuesday through Sunday for lunch and dinner.

# CHAPTER 10

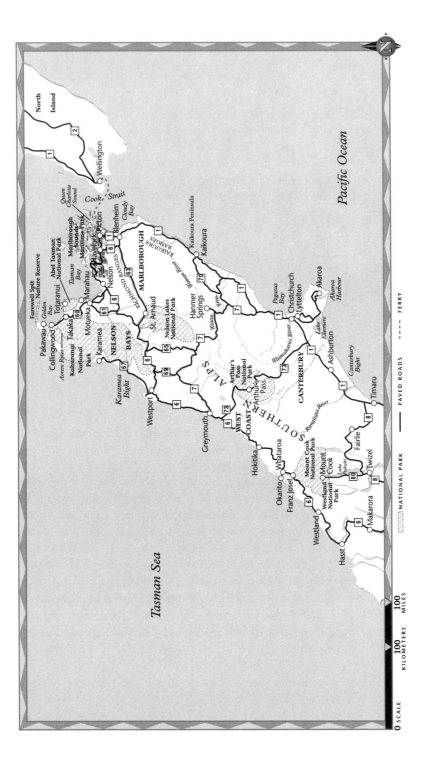

# Christchurch and the Pacific Coast

Arriving at Picton on the ferry across Cook Strait, you can travel overland to Kaikoura, Christchurch, and the Pacific coast. You'll pass through Blenheim, a pleasant town in the Marlborough wine-making region. Follow Highway 1 south (not hard—it's the only highway south), and the road soon skirts the Pacific coast, while the Richmond Ranges, which rise to 1,760 meters, fall away behind you. West, behind the Kaikoura Ranges, are scattered rugged mountain ranges that extend northeast to Nelson Lakes National Park. Continue south toward Kaikoura, and the coastline becomes rockier, with small bays and estuaries rich with bird life.

The village of Kaikoura, with about 3,500 residents, has become an important year-round mecca for wildlife observation. Kaikoura nestles beside a peninsula with the Pacific Ocean beyond. Offshore, a sub-trench from the longer Hikurangi Trough reaches close to land, forming an environment that attracts marine mammals.

Continue along the highway south of Kaikoura and you'll cross the Waiau River, flowing from Hanmer Springs, the center of the largest thermal region on South Island. Farther south, along the coastal highway to Christchurch, the stunning snowcapped Southern Alps rise to the west.

In the Christchurch area, two sloped, rounded, and extinct

cones were formed at different times by eruptions of the Lyttelton and Akaroa volcanoes. Christchurch has a network of hiking trails that links gardens and parks. Extending out to the ocean from Christchurch is the Banks Peninsula, where ridges formed by volcanic action reach the sea from 700-meter mountains. Long narrow bays fill the gaps between these ridges.

Mount Cook National Park, accessible through Burke Pass and a road leading north alongside Lake Pukaki, has 19 mountains over 3,000 meters high. Named Aorangi by the Maoris, majestic Mount Cook itself stands 3,764 meters high; its jagged peaks and sloped faces are piled with masses of snow. Glaciers feed rivers and elongated lakes below the mountain, while taller peaks and surrounding ranges embrace a drier center. Nearby mountains include 3,498-meter Mount Tasman. The Tasman is one of several long glaciers in the park and New Zealand's longest. Only a few thousand people inhabit the awesome landscape around Mount Cook.

North and northeast of Mount Cook National Park are remote rugged forest parks and scattered lower mountain ranges, lakes, and rivers. Arthur's Pass National Park, northwest of Christchurch and 155 kilometers away, has a road and a scenic train running through the highest alpine crossing in the Southern Alps. If you follow Highway 73, a road along the Waimakariri River, and cross at 924-meter Arthur's Pass, you can reach Greymouth on the west coast. An alternate route skirts the edge of the Canterbury Bight, passes through Ashburton, and crosses the Rangitata River.

## HISTORY, CULTURE, AND CUSTOMS

Early Maoris hunted moas in the area southeast of Mount Cook; evidence of Maori habitation can be seen in drawings on the walls of limestone caves near the town of Fairlie. On the Kaikoura Peninsula, Maoris hunted moas and ate crustaceans, fish, and seals (*kaikoura* means "meal of crayfish"). Remains of several *pa* sites can be seen.

European sealers and whalers on sailing vessels eventually joined Maori hunters. New Zealand fur seals were hunted nearly to extinction (their numbers are now slowly increasing). Whalers also reduced the area's large whale populations dramatically.

Captain Cook visited the Banks Peninsula in 1770. Unaware of the land link to the mainland, he named it Banks Island. Maoris inhabited the peninsula long before the French settled there in 1840. *Akaroa* means "long harbor" in Maori; the French influence can still be seen in the charming seaside town.

European colonization of Christchurch began in April 1850 when a sailing vessel loaded with English settlers landed in Port Lyttelton. Four more ships arrived in December. Although the early residents planned to re-create an English town, they found it very difficult to do so. They were not prepared for the challenges of life in this remote land and ultimately focused more on survival than on town planning. The city's economy was first based on agriculture, but has grown to include industry, commerce, and tourism.

Some local history and many legends have evolved around James McKensie, a Scottish sheep drover found in the company of a huge flock of sheep in 1855 and sent to prison for stealing them. There are many versions of this tale: he never admitted the crime . . . he did steal the sheep . . . he was imprisoned unjustly. In any case, he is known for making a series of difficult escapes. The region known as Mackenzie Country bears his name, if not the original spelling.

Arthur's Pass was surveyed in 1864, and the road across the Southern Alps was cut soon after, using explosives and hand tools. The first ascent of Mount Cook was made in 1894. During the early twentieth century, mountain climbing, much in vogue among the wealthy, brought a few climbers to New Zealand. Some tackled the challenging climbs in what is now Mount Cook National Park. The national park was established in 1953.

## NATURE AND ADVENTURE ACTIVITIES

Marine-mammal watching, boat cruises, urban and wilderness hiking, and exploring alpine national parks are popular activities here. The region has an array of fascinating natural areas.

In the Marlborough wine region, you can visit winery tasting rooms (now, there's a soft adventure!) or book homestays on rural farms. Along the Pacific coast, you can explore tidal estuaries and view flocks of wading birds and gulls. You can walk along the cliffs, rocks, and beaches of the Kaikoura coast, the habitat for many kinds of wildlife.

The village of Kaikoura, known for its crayfish and seafood restaurants, is also a mecca for marine-mammal watchers. You can photograph dolphins from a boat or go whale watching via boat, airplane, or helicopter. The village even has a colony of seals—you can walk to the lookout and watch them napping on the rocks. At least one tour company has organized a seal-swimming experience. Another takes you to see pelagic birds.

*Lodging is plentiful near Cathedral Square in Christchurch.*

In Christchurch, you can ride a bicycle, hike to gardens and museums, or go punting on the Avon River. Port Hills and other nearby areas have many hiking trails. South of the city, on Lake Ellesmere, you can photograph black swans and other waterfowl. From Akaroa on the Banks Peninsula, you can hike alone or with a guide or paddle a kayak on one of many long bays. The peninsula also has dolphin- and bird-watching tours.

Mount Cook has long been a focus for exploration; the area has drawn visitors since the early twentieth century. You can ski there in winter. Lake Tekapo is a center for summer activities: hiking, rock climbing, snowshoeing, and rappelling. Arthur's Pass also has hiking trails and an alpine environment. Hanmer Springs, nearer Christchurch, is a mountain resort with thermal baths.

## FLORA AND FAUNA

With a mixture of warm currents and cool southern seas, the area's Pacific coast waters—especially near Kaikoura—are a rich source of phytoplankton, the basis for a food chain that supports crustaceans, birds, and mammals. At Kaikoura, baleen whales, including hump-backs, come very close to shore. Throughout the year, huge sperm whales can usually be seen. Other species are spotted at different times, depending on the season.

You can also see pilot and orca whales, along with three species of dolphins: dusky, bottle-nosed, and Hector's. Kaikoura is also a good place to see New Zealand fur seals. There is a colony farther north at Ohau Point and others along the coast. They feed on fish at night and dry out their coats on sun-warmed rocks during the day.

In winter (May through September), guests on an Ocean Wings tour often see 20 to 30 different species of birds. Throughout the year, albatross, mollymawks, herons, shearwaters, petrels, shags, gulls, and terns can be seen, as well as the little blue penguins. The rich bird life is made possible by luxuriant food sources.

West of Kaikoura, in the higher parts of the Kaikoura Ranges, you can see "vegetable sheep"—dirty-white wooly masses comprised of three interdependent plant species. The range known as the Inland Kaikouras has dense coastal forest. In the valleys, you'll see dotterels and black-fronted terns, with warblers and bellbirds in the forests.

Near Christchurch, the Banks Peninsula also has rich bird life, and dolphins can be seen offshore. The region's lakes are stocked with brown and rainbow trout. You'll see Australasian black swans, along with geese and ducks swimming on Lake Ellesmere.

The Maoris name for Mount Cook was Aorangi, which means "Cloud in the Sky." The Europeans named the mountain for the great seafaring captain. Although difficult to reach, Mount Cook's high-stress alpine, glacial, river, and lake environments are lush with variant plant species that somehow manage to survive. The Tasman glacier and river feed Lake Pukaki; the Godley glacier and river feed Lake Tekapo. In the park, you might see a crested grebe or silvereyes, fan-tails, or the tiny rifleman.

The Mount Cook lily, actually a large white buttercup with a yel-low center, is the best known of many flowers in Mount Cook National Park. Other species of buttercups, many kinds of hebes, and gentians bloom here. As if to mimic the snowscape, many of the blos-soms are white.

# VISITOR INFORMATION

Christchurch, the location of many foreign consulate services, has a visitor information center downtown near the cathedral, at the corner of Worcester Street and Oxford Terrace beside the Avon River, P.O. Box 2600, 03-379-9629, fax 03-377-2424. There are two more centers at the domestic and international airline terminals. The New Zealand immigration office is located at Carter House, 81 Lichfield St., 03-365-2520.

Most smaller South Island communities also have visitor information centers. In the center at Kaikoura, you can watch an excellent multimedia show about whales, which also provides information on bird life and other marine mammals seen in the area. The center is located on the Esplanade, 03-319-5641, fax 03-319-6819.

North of Kaikoura, you'll find the Blenheim visitor center in the Forum Building, Queen St., 03-578-9904, fax 03-578-6084. Other centers near important nature areas are Arthur's Pass, Main Rd., 03-318-9211, fax 03-318-9271; Mount Cook, Bowen Dr., 03-435-1818, fax 03-435-1080; Twizel, Wairepo Rd., 03-435-0802; and Hanmer Springs, Amuri Ave. and Jack's Pass Rd., phone/fax 03-315-7128. On the Banks Peninsula, the Akaroa Information Office is located at the corner of Lavaud and Balguerie Sts., 03-304-8600.

You can check your e-mail at CyberCafe Christchurch, located downtown at 127 Gloucester St., 03-365-5183, fax 03-365-9037, info@cybercafe-chch.co.nz. They can also handle low-cost international phone calls, send faxes—even take a digital photo that you can attach to your e-mail message.

# GETTING AROUND

To reach the region from Wellington on North Island, you can take the Wellington to Picton InterIslander ferry, 0800-658-999, with service four times a day. There's a free shuttle bus from the Wellington railway station to the ferry dock. Book the ferry well ahead, especially during peak travel times. Ask about discounts; advance bookings lower your price. The ferry handles cars, campers, and bicycles, along with passengers, for various charges. The vehicle cost is NZ$100 to NZ$150. The faster Lynx, which runs only in summer, also takes vehicles, equipment, and passengers. For information call 0800-658-999.

Several bus lines serve Picton, Blenheim, and Kaikoura. Bus schedules are coordinated with ferry arrivals and departures. Phone Mount Cook Landline at 03-573-6687 or InterCity at 03-573-6855. Both bus lines have extensive South Island service.

In Kaikoura, T.J.'s Shuttle & Tour Service connects with buses, trains, lodging, sites, and the local airfield. Transport runs NZ$4 to NZ$6 per person to local destinations and NZ$10 to NZ$20 per person to the Hinau and Fyffe Palmers hiking trails. Call Terry, 03-319-6803, mobile 025-855-414, for more information.

The Hanmer Connection Ltd., Amuri Ave., Hanmer Springs, 0800-377-378 or 03-315-7575, fax 03-389-0160, mobile 025-332-088, an official InterCity bus, has service linking Kaikoura, Hanmer Springs, and Christchurch. It operates every day of the year except Christmas. Costs are NZ$22 to NZ$25 one way, with savings if you buy return fare.

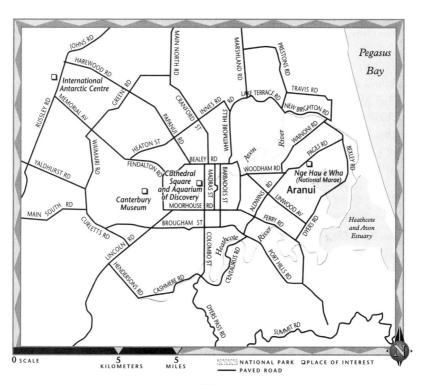

Between Christchurch and Dunedin, InterCity and Mount Cook Landline have bus service, along with the smaller Supa KutPrice Shuttles, which claims "we will not be beaten on price." The fare between the larger cities is NZ$20.

From the airport in Christchurch, take SuperShuttle, 03-365-5655, located outside the baggage area, or call P.B.S. Shuttles, 03-355-1111. Taxi services include Blue Star, 03-379-9799, and Gold Band, 03-379-5795.

## NATURE AND ADVENTURE SIGHTS IN CHRISTCHURCH

### Aquarium of Discovery

The aquarium houses specimens of South Island's diverse freshwater and marine species, including trout, eels, and sharks, which you can watch being fed. Habitats range from the offshore waters of New Zealand's east coast to the river estuaries on the west coast.

*Details: Located on Cathedral Square, 03-377-3474. Open daily.*

### Avon River

The Avon is a lovely little stream that curves through downtown Christchurch. You can ride in a narrow, upholstered wooden punt, while a nattily dressed man pushes you along beneath the overhanging willow trees. There are landings at the visitor center, Town Hall, and the Thomas Edmonds Restaurant.

*Details: Punting on the Avon, Worcester Blvd. and Oxford Ter., P.O. Box 2600, Christchurch, 03-379-9629, fax 03-377-2424. Punting in the Park, Antigua Boatsheds, 2 Cambridge Ter., Christchurch, also offers rides and rents canoes and paddleboats. Call 03-366-0337 for information.*

### International Antarctic Centre

Many Antarctic expeditions have been staged from Christchurch and the port of Lyttelton. Visit the International Antarctic Centre, and you'll not only learn more about Antarctica, but you'll also get a sense of what it's like to visit there. The center houses research programs operated by New Zealand, the United States, and Italy, along with an information center for researchers.

Enter the visitor center and you'll be welcomed by a display of photographs. Next, you'll learn how the four seasons vary on the continent, not only in temperature but also in the swing from winter darkness to long summer daylight. At the Scott Base exhibit, you'll use interactive technology to learn more about the people who live and work in Antarctica—some of them through the winter. You can see the special clothes they wear and learn more about Scott Base and New Zealand research programs in the area.

In another gallery, you can learn more about the International Antarctic Treaty, travel to and from the continent, ozone layer research, and the continent's wildlife and habitats. You'll get to look at a polar campsite and the snowmobiles used to get around; at the visitors center, you can even ride in one. An audio-visual program re-creates the sights and sounds of the "Great White South." Your visit culminates in a chilly experience when you slide down a snow slope, explore a snow cave, and feel an icy wind.

Commentaries and brochures are available in six languages. The "Antarctic Heritage Trail" brochure, available at the IAC and at Christchurch tourism centers, reviews the history of Antarctic expeditions staged from Christchurch and describes other Christchurch sites related to Antarctic exploration. (These include the Hall of Antarctic Discovery in the **Canterbury Museum,** 03-366-8379, and the Antarctic Gallery at the **Lyttelton Museum** in Gladstone Quay.) Located at the airport, the Antarctic Centre can be reached via the city-airport bus. SuperShuttle also stops at the center on request. The center is wheelchair accessible; wheelchairs are available.

***Details:*** *Orchard Rd., P.O. Box 14-001, Christchurch, 03-358-9896, fax 03-353-7799, infor@iceberg.co.nz, www.iceberg.co.nz.*


## *Nga Hau E Wha National Marae*

The largest marae in New Zealand is six kilometers from Christchurch city center. Called the Nga Hau E Wha National Marae (Marae of the Four Winds), it is a center for Maori customs and culture, a place where people from all points of the compass meet one another. The marae, with its ornate gate and red-roofed meetinghouses, is open every day. It offers guided tours, dinners, and Maori cultural performances.

*Details: 250 Pages Rd., Aranui, 03-388-7685 or 0800-456-898.*

## Willowbank Wildlife Reserve

The reserve features specimens of native and introduced species in natural settings. There are opportunities for animal contact, including a daytime viewing area for the nocturnal kiwi.

*Details: Hussey Rd., Christchurch, 03-359-6226, fax 03-359-6212.*

# NATURE AND ADVENTURE SIGHTS ON THE PACIFIC COAST

## Banks Peninsula

The Banks Peninsula coast has a resident population of Hector's dolphins, the smallest oceanic dolphins in the world, found only in New Zealand. The species is threatened—only an estimated 3,000 to 4,000 exist, 600 to 700 of them near the Banks Peninsula. Short and thick-looking, the mammals have a rounded dorsal fin and are usually seen swimming in pods of two to eight. The Banks Peninsula is also one of two known breeding locations for the white-flippered blue penguin.

Based in Akaroa Harbour, Dolphins Up Close operates scenic and wildlife catamaran cruises around the peninsula, visiting **Onuku**, **The Blowhole**, **Cathedral Cave**, **Lighthouse Point**, and a salmon farm at **Lucas Bay**. From the deck, you can expect sightings of Hector's dolphins, New Zealand southern fur seals, little blue penguins, spotted shags, red-billed gulls, and white-fronted terns. You might also see pied or little black shags, white-throated shags, giant petrels, or kingfishers. The company reports a 98 percent success rate for dolphin sightings. You'll find Dolphins Up Close at the Main Wharf, Beach Rd., 0800-43657-4467 (0800-4-DOLPHINS) or 03-304-7641, fax 03-304-7643. Cruises take place on the *Canterbury Cat*. The cost is NZ$65 for swimmers, NZ$29 for spectators.

With Dolphin Experience Akaroa, 61 Beach Rd., Akaroa, phone/fax 03-304-7866, you can either swim with the dolphins—

Sally McKinney

*Boats offer leisurely punting opportunities on the Avon River.*

wetsuits are provided—or just ride along to watch. The wetsuits are buoyant; no swimming experience is required. You will be supervised throughout. The cost is NZ$68 for swimmers, NZ$29 for watchers, including equipment, hot showers, and refreshments.

Canterbury Sea Tours, P.O. Box 17587 Christchurch, phone/fax 03-326-5607, mobile 025-344-770, operates a twin-engine Naiad tourcraft and can add a horse trek, barbecue lunch, and farm visit to your dolphin-watching tour. Canterbury offers two tours daily, departing from Lyttelton and Sumner. You can also arrange for the company to pick you up in Christchurch.

*Details: Christchurch-Canterbury Visitor Centre, P.O. Box 2600, 03-379-9629, info@christchurchtourism.co.nz.*

## Banks Peninsula Track

Beginning and ending in the historic village of Akaroa, 80 kilometers from Christchurch, this track follows 35 kilometers of the peninsula's unusual volcanic coastline. Along the way, you'll find wide-open spaces, swimming beaches, waterfalls, beech forests, regenerating coastal bush, rocky cliff faces, and open pastures. You see a variety of birds, and you could see penguins, seals, and Hector's dolphins in or near the bays. There are no problem insects on the hike.

The track climbs from sea level to more than 600 meters in two different places and crosses rugged exposed headlands. The trek takes four days and nights; a two-day option is available. This is a private track, and you'll stay in cozy private huts. Since the number of hikers is limited, the trail is not crowded.

The first night's hut, at **Onuku Farm**, has a view of Akaroa Harbour. The second night's lodging is a charming cottage with a verandah overlooking the sea. On the third night, you'll stay in the **Stony Bay** hut, with its open fireplace and log burner. On the fourth night, you'll stay at **Otanerito Beach**, in a cozy farmhouse about 50 yards from a sandy beach with safe swimming.

Food is available at shops in Stony Bay and at Otanerito Beach along the route, so you don't have to carry everything (you might try the local cheese). You must bring a sleeping bag and clothing for variable weather. The season runs from October 1 through April 30.

*Details: Banks Peninsula Track Ltd., P.O. Box 50, Akaroa, 03-304-7612, fax 03-304-7738. Four-day trek NZ$120 or NZ$140; two-day trek NZ$75. Cost includes transportation and lodging.*

## Hanmer Springs

Although many New Zealand adventures are challenging and strenuous, they don't all have to be. The mountain resort community of Hanmer Springs offers a combination. At Thrillseeker's Canyon you can rent kayaks and river bugs or go river rafting. You can tour vast sheep stations in the area by four-wheel-drive vehicle. Afterward, you can relax in one of seven open-air thermal pools, four private thermal pools, or a 25-meter freshwater heated pool. A picnic area and a café with bar facilities are nearby. You can also get a therapeutic massage, use a fitness and health center, take a Scandinavian-style sauna bath, or use the steam rooms.

Hanmer Springs has a long history. Maoris first used the natural thermal pools after strenuous west coast hunting trips for *pounamu* (greenstone—the New Zealand jade). The resort community was launched in the 1860s, when people believed that bathing in thermal springs would help heal various ailments.

Surrounded by mountains, Hanmer Springs lies within a region of livestock grazing and farming. The climate is dry and the air is clear. While in the area, you can take a Rainbow Horse Trekking ride, Jacks Pass Rd., Hanmer Springs, phone/fax 03-315-7444, mobile 025-227-5347, or rent a mountain bike from Dust 'n' Dirt, 20 Conical Hill Rd., phone/fax 03-315-7233, mobile 025-221-1568.

*Details: Hanmer Springs Thermal Reserve, Amuri Rd., P.O. Box 30, Hanmer Springs, 03-315-7511.*

## Kaikoura Coast

Dusky dolphins, the most acrobatic of the dolphin species, swim along the coast in masses. Every day, they migrate to Goose Bay, south of the Kaikoura Peninsula. The coast also has an unusually high concentration of seabirds—over 40 species can be seen off Kaikoura at various times of the year.

Canterbury Tourism Council

*World-renowned Hanmer Thermal Reserve*

Despite extensive hunting in earlier centuries, several species of whales can be seen off the Kaikoura coast, including humpback and occasionally blue whales. Sometimes, a pod of orcas appears, and pilot whales also visit the area occasionally. Although it's unusual for whales to come this close to shore, a sub-trench 1,000 meters deep reaches inland from the longer Hikurangi Trench. Here, cool Antarctic waters rich in nutrients mix with warmer currents from the north. With the help of the sun, phytoplankton grow in massive quantities, creating a base for a food chain that links tiny fish and small crustaceans, crayfish, birds, and marine mammals,.

Kaikoura's Dolphin Encounter, 58 West End Rd., 03-319-6777, fax 03-319-6534, info@dolphin.co.nz, www.dolphin.co.nz, pioneered dolphin swimming in New Zealand. Its cruise tour, offered twice daily, focuses on sighting dolphins and swimming with them in their Pacific habitat. The tour has been compared to a biology field trip on water. Dolphin Encounter provides a commentary during the tour, operates within guidelines from the DOC, and arranges encounters that will create the least disturbance for dolphins. Four long-time residents of Kaikoura own the company. You don't have to swim—you can join a tour at a lower rate to simply watch wildlife, take photos, and enjoy the scenery. The adult swimmer rate is NZ$85, the spectator rate is NZ$48. Book ahead for November to April tours.

The **Kaikoura Wildlife Centre** on West End Road also operates tours on the high-tech craft *Kotuku* that allow you to swim with, photograph, and view dusky dolphins. Hydrophones allow you to hear the dolphins communicate. The center also offers seal snorkeling tours (they will teach you how to snorkel), bird-watching, scuba diving (for beginners and experienced divers), and whale watching from the air. Contact New Zealand Wildlife Eco-Tours at Kaikoura Wildlife Centre, P.O. Box 85, Kaikoura, 03-319-6622, fax 03-319-6868, nzsa@southern.co.nz, www.scubadive.co.nz.

Also based in Kaikoura and associated with Dolphin Encounter, Ocean Wings will take you on a bird-watching cruise. Skipper Gary Melville has 22 years of experience on the water in and around the peninsula. An ex-fisherman, he shares a specialized knowledge of bird life and other marine creatures on this cruise. Ocean Wings has a lengthy checklist of birds you might see, including 3 varieties of royal albatross, 6 varieties of mollymawk, 7 varieties of shearwaters, 14 varieties of petrels, and 4 varieties of shag. Your guide can help you sort out the Hutton's shearwater from the Westland petrel and confirm that the large soaring bird is a royal, not a wandering, albatross. The trip operates year-round, three times a day, and lasts two or three hours. During winter, between May and September, it's possible to see 20 to 30 different species on one tour. During summer, some species are gone—breeding in more southern locations.

You'll cruise on a small boat that carries up to 15 passengers. The small motor cruiser has a roof, but is open to the air. In winter, a larger vessel, the *Lissodelphis*, carries up to 36 passengers. Contact Ocean Wings Pelagic Birdwatching at 58 West End, Kaikoura, 0800-733-365 or 03-319-6777, fax 03-319-6534, info@oceanwings.co.nz, www.oceanwings.co.nz. The cost is NZ$65 per adult.

Whale Watch TM Kaikoura Limited, P.O. Box 89, Kaikoura, 0800-655-121 or 03-319-6767, fax 03-319-6545, res@whalewatch.co.nz, operates up to six tours a day, taking visitors to witness whales surfacing and diving into the deep water of a trench about 1,000 meters offshore. What you see depends on the season, and the company gives a partial refund if no whales are sighted.

You can also spot whales from an airplane or helicopter. Wings Over Whales, P.O. Box 55, Kaikoura, 03-319-6580, fax 03-319-6668, W.O.W.@xtra.co.nz, offers half-hour scenic flights from Kaikoura Airport. Prices start at NZ$95 per adult. For reservations call 0800-2C-MOBY. Kaikoura Helicopters, Railway Station Road, P.O. Box 5, Kaikoura, 03-319-6609, fax 03-319-5955, will take you on a whale-watching helicopter ride. Kaikoura's rugged coastal scenery provides a backdrop for your whale watching.

*Details: Kaikoura Information Centre, Westend, 03-319-5641, kbzuin @nzhost.co.nz.*

## Kaikoura Coast Track

This 43-kilometer trek is private, not public—hikers must join the tour organized by Sally and David Handyside and their neighbors. The trek begins and ends at the Staging Post in Hawkswood, near the Hawkswood Range. It is a three-day journey for reasonably fit hikers. The season runs from October through April.

The tour combines daily hikes with farmstay lodging. You'll sleep in warm clean cottages with fully equipped kitchens, bathrooms, and hot showers. Fresh farm produce is available, and you can arrange to have home-cooked meals.

First-night lodging at a historic sheep station allows you to rest up for the first day of perhaps five to seven hours of hiking. You'll cross the Hawkswood Range on the way to the top of 600-meter **Mount Admiral**. After enjoying wonderful views of mountains and ocean (on a clear day you can see the Banks Peninsula), you'll descend through tussock and bush to reach the Ngaroma homestead. The hosts have a swimming pool and barbecue.

The second day's route, perhaps three to five hours, runs along a beach beneath cliffs embedded with ancient tree stumps and fossils. You could see dolphins offshore before your lunch beside a stream. You'll then continue over farmland and walk through regenerating bush to **Medina**, a remote homestead on a sheep station, nestled between the mountains and the sea.

The third day, you'll walk for maybe four to six hours through Medina farmland and over slopes of the Hawkswood Range to reach **Mount Wilson**, which is 642 meters high. The view includes the Southern Alps in the distance and the Staging Post down below.

*Details: Kaikoura Coast Track, Medina, RD Parnassus, North Canterbury, 03-319-2715, fax 03-319-2724.*

## TOUR OPERATORS

For guided hiking tours in the Christchurch area, consider **Ian Mcleod's Walkaway Tours**. On the Volcanoes Tour, you'll investigate Maori archaeological sites, learn about history, and visit an herb farm, a cheese factory, or a winery. The Sea Tour takes you through native bush and along the crater rim. The tour combines local history with a visit to sea caves and occasional wildlife sightings; you could see Hector's dolphins or gannets. Mcleod also takes tours to Port Hills, Arthur's Pass, and the Otira Gorge. Prices range from NZ$25 to NZ$157. Contact Walkaway Tours, P.O. Box 22-398, Christchurch, 03-365-6672, fax 03-365-9140.

**Alpine Recreation Limited**, P.O. Box 75, Lake Tekapo, 03-680-6736, fax 03-680-6765, alprec@voyager.co.nz, www.canterburypages.

co.nz/climb/alpred/index.html, offers a four-day course for hikers and rock climbers with little or no mountaineering experience. The course teaches the basics of climbing amid rock, snow, and ice. You'll also learn glacier travel, belay techniques, and methods for finding your way, evaluating the weather, and surviving in an emergency. The guide-to-client ratio is four to one. The course takes place at Caroline Hut, the only private hut in Mount Cook National Park, located in the lee of Mount Cook for better weather and warmed by a wood stove. All company guides have been trained through the New Zealand affiliate of IFMGA, the International Federation of Mountain Guides Associations.

The company also offers a challenging three-day Ball Pass Trek, suitable for experienced hikers who can walk over steep, rugged, and trackless terrain for several hours a day. The trek begins at the Tasman Glacier, at an altitude of 850 meters, and includes panoramic views of Mount Cook, Mount Tasman, the glacier, and Lake Pukaki. Lodging is also at Caroline Hut. On the third day you'll cross Ball Pass, 2,130 meters high, for spectacular views of mountains, glaciers, and lakes. Conditions may require use of crampons and ice axes; you'll be shown how to use them. The end of the route passes through some of the most luxuriant vegetation in the national park. You'll be provided with a lengthy list of equipment and should train by doing six-hour hikes over rugged terrain.

**Up, Up, and Away Ballooning Adventures**, P.O. Box 14160, Christchurch, 03-358-9859, fax 03-358-9829, mobile 025-325-611, upupandaway@xtra.co.nz, has the largest balloon fleet in New Zealand. From the air, you will see the famous cathedral square in Christchurch's city center, the wide expanse of city buildings, snow-capped mountain ranges in the west, and the Pacific Ocean in the east. Tours are often launched from the city parks, although launch sites depend on winds and weather.

Flights typically last one hour. Some of the best ballooning experiences begin at dawn—which can be as early as 4:30 in summer and as late as 7:30 in winter. Landing could well be in a farmer's field, where you'll enjoy a glass of chilled New Zealand Methode Champenoise. On request, the company can fly up to 36 passengers at a time in up to four balloons. They will provide transportation to and from your accommodation in central Christchurch at no extra

Canterbury Tourism Council

*Hot-air balloons over the Canterbury Plains*

charge. Note that the cost of ballooning here is about 30 percent less than in other countries.

**City Cycle Hire**, Canterbury Information Centre, corner Oxford Ter. and Worcester Blvd., will deliver bicycles to your accommodations (within Christchurch) and collect them when you've finished. They also have helmets, water bottles, locks, and maps of the city. Call 0800-343-848, mobile 025-222-9893.

In Kaikoura, Sue and Peter McInnes, 03-319-5069, mobile 025-353-904, operate **Fyffe View Horse Trek** at the edge of the village. You'll ride through an area of farmland and native forests, set against a stunning backdrop of mountains and sea. The cost is NZ$40 for a two-hour ride. Sue, a certified massage therapist, also offers a 15-minute neck and shoulder massage for NZ$10 or a 45-minute neck, back, and shoulder massage, using aromatherapy oils, for NZ$25.

At the **Kaikoura Aero Club**, P.O. Box 68, Peketa, Kaikoura, phone/fax 03-319-6579, you can take a trial flight in a small plane for 30 minutes and do a bit of the flying yourself. An instructor will take you without experience, no matter what your age. Prices start at NZ$69 for the trial flight.

Bob Wilkinson of **Boots Et All Adventures**, phone/fax 03-332-7296, trek@ihug.co.nz, will guide you on a day walk or a trek up to five days long. Areas include the Banks Peninsula, the Southern Alps, the Arthur's Pass region, or South Island's west coast. Wilkinson serves as driver, guide, and chef and organizes camping. After learning more about your experience and requirements, he'll suggest a trek you can handle and describe the area's unique features while you walk.

# CAMPING

**Kaikoura Searidge Holiday Park**, 34 Beach Rd., Kaikoura, phone/fax 03-319-5362, is a family park near town center and activities. The place has 100 tent sites and 50 powered sites, along with a children's playground and trampolines, set in spacious grounds.

**Esplanade Holiday Park**, 128 Esplanade, Kaikoura, 03-319-5947, fax 03-319-5947, also a short walk to town, is a smaller campground with panoramic views of the mountains and the Pacific Ocean. Your hosts can arrange various nature tours for you. They also have cabins that sleep up to six people.

**Mountain View Holiday Park**, Main Rd., P.O. Box 169, Hanmer Springs, 03-315-7113, fax 03-315-7113, is only 400 meters from the thermal pools and town center. You will camp in a parklike setting with views of forest and mountains. The park has 30 tent sites, 50 RV sites, cabins, tourist flats, a kitchen, dining rooms, a play area, trampoline, squash court, and nearby forest walks. Tent sites cost NZ$18 for two people; powered sites are NZ$20. Cabins cost NZ$35 to NZ$49; flats are higher.

**Pines Motor Camp**, at the corner of Jacks Pass and Argelins Rd., P.O. Box 193, Hanmer Springs, 03-315-7152, fax 03-315-7152, has 20 tent sites and 34 powered sites in quiet surroundings. You can walk to town center and the thermal pools. Nearby are horse treks and other mountain activities.

**Meadow Park Holiday Park**, 39 Meadow St., P.O. Box 5178, Christchurch, 03-352-9176, is located four kilometers north of downtown on Highway 74. The park has 80 tent sites and 90 powered sites,

# NEW ZEALAND TRIVIA QUIZ

1. What large marine mammal, a prize catch during the nineteenth century, has been hunted for its spermaceti, blubber, and ambergris? *The sperm whale, or paraoa in Maori.*

2. The world's smallest marine dolphin (it grows up to 1.6 meters long) lives only in New Zealand waters. What is it called? *Hector's dolphin, or tupoupou in Maori.*

3. What New Zealand author, known for her mystery novels, has the given name of a native flower? *Ngaio Marsh.*

4. What Wellington-based filmmaker's studio shares its name with a giant insect? *Peter Jackson's WETA (Wingnut Effects and Technical Information) Studios.*

5. What rare New Zealand creature descended from reptiles that lived in the Mesozoic era? *The tuatara.*

6. Not far from Rotorua is the world's largest hot-water spring, which measures 200 degrees Celsius at its deepest point. What is it called? *Frying Pan Lake.*

7. Near Nelson is a spring that generates 2,160 million liters of water every day. What is the spring called? *Waikoropupu Springs (also known by its nickname, Pupu Springs).*

8. What is the name of New Zealand's flightless parrot? *The kakapo.*

9. South Island has an extensive area of petrified forest, estimated to be 180 million years old. Where is it located? *At Curio Bay, on the coast east of Invercargill.*

10. New Zealand has three varieties of ornamental greenstone that Europeans call nephrite, or jade. The Maoris call it pounamu. Which national park is named for one of the three varieties? *Kahurangi National Park. (The other two varieties are kawakawa and inanga.)*

grassy sites, and an array of facilities including a swimming pool and sauna. It also has an 88-bed lodge.

**South New Brighton Motor Camp**, on Halsey St. off Estuary Rd., is located on a peninsula in South Brighton, about 10 kilometers from Christchurch. The campground has 35 tent sites and 98 RV sites in a sheltered park reserve beside a tidal estuary. A beach is 300 meters away; New Brighton Pier shops are three kilometers away. The campground has playgrounds, trampolines, and various sports fields and equipment. A café/bar is around the corner.

**Le Bons Bay Motor Camp & Holiday Park**, Valley Rd., RD 3, Le Bons Bay, Banks Peninsula, is a campground on a sheep farm in a sheltered valley. It has 41 tent sites and 16 RV hookups. The park offers pony rides and horse treks, and guests can enjoy a store, clothes dryer, barbecue, and pool. Tramping tracks, forest reserves, and swimming beaches are nearby.

**Glentanner Park**, SH 80, P.O. Box 23, Mount Cook, is a large camp 20 kilometers from Mount Cook Village. There are 100 tent sites and 60 powered sites at this base for hiking, horseback riding, mountain biking, and fishing.

For the huts in the Copland Pass alpine crossing, call the **Mount Cook DOC Field Centre**, 03-435-1819. Crampons and ice axes are needed all year for the crossing; the DOC advises going with a guide. The Hooker Hut Track in Mount Cook National Park is accessed from Mount Cook Village. Call the Mount Cook Field Centre for more information.

# LODGING

The village of Kaikoura has several motels, including the **Kaikoura Motel**, 11-15 Beach Rd., phone/fax 03-319-5999, kaimotel.@ voyagernz. The **Alpine View,** 146 Beach Rd., 03-319-5429, fax 03-319-6679, has rates of NZ$70 to NZ$80. The **Colonial Motel**, 205 Beach Rd., phone/fax 03-319-6037, charges NZ$80 for double rooms.

On the Esplanade, you'll find the **Norfolk Pine Motel**, 124 Esplanada, 03-319-5120, fax 03-319-6405. Rates are NZ$80 for a double room. The **Blue Seas Motel**, 222 Esplanada, 03-319-5441, fax 03-319-6707, blue.seas@xtra.co.nz, has rates from NZ$75 to NZ$130.

The **ParkRoyal**, at the corner of Kilmore and Durham Sts. across from the convention center, P.O. Box 1544, Christchurch, has a large atrium lounge with a glass roof and 296 luxurious rooms and suites. You'll also find a gym and sauna, the brasserie-style Victoria Street Cafe, a formal dining room, and two bars. Food is made from fresh local ingredients, and the wine list includes New Zealand and imported wines. Rates are expensive.

The **Elms Hotel**, 456 Papanui Rd., Christchurch, 03-355-3577, fax 03-352-0290, reservations@the-elms-hotel.co.nz, has a garden setting and a location between the airport and city center. There are 90 studio rooms and nine luxury suites, all nicely decorated. Bogart's Restaurant and Bar, on the premises, is open daily.

Christchurch backpackers' lodgings include **New Excelsior Backpackers** located in a historic building at the corner of High and Manchester Sts., 03-366-7570, fax 03-366-7629. It is near the bus station, cafés, a supermarket, and Cathedral Square. **Dreamland**, 21 Packe St., St.Albans, Christchurch, 03-366-3519, has a homey atmosphere with fireplaces and gardens. It has twin, double, and shared rooms; will pick up guests in the inner city; and will rent bikes for NZ$1. **Christchurch Central YHA**, 273 Manchester St., 03-379-9535, fax 03-379-9537, yhachch@yha.org.nz, has a convenient location and rates from NZ$19.

**Mount Cook YHA**, Bowen and Kitchener Drs., Mount Cook National Park, 03-435-1820, fax 03-435-1821, yhamtck@ha.org.nz, is located within the park. It has cozy lounges, a sauna, a shop, and clean bunkroom accommodations starting at NZ$20 a night.

At Arthur's Pass, about 130 kilometers west of Christchurch on SH 73, you'll find the wonderful but expensive **Wilderness Lodge**, P.O. Box 33, Arthur's Pass 8190, Canterbury, wlodgeap@xtra.co.nz. Developed by an ecologist, it combines high-quality hospitality with eco-sensitivity. Designed by architect Gary Hopkinson, the lodge has 20 guest rooms, all with private baths and mountain views, plus a restaurant, lounge, library, and conference room. Views from the lodge reach for 60 kilometers in all directions. You can see the Binser Range, the Waimakariri River Valley, mixed beech forests, and even Mount Rolleston, at 2,275 meters the highest mountain in the area. The owners work with the DOC to protect special plants and animals in the area and on a farm management program to improve land quality. Guests can take part in high-country adven-

*Canterbury Tourism Council*

*Hiking in Arthur's Pass National Park*

tures including canoeing, a cave visit, a historic walk, alpine hiking, and a visit to a sheep station. Activity charges range from NZ$48 to NZ$68 per person. Lodge rates, which include full breakfast and four-course dinners with vegetarian options, are NZ$195 per person for a shared lodge room and NZ$260 per person for a single-occupancy lodge room.

## FOOD

Kaikoura is known for its crayfish meals. The crustacean is served hot or cold, with chips, salad, rice, or vegetables, or made into crayfish Mornay. Restaurants specializing in crayfish include **Caves Restaurant** on SH 1 south of town, phone/fax 03-319-5023; **Continental Seafoods**, 47 Beach Rd., 03-319-6041; **Craypot Cafe**, West End Rd., 03-319-6027; **Fyffe Gallery/Fyffe Country Inn**, RD 2, SH 1 south of Kaikoura, 03-319-6869; and **Hislops Cafe**, 33 Beach Rd., 03-319-6971.

In Christchurch, **Blue Jean Cuisine Restaurant & Bar**, 205 Manchester St. (just north of Hereford), 03-365-4130, creates sophisticated food in an informal setting of exposed brick walls, decorated in "Early Attic." The restaurant serves a kumare, carrot, and sour cream soup and gourmet pizzas (such as chicken, tomato, cream cheese, and broccoli). Very popular for business and social lunches, the restaurant also offers an array of starters, pasta, salads, sandwiches, and main dishes, including a popular char-grilled New Zealand lamb. A typical dinner might be fish baked in an infusion of capers, spring onion, and capsicum. New Zealand beers and wines are available, and the music is classical jazz. Prices are moderate.

**Annie's Wine Bar & Restaurant**, located within the Arts Centre at the corner of Hereford and Rolleston, 03-365-0566, is a *Gourmet* magazine award winner. It serves complex, intriguing food in an old country tavern setting with heavy wooden furniture. You might have Annie's Oven Roasted Bread with seasoned oil for a starter, then go on to prime beef fillet with cilantro and cherry tomatoes or seared Canterbury smoked chicken breast with summer berry salad. Dessert? They serve vanilla ice cream with chocolate fudge and fresh sweet berries. The emphasis is on New Zealand wines, especially the whites— one of the owner's reasons for opening Annie's. Prices are expensive.

On Oxford Terrace, down from the visitor center and across from the Avon River, you'll find an entire block of indoor/outdoor cafés. **All Bar None**, 130 Oxford Ter., 03-377-9898, serves breakfast all day, along with tasty and rather familiar dishes in a comfortable "old shoe" atmosphere. The menu, which changes often, might list penne pasta with seafood and tomato in a sweet chili cream, lamb fajitas, pan-fried tarakihi fish with veggies, or a seasonal fruit platter with whipped cream. Hours are 11 on weekdays and 10:30 on weekends until about 10 at night. However, meal service halts between 3:30 and 5:30 p.m., when they serve just snacks and drinks.

**Drexel's**, 106 Hereford St., Christchurch, 03-379-8089, takes reservations for their freshly made and promptly served meals. Owners Norman and Veronica Drexel, the chef, decided to open this place when they had a disappointing anniversary breakfast in a "recommended" hotel dining room. The restaurant's breakfasts (and other meals) are extremely popular, served in a diner setting.

# APPENDIX A
## TRAVEL BASICS

The early Maoris sailed to what is now New Zealand in large double-hulled canoes. The country's early European colonists arrived in classic sailing vessels. Modern air transportation has changed all that; most visitors now arrive on one of the major airlines, usually flying into Auckland or another large city. In season, a few cruise ships call at Auckland's Waitemata Harbour. Intrepid yachties also make the journey to New Zealand under sail.

There are direct flights to Auckland from major cities around the Pacific Rim; some of these flights continue on to Australian cities. Trips to New Zealand combine well with visits to Fiji or Australia. Flying to and from New Zealand is also popular with New Zealanders, who are great travelers. Thus, airline seats are often booked well ahead, and significant discounts are rare.

High season is the austral summer (December through March)—especially between mid-December and early January and during the Easter holidays, when New Zealanders take long vacations. If you're touring during high season, plan well ahead. Using the detailed phone/fax/e-mail information in this travel guide, you can easily make reservations and guarantee them, if necessary, with a major credit card.

## BUSINESS HOURS

New Zealand offices and businesses usually operate Monday through Friday between 8 and 5. Banking hours are usually Monday through Friday 9 to 4:30. Shops are open 9 to 5 weekdays, with extended hours (sometimes) on Friday or possibly Thursday, but with earlier closings—if the shops open at all—on weekends. Post offices are open Monday through Friday between 9 and 5, with some Saturday openings from 9 to 1. The New Zealand version of a convenience store is called a dairy. These stores, which sell bread, fresh veggies, canned goods, flowers, and newspapers, in addition to dairy products, are open 7 a.m. to 10 p.m. seven days a week.

## CLIMATE

New Zealand's variable maritime climate—with rain falling throughout the year—contrasts with that of neighboring Australia, with its regional variations in rainfall and its vast arid center with wide seasonal temperature swings. New Zealand's general patterns include higher west coast rainfall, brought by westerly winds across the Tasman Sea, and decreasing temperatures at higher altitudes and more southerly latitudes.

Yet the country's volcanic landscapes contain myriad microclimates. One New Zealand tour operator claims visitors may discover more variation in one location within one day than they will variations between locations during the same day. Expect variations in temperature and always be prepared for rain. Mean daily temperatures for the North Island city of Auckland are 23.8 degrees Celsius in January and 15.1 degrees Celsius in July. The city receives 2,071 hours of bright sunshine a year and a mean annual rainfall of 1,106 millimeters. On South Island, Dunedin has a mean daily maximum temperature of 18.9 degrees Celsius in January and 9.9 degrees Celsius in July. The city gets 1,595 hours of sunshine a year and 799 millimeters of rainfall.

Consider the extremes: rainfall of 14,108 millimeters one year at Waterfall Creek (on the west coast of South Island) and only 10 millimeters another year in the community of Clyde (also on South Island). The highest recorded temperature was 39.2 degrees Celsius at Ruatoria on North Island, and the lowest recorded temperature was a chilly 21.6 degrees Celsius at Ophir (South Island) in July 1995. Wind gusts on the main islands have been recorded at 250 kilometers per hour.

## SEASONS

After summer comes autumn (March to June), then winter (end of June through most of September), and spring (September through most of November). The South Pacific yachting season runs generally from May to October, with hurricanes most likely between November and March. Bicyclists can expect year-round rainfall and, usually, southwesterly winds, with stronger winds as you go farther south. Trampers (hikers) need to prepare for variations in temperature, unexpected rainfall, and weather that's worse than what you'd expect for that season.

## WEATHER INFORMATION

New Zealand has several sources for updated weather information, including television. The AM National Radio station gives a weather report at 1 p.m. daily, preceded about a half-hour earlier by a five-day forecast. Two phone lines provide weather information. Call the mountain weather forecast on 0900-99966. Use the MetPhone line for specific area forecasts: 0800-500-669.

Useful Web sites include Weather and Related Phenomena, www.highfiber.com~jrssmith/weathercache.html#; Weather Underground, www.wunderground.com/globalNZ.html; and WorldClimate, www.worldclimate.com (which allows you to track trends historically).

## CUISINE

Once known for its hearty, straightforward, meat-and-potatoes meals—the legacy of its agricultural heritage—New Zealand now features lighter, tastier cuisine influenced by its neighbors around the Pacific Rim. Locally produced meats, fruits, and vegetables and regionally harvested seafood are often fashioned into Asian-, European-, or California-style dishes. Away from the large cities, however, a typical meal might be lamb with roasted potatoes and colorful veggies, all of it smothered in brown gravy.

Many of the country's restaurants and cafés have outdoor seating rather than air-conditioning; your table may be cooled by a sea breeze. As an eco-traveler, you are encouraged to select regionally produced foods, to avoid over-harvested species of seafood, and to recycle leftovers, preferably carrying them home in your own container (note that fish-and-chips shops use thick paper wrappings, and some restaurants use foam containers for leftovers). Plan ahead—most backpackers' lodging and some motels have refrigerators for leftovers and microwave ovens for reheating meals. For more information about food, check out Whitcoull's and other book shops, where you'll find colorful illustrated cookbooks describing New Zealand cuisine.

## MONEY AND BANKING

The country's currency is the New Zealand dollar. One dollar is equal to 100 cents; there are 50-, 20-, 10-, and 5-cent coins, as well as gold-colored one- and two-dollar coins. These larger coins are often given as change; make an effort to pay with them, and you won't acquire a heavy collection of coins in your pocket.

Generally, two New Zealand dollars equal one U.S. dollar. The U.S. dollar and other foreign currencies are not used in New Zealand, but it's fairly easy to exchange currency. Exchange services are open in the airports after international flights arrive, and large hotels have exchange desks. It's also convenient to order a few New Zealand dollars before you leave home—enough to get you through, say, a Sunday when banks are closed.

New Zealand banks offer the most favorable exchange rates. The Bank of New Zealand (BNZ) buys U.S. currency without charging a fee—you can thus exchange small amounts economically. Other New Zealand banks include ASB, ANZ, and WestPac. (Note that z is called *zed* here.) There are no restrictions on foreign currency brought in or taken out of New Zealand.

Automatic teller machines linked to the Cirrus, Plus, and other systems can be found around New Zealand. You'll need a pin number and a debit or credit card to use them. The ATMs dispense cash in New Zealand dollars, even if your debit card accesses a checking account in another currency. The ASB machines print out your bank balance in New Zealand dollars. Note that as the exchange rate shifts between New Zealand and your home country, this balance will rise or fall, even though the balance in your home bank stays the same. Take along your home bank's non-800 customer-service phone number in case you lose your card or otherwise need to phone them.

Large hotels and many businesses, restaurants, and tour companies accept major credit cards—Visa, MasterCard, American Express,

Diners Club, and others. Smaller tour companies and cafés, however, may prefer cash to credit cards, which delay payment. Whenever possible, use a card to make a reservation, but pay small businesses in cash. New Zealand's Eftpost system, operated by major banks, involves a card used for purchases and to obtain cash.

The bank that issued your credit card handles the reissue of a lost or stolen card—but service might not be as swift as that described in commercials. Courier shipments to or from North America and New Zealand normally take three to five business days. Always have a back-up plan; replacing a card could take from a few days to a couple weeks. You might carry "desperation currency" in a money belt— enough to get by on for two weeks. You might also leave banking information with someone at home who can make emergency deposits into your account that can be accessed by an ATM. Also, just because a village is represented by a dot on a map, it doesn't mean that village has banking services. Some remote areas have no towns, and small towns may have no ATM at all.

Traveler's checks are another option, carried in a waist bag or money belt along with small amounts of currency, photocopies of your passport, visa, credit cards, and so on. In New Zealand, rain falls throughout the year, so enclose these papers in a waterproof pouch or plastic bag. Be aware that a departure fee of $NZ20 must be paid before you leave the country; a major credit card can be used.

A goods and services tax (GST) of 12.5 percent is generally included in the price of purchases.

## ELECTRICAL CURRENT

In New Zealand, you'll plug into 240-volt AC, 50-cycle power with a three-pronged plug. You'll need a transformer to operate equipment that uses different voltages, though many hotels and motels have 110-volt outlets for razors and hair dryers. Note that outlets in New Zealand have on/off power switches.

In the United States, contact Walkabout Travel Gear, 800/852-7085 or www.walkabouttravelgear.com, for information from their Worldwide Electricity Index and help with equipment. If you're already in New Zealand, walk into the nearest Dick Smith store, an electronic equipment shop with a knowledgeable staff.

## ENTRY AND EXIT REQUIREMENTS

All visitors to New Zealand are required to hold passports. American and Canadian passport holders may stay up to three months without a visitor's visa, if they have sufficient funds and a ticket for onward transportation (home or to another country). To apply for a visitor's visa or permit, you'll need the completed signed application form (sometimes available at large travel agencies), the application fee, and your passport, which must be valid for at least three months after the date you plan to leave New Zealand. You'll also need a recent passport-size photograph and evidence of financial support while you're in New Zealand—the equivalent of NZ$1,000 per month. Without sufficient funds, you'll need a guarantee of accommodation and maintenance from a sponsor living in New Zealand. You may also be asked to show evidence of an airline ticket, or other means for onward travel to a country to which you have right of entry, or document sufficient funds to purchase that ticket. The application goes to the nearest New Zealand embassy or High Commission office overseas.

In New Zealand, mail the application to New Zealand Immigration Service, Application Processing Centre, Private Bag, Wellesley St., Auckland. For information phone 09-914-4100. This office will accept MasterCard, Bankcard, or Visa payment for the fee. Currently, the office also charges a NZ$60 application fee for visa extensions.

If time is short, a passport agency can expedite the visa application process. I recommend Passport and Visa Express, 701 E. 18th St., Plano, TX 75074. Agent Don Goyal noticed immediately that two pages in my application were missing and asked the embassy to fax them (before I even knew there was a problem). He sent the completed visa/passport via courier to a business address in Southern California, then phoned to make sure it had arrived. Call 800/344-2810 for more information.

New arrivals to New Zealand must fill out a form declaring they're not bringing in prohibited food, plants, or animal material. There are stiff penalties for bringing in illegal drugs. Visitors are allowed to bring in personal effects and purchases up to a combined value of NZ$700 duty-free and exempt from goods and services tax. Visitors over 17 years of age may also bring in a limited amount of cigarettes, cigars, tobacco, and alcohol.

# LODGING

New Zealand offers an array of choices, from the most basic bunk bed to lavish suites. You can save money—and protect resources—if you live as simply as possible while traveling and book no more space than you need. Backpackers' lodges (also called hostels) can be found around the country. Some have single and double rooms; all have shared dorms sleeping around four to eight people. Although most hostels are well run, the worst are awful. Information about good backpackers' lodges will come from other travelers and the *Budget Backpacker Hostels Accommodation Handbook*. Lodgings are organized by region; most have travelers' ratings. Contact BBHNZ at 99 Titiraupenga St., Taupo, phone/fax 07-377-1568, bbh@backpack.co.nz, www.backpack.co.nz.

Youth Hostel membership gives you discounts on a network of hostels throughout the country, plus discounts on domestic transportation. Contact the YHA National Reservations Centre, P.O. Box 68-149, Auckland, 09-303-9524, fax 09-303-9525, book@yha.org.nz, www.yha.org.nz. Lodging at selected hostels can also be booked up to six months ahead using the International Booking Network, a computerized reservation system for members only (202/783-6161 in the United States; hiahserv@hiayh.org, www.hiayh.org). Book well ahead for travel during the New Zealand summer holidays.

Farm holidays and homestays let you experience the essence of New Zealand and its people. Contact Rural Holidays N.Z. Ltd., P.O. Box 2155, Christchurch, 03-366-1919, fax 03-379-3087, farmstay @ruralhols.co.nz, www.ruralhols.co.nz. New Zealand Farm Holidays Ltd. is similar; contact P.O. Box 256, Silverdale, Auckland, 09-426-5430, fax 09-426-8474, farm@nzaccom.co.nz. The U.S. toll-free number is 800/351-2323.

DOC huts and cabins can be booked at DOC offices throughout New Zealand. Book huts for Great Walks well in advance of summer season. Note that tracks that cross alpine passes may not be open during the austral winter.

For B&B accommodations, contact New Zealand's Federation of Bed and Breakfast Hotels, 52 Armagh St., Christchurch, 03-366-1503, fax 03-366-9796, www.nzbnbhotels.com. New Zealand families run many motels in the Budget Motel Chain. The average rate is NZ$62. For a free directory, write Bentley Services, 580 Market St., Suite 350, San Francisco, CA 94109, 800/986-9037, fax 415-986-5064. Travel Interlink, 800/888-5898, travelink@aol.com, offers reduced rates on not-yet-booked hotel rooms.

Several organizations publish pocket guides to campgrounds and holiday parks. Contact Holiday Accommodation Parks N.Z., P.O. Box 394, Paraparaumu 6450, 04-298-3283, hapnz@kapiti.co.nz; Kiwi Holiday Parks, 885 Carrington Rd., RD 1, New Plymouth, 06-753-5697, david@kiwi-camps.co.nz; or Holiday Parks and Camp-grounds, P.O. Box 9390, Newmarket, Auckland 1031.

## LIVING AND WORKING IN NEW ZEALAND

Long-term visitors need official permission to work in New Zealand. The *New Zealand Herald* and other metropolitan newspapers list furnished and unfurnished apartments for rent. Real estate agencies handle rentals of more expensive apartments. The length of stay in an apartment is often negotiable; a deposit, called a bond, is usually refunded if you leave the place in good condition. You'll also find widespread sharing of apartments; check the classified section under "Flatmates Wanted."

In Auckland, the Kiwi Bed Company, 0800-549-423, offers a Dial-A-Bed Service. You can arrange to have a bed delivered, pay the driver with a check or cash, and even sell the bed back to the company (at half price—keep your receipt) before you leave.

## METRIC CONVERSION

New Zealand uses the metric system. One kilometer equals .6 of a mile or 1,093 yards; one meter equals 3.28 feet; one centimeter equals .39 of an inch; one kilogram equals 2.2 pounds; one liter equals .22 gallons; and one hectare equals 2.47 acres. Temperatures are given in degrees centigrade, in which zero degrees represents the freezing point (32°F) and 100 degrees stands for the steam point (212°F).

# COMMUNICATIONS

## *Internet Access*

About one-fifth of New Zealand's population has access to computers; e-mail addresses and Web sites are often used in the New Zealand tourism industry. Large cities have cyber-cafés; some budget backpackers' lodges make computer use available for guests— sometimes at no extra charge. (At least one lodge has a coin-operated computer!) The charge per hour for computer use is typically NZ$10 to NZ$12. Ask at your lodging for the nearest cyber-café; this guide lists a few. Some public libraries offer computer access—for NZ$10 an hour, but without the double lattes. Internet Outpost is an "e-mail center for travelers," with locations in Queenstown, Kaikoura, Franz Josef, and Bay of Islands.

## *Postal Services*

New Zealand Post Shops, which handle domestic and international mail, are located throughout the country. Affiliated with DHL International, they also offer courier shipping. They sell stamps, packaging materials, newspapers, magazines, and greeting cards. In rural areas, you might find a tiny post shop within a general store. Usually open 9 to 5, some stores also have Saturday morning hours. Many post shops offer fax service as well.

International air mail is called Air Post; domestic priority mail service is called Fast Post. Post cards to North America cost NZ$1 to send; an airmail letter goes for NZ$1.50. I found it convenient to carry stamps in these denominations, along with post cards, sheets of paper, and business-size envelopes.

New Zealand operates a service for holding your mail at post offices throughout the country. Tourism offices in gateway cities have a complete list of Poste Restante addresses, but here are a few useful addresses in key cities:
• Bledisloe Building, 24 Wellesley St., Auckland, 09-379-6714

- 15-31 Cathedral Square, Christchurch, 03-353-1814
- Trafalgar and Halifax Sts., Nelson, 03-546-7818
- 2 Williams Rd., Paihia, 09-402-7803
- 15-19 Camp St., Queenstown, 03-442-7670
- 79-85 Hinemoa St., Rotorua, 07-349-2397

Lacking an address, have mail addressed to you c/o Poste Restante at the central post office in any New Zealand city or town. When collecting your mail, ask the agent to check mail filed under both your first and last initials.

## Telephone Service

New Zealand has phone boxes (booths) in populated regions throughout the country. Although the telephone industry has undergone deregulation, New Zealand Telecom—which is enormously profitable—is still the major company. Phone booths often contain phone directories and doors you can close against wind, rain, and the drone of traffic. Calls can be made with coins or credit cards. Follow posted instructions.

International operator-assisted and direct-dial numbers are posted in the booths. Large post offices and public libraries are sources of domestic phone numbers. From New Zealand, dial 001 to make a direct international call, 0170 for the international operator, and 0172 for international directory assistance. In general, make long-distance calls during evening and weekend hours to get the lowest rates. Useful New Zealand area codes are

09: Paihia, Bay of Islands, and Auckland
07: Rotorua and Taupo
04: Wellington
03: South Island

When calling a New Zealand number from outside the country, dial the international operator, the country code (64), then the area code—without the zero. Within New Zealand, emergency services—police, fire, or ambulance—can be reached by dialing 111. To repeat, dial 111 and *not* the 911 used in the United States.

Prepaid phone cards (those offered by Smartel are a better value than Telecom prepaid cards) offer a bundle of services. You can use them not only to make domestic and international phone calls, but also to receive voice-mail messages. I bought a Smartel phone card at a post shop for an initial NZ$40 and recharged it by telephone using a credit card. I could dial a freephone number and access voice mail messages wherever I traveled. Cards can also be purchased at hostels, backpacker lodges, holiday parks (campgrounds), and some tourist attractions.

## TIME ZONE

Located west of the International Date Line, New Zealand is 12 hours ahead of Greenwich Mean Time. The country adopts daylight saving time during summer. Generally, New Zealand is 12 hours ahead of London, 16 hours ahead of New York, and 19 hours ahead of Los Angeles. The country is also two hours ahead of Sydney, three hours ahead of Tokyo, and four hours ahead of Singapore.

## WHAT TO BRING

Essential clothing includes quick-dry underwear, T-shirts, shorts, long pants, fleece or wool layers for warmth, and rain gear, including a waterproof jacket and pants. Polypropylene, or the latest technical fabric, is good next to skin. Avoid all-cotton jeans and Ts, which are frustratingly slow to dry. Take broken-in hiking boots (Gore-Tex linings preferred), sport sandals such as Tevas, and some low-top shoes you can walk miles in—and also wear in town. You'll also need a swimsuit, sun hat, sunglasses (remember the ozone hole), Polartec or wool hat, and gloves for higher altitudes and unexpected snowfalls.

Whether you take a frame pack, biking shorts, deck shoes, paddling gloves, or other equipment depends on the activities you choose. For everyday items, consider a daypack or waist bag (as well as a hidden money pouch). You'll want to carry a watch (or tiny travel alarm clock) for meeting schedules, disinfectant swabs and bandages, a mild painkiller such as Tylenol, camera, film, and a waterproof film bag, a small bar of soap, plastic bags, tissues, insect repellent, and a copy of *New Zealand: Adventures in Nature*.

Take along contact addresses for friends and family, as well as telephone and fax numbers and e-mail addresses. Pack a list of passport, credit card, bank account, e-ticket, and other numbers or make photocopies (for 100 percent accuracy) of such numbers. Travel with one copy in your money belt and another in your purse or waist bag and leave a third copy in the care of a well-organized friend back home. You'll also need to bring non-800 phone numbers of the banks that issued your credit cards.

If you don't have an e-mail address, sign up for a free one at www.hotmail.com. You can use it while touring New Zealand and anywhere else you go.

## HEALTH ISSUES

New Zealand has no requirements for vaccinations or immunizations. You'll be touring a country whose residents enjoy a healthy lifestyle; expect to find high standards of cleanliness in handling food. You'll find good hospitals in the larger cities and medical clinics in smaller towns. The chemist (pharmacist) in a chemist shop can help you find a physician or recommend non-prescription medication. The chemist can also recommend a good insect repellent. The U.S. Centers for Disease Control and Prevention has information about health concerns for international travelers. Phone the agency at 404/332-4559 or 404/332-4565.

Tap water in New Zealand is safe to drink; city water is chlorinated and fluoridated. Most frozen and refrigerated food is handled carefully before you buy it, though I encountered a couple instances of poorly refrigerated ice cream—once at a festival, another time in a restaurant. So if the food's color, texture, or aroma seems "off," leave it on the plate. As you would anywhere, be alert to the freshness of food. Eat where the locals eat, and you're not likely to have problems.

Campylobactor—contamination of raw poultry—has been on the increase in New Zealand, so cook chicken thoroughly. This food-borne illness causes diarrhea—not what you want on a holiday. Cryptosporidium, a protozoan parasite that causes fever, cramping, and profuse watery diarrhea, is widespread in New Zealand waterways. The E coli and meningococci bacteria, and the virus that causes hepatitis

C, have also migrated into New Zealand and occasionally infect people. If you have any doubts about sanitation anywhere, eat only cooked food, peel fruit yourself, do without ice, and drink only bottled water. And always wash your hands.

Giardia, usually spread by small mammals, can infect humans through contaminated water and poor personal hygiene or food handling. Giardia lives in many New Zealand lakes, rivers, and streams. The DOC recommends that you treat suspected water by boiling, filtering, or treating it with an iodine solution. Chlorine-based purification tablets are said to be less effective. Always wash your hands thoroughly with soap before eating, no matter how difficult it is to do so.

### Insect Pests

Sand flies are a problem in many areas; avoid sitting directly on the ground, cover exposed skin with clothing, and use insect repellent liberally. The DOC recommends spreading a mixture of Dettol—a household disinfectant—and baby oil over exposed skin (mix in a 1:1 ratio).

Mosquitoes—some species have been immigrating—can also be a problem. For the most protection, use repellent on skin underneath your clothing and wrap your head, pirate-style, with a scarf.

### Sun Damage

Because the thinning ozone layer over the Antarctic shifts seasonally to the upper atmosphere above New Zealand, it's really important to protect your body from ultraviolet rays, especially in spring. A sun hat, protective clothing, and sunscreen are all vital equipment. During summer, sunburn times—given in minutes and announced periodically on New Zealand television—are surprisingly short. Be aware of the risk.

### Safety Outdoors

New Zealand's golden sand beaches, rugged cliffs, and clear, lyrically blue water offer their share of risks. Sudden snowstorms can cause white-out conditions for trekkers crossing high mountain passes. Even experienced swimmers can drown in riptides. Fortunately, New Zealand's tour operators are quite safety-conscious and so are various government agencies. You'll find many cautionary brochures displayed in tourism and DOC offices.

Hypothermia, a condition in which the vital organs of the body become colder than 37 degrees Celsius, is the main danger people face outdoors in New Zealand. The condition develops as a result of cold and some combination of the following: wind, wet clothing, hunger, fatigue, injury, anxiety, or illness. Warning signs include chills, shivering, lethargy, clumsiness, slurred speech, irritability, and irrational behavior. Action should be taken to prevent further heat loss and to rewarm the victim. The afflicted person should *not* be encouraged to "push onward." The best policy is to stop and find shelter, get out of the wind, get the victim into dry clothes and a sleeping bag, and give him or her a sweet warm drink. Do not rub the victim or give him or her alcohol. Do not try to reheat the person rapidly. If breathing stops, start resuscitation. Full recovery can take up to two days.

The New Zealand Mountain Safety Council, P.O. Box 6027, Te Aro, Wellington, 04-385-7162, fax 04-385-7366, publishes a series of pamphlets with excellent safety suggestions. The materials cover general outdoor safety, bushcraft, mountaineering, hypothermia, skiing, outdoor first aid, and survival.

### Plan Ahead

Your outdoor gear should include a flashlight with spare bulb and batteries, a water bottle, toilet paper, map, and compass. You should also carry the following survival items (packed with double protection from rain):

- waterproof matches
- waterproof paper and a pencil
- half a candle
- a pocket knife (or single-edge razor blade
- a small roll of Leucoplast tape
- fish hooks and a few meters of line
- a length of cord
- a survival bag or blanket
- a whistle

If an earthquake, tsunami (series of tidal waves), volcanic eruption, flood, or storm (winds more than 87 kilometers per hour) occurs during your visit to New Zealand, officials may declare a Civil Defense Emergency. Police and other personnel would then have authority to evacuate buildings, restrict entry, close roads, remove vehicles likely to impede emergency services, and requisition items they need. In such an emergency, grab your rain gear, sun protection, camping gear, and survival supplies—including a first-aid kit, bottled water, canned food, and a can opener—and head for safer ground. Pitch in to help others, as needed.

International SOS Assistance offers medical, personal, travel, legal, and security assistance to people living or traveling outside their home countries. Reports on the SOS Web site (www.intsos.com) summarize health and safety advice for specific destinations. The service, offered in more than 30 languages, is accessed by a telephone call to a team of coordinators, nurses, and doctors. Among other things, they can help determine whether a hospital is qualified to handle a particular case and keep a traveler's family informed during a medical emergency. Members also get help with trip planning, translation, emergency replacement of medication, emergency cash service, medically supervised repatriation, and so on. For more information visit www.intsos.com. Within the United States call 800/523-8662. The lowest-priced service is NZ$55 for individual coverage during a two-week trip, NZ$96 for a couple, and NZ$151 for a family. You can even sign up for membership online.

## TRANSPORTATION

Major airlines serving Auckland are British Airways, Lan Chile, Singapore, Lufthansa, Thai Airways, Air Pacific, Air Canada, American, Canadian, Japan, Qantas, United, Air New Zealand, and Cathay Pacific. I found the best value with a United Airlines round-trip ticket between Los Angeles and Auckland (phone United at 800/538-2929 to make international reservations). The OAG Web site (www.oag.com) lists 27 airlines serving Auckland, where most travelers arrive.

At Christchurch International Airport, British Airways, Air New Zealand, Japan Airlines, Qantas, Singapore Airlines, Lufthansa, United, and other airlines provide service. Air New Zealand and Ansett have service to Rotorua. To fly into Wellington, check with British Airways, Singapore Airlines, Air New Zealand, United Airlines, Qantas, or one of several others. During cruise season (October through March), ships from several cruise lines call at Auckland's Waitemata Harbour.

In the United States, you can make international reservations at the following numbers:
- Air New Zealand, 800/262-1234
- American Airlines, 800/624-6262
- Canadian Airlines International, 800/426-7000
- Qantas, 800/227-4500
- Singapore Airlines, 800/742-3333
- Thai Airways International, 800/426-5204
- United Airlines, 800/538-6877

Average international flight times to New Zealand are 24.15 hours from London, 3.2 hours from Sydney, 10 hours from Singapore, 10.35 hours from Hong Kong, 12 hours from Los Angeles, and 16 hours from Vancouver.

Study ads in the travel section of a large metropolitan newspaper, phone the most promising, and compare fares. Plan ahead to get the best deals; consider getting a low airfare by booking a package tour— you don't have to take the tour. Consult the guidebook *Fly For Less: The Ultimate Guide to Bargain Airfares* by Gary E. Schmidt. Schmidt explains the airfare structure, offers advice on picking a travel agent, and discusses shopping for the best "cyber-fares" online.

### Leaving the Airport

The Auckland Airport has the best selection of car rentals in the country; you'll find Avis, Budget, Hertz, National, and Thrifty. Budget also rents campers, as does Leisureport, Maui, and many other companies. Approximate cost for a mid-size car is NZ$80 to NZ$110 a day.

Low-cost shuttles and higher-priced taxis can be found outside the baggage claim area. The Airbus leaves every 20 minutes for the Downtown Airline Terminal and makes other stops along the way. Phone Buz-A-Bus, 09-366-6400, for information about the vast network of city buses, including service to and from the airport. Taxi service from the airport to downtown Auckland runs about NZ$35. A taxi from downtown to a nearby neighborhood like Parnell, Mission Bay, or Ponsonby will run NZ$6 to NZ$12. Ferries to Devonport, Waiheke Island, and other Hauraki Gulf islands depart from the Ferry Building on Quay Street in downtown Auckland. For more information on getting around the city, consult the Auckland chapter.

## Getting Around the Country

Air New Zealand, Australian-based Ansett New Zealand, and other airlines provide domestic air service. Mount Cook, Air Nelson, and Eagle Air, in an arrangement with Air New Zealand, fly under the umbrella name Air New Zealand Link. Smaller planes and seaplanes that service smaller airports complete the connective network. Ask about air passes for overseas visitors.

InterCity, New Zealand's major busline, 09-913-6100, info@intercitycoach.co.nz, has a large terminal in downtown Auckland within the Sky Tower complex. Newman's and Northliner Express buses offer service around North Island and operate from Auckland's Downtown Airline Terminal. InterCity and Mount Cook Landline, along with smaller companies, provide service on South Island. Ask about student, backpacker, senior, and other discounts.

For information on trains departing from Auckland, phone 0800-802-802. The daily Overlander connects Auckland and Wellington; the journey takes 12 hours. An overnight train is called the Northerner. Discounts often apply.

Daily ferry service across Cook Strait connects Wellington and the South Island port of Picton. The InterIsland ferry serves good food, although some crossings can be rough. Book ferry passage weeks in advance for the lowest fares. (See the Nelson chapter for more information about sea and air connections between North and South Islands.) Savvy bicyclists sometimes take ferries from downtown Auckland across the Hauraki Gulf to Coromandel, to avoid pedaling through Auckland traffic.

## "Not a Tour" Tour Buses

Magic Travellers Network and Kiwi Experience, known as "backpacker buses," operate networks of buses that follow loop routes in various parts of the country. Passengers, who book their own lodging, pay more than they would for public bus service and less than they would for a tour. They can stop anywhere along the route and, with notification, board the next or a later bus whenever they choose. Drivers drop passengers—and their luggage—at selected lodgings and pick them up the next morning or several days later.

Magic and Kiwi Experience combine some of the best features of public bus service and package tours. They make photo stops at interesting historic spots and natural features (dramatic gorges, waterfalls, mountain vistas, etc.) and allow passengers 15 minutes or half an hour to explore. You might get to hike through a forest or across a bridge. There are lunch, shopping, and banking stops and periodic tea breaks. You'll move from one place to another; the journey is the goal.

Unlike a lock-step tour, you can get off in, say, Turangi and spend several days hiking in Tongariro National Park, then board another bus. You can eat in restaurants or prepare your own food; some drivers allow you to lunch during the bus ride. You can stay in backpackers' lodges affiliated with the bus network (most passengers do) or choose another type of lodging. Optional activities, like skydiving or a helicopter excursion to a glacier, can be done for extra charges. However, no activity is required.

Traveling with Magic, I liked the savvy drivers, who also served as tour guides. The drivers played music—often on CDs provided by passengers. The passengers, while mostly young, included a sprinkling of active 70-year-olds and represented a wide range of nationalities. For a solo traveler, the sociability is a plus—if you enjoy meeting people. Magic holds occasional barbecues (Kiwi Experience does something similar) that include a low-cost meal; no one is required to go.

Contact Magic Travellers Network at Union House, 136-138 Quay St., Auckland, 09-358-5600, fax 09-358-3471, info@magicbus.co.nz, www.magicbus.co.nz. Contact Kiwi Experience at 170 Parnell Rd., Parnell, Auckland, 09-366-9830.

Certain other lines provide extensions to the basic Magic and Kiwi Experience loops. Sam's East Cape Escape begins in Rotorua and visits the town of Whakatane, the country's largest pohutukawa tree, and lovely east coast beaches. Maori drivers help make this tour a cultural experience. The Auckland number is 09-366-9830. The Rotorua number is 07-345-6645.

On South Island you can take the Bottom Bus, which offers various loop trips in the region south of Milford Sound and Dunedin. The Bottom Bus can also take you over segments (Te Anau to Dunedin, for instance). Affiliated with Kiwi Experience in New Zealand and the Oz Experience in Australia, the Bottom Bus has an office at 37 Shotover St., Queenstown, 03-442-9708, fax 03-442-7038.

## Driving in New Zealand

New Zealand's main highways are paved. Speed limits on the open road are 100 kilometers per hour; speed limits on town roads are 50 kilometers per hour. (Note that one mile equals about 1.6 kilometers, and one kilometer equals about .6 miles.) Traffic patterns are opposite those in the United States (cars drive in the left lane), and the driver sits in the right seat.

Drivers can expect to make 80 kilometers an hour in New Zealand, less during congested periods around cities on Friday and Sunday evenings. From Auckland, Kaitaia in Northland is 324 kilometers away, Whangarei is 170 kilometers, Rotorua is 234 kilometers, and Wellington is 660 kilometers. On South Island, it's 350 kilometers from Picton to Christchurch, 479 kilometers from Christchurch to Queenstown, and 189 kilometers from Queenstown to Milford Sound. New Zealand Tourism suggests you allow four hours, forty minutes for a drive from Picton to Christchurch, six hours from Greymouth to Haast, and two hours, twenty minutes from Queenstown to Invercargill.

## Road Safety

New Zealand ranks below the United States in road safety and also ranks in the lower half of all OECD nations. Auckland drivers, in particular, seem focused only on their destinations—not on anything that might get in their way. New Zealand drivers have problems with speed, drunk driving, and neglecting to use seat belts. Although a Ministry of Transport campaign emphasizes road safety, many unsafe drivers are still on the road.

That said, be aware that motor vehicles move forward on the left side of roads and highways. American drivers will find that rental cars have not only a steering wheel on the right side, but also many reversed controls. When crossing streets, American pedestrians need to be aware of vehicles coming from the right and must watch for vehicles turning toward them from unexpected directions at intersections and roundabouts.

Avoid driving a rental car, especially at night and when jet-lagged, to find lodging in an unfamiliar neighborhood. You'd be better off letting an airport shuttle or taxi driver take you to your lodging. It's much easier and safer to learn new driving patterns in broad daylight, after you've rested.

New Zealand's Land Transport Safety Authority has an excellent brochure, written in English, German, and Japanese, that describes safe driving practices. Look for it at tourist offices throughout the country; consult it for details about speed limits and right-of-way protocol at intersections and roundabouts.

Bicyclists are allowed on roads, but not on freeways. All cyclists must wear safety helmets. Major cities have bike shops that will rent the necessary gear.

# APPENDIX B
## ADDITIONAL RESOURCES

New Zealand Tourism Board offices overseas include one in the United States at 501 Santa Monica Blvd., Suite 300, Santa Monica, CA 90401, 310/395-7480, fax 310/395-5453. Other offices are located at
- 35 Pitt St., Sydney, New South Wales 2000, Australia
- 888 Dunsmuir St., Vancouver, British Columbia V6C 3K4, Canada
- New Zealand House, Haymarket, London SW1Y 4TQ, England
- Shinjuku Monolity, 2-3-1 Nishi Shinjuku, Shinjuku, Tokyo 163-09, Japan

Within New Zealand, contact the New Zealand Tourism Board at Level 7, 89 The Terrace, P.O. Box 95, Wellington, 04-472-8860, fax 04-478-1736. The Board's Web site, www.purenz.com, offers useful facts and information, plus links to more than 100 New Zealand tourism Web sites.

New Zealand operates more than 80 offices affiliated with its Visitor Information Network (VIN). Besides providing brochures, VIN offices help with itinerary planning and sell maps, gifts, stamps, and phone cards. Using the NZHOST National Tourism Database, agents can book your accommodations, transportation, and visits to attractions. (Be aware that VIN promotes only certain tourist businesses and operators—those that have contracted with the network. Survey brochure racks in your lodge or other locations to discover little-known tours and small operators that may not have the income to promote their tours widely.)

Auckland has VIN centers in its international and domestic airline terminals, at Queen Elizabeth Square, 09-366-0691, reservations@ aucklandnz.com; at Aotea Square, 09-366-6888, reservations@ aucklandnz.com; and at Viaduct Harbour.

Christchurch has centers in both the international and domestic airline terminals and in city center near Cathedral Square, Worcester Blvd. and Oxford Ter., 03-379-9629, info@christchurchtourism.co.nz. Other centers are
- **Kaikoura:** Westend, 03-319-5641, kbzvin@nzhost.co.nz

- **Paihia:** the marina on Marsden Road, 09-402-734, paivin@nzhost.co.nz
- **Picton:** on the foreshore, 03-573-7477
- **Queenstown:** Tower Centre, Shotover and Camp Sts., 03-442-4100, qvc@xtra.co.nz
- **Rotorua:** 1167 Fenton St.07-348-5179, gdela@rdc.govt.nz
- **Stewart Island:** Main Rd.Halfmoon Bay, 03-219-1218, stewartislandfc@doc.govt.nz
- **Taupo:** 13 Tongariro St. 07-378-9000, tuovin@nzhost.co.nz
- **Te Anau:** Te Anau Ter. (on the lakefront), 03-249-8900, teuvin@nzhost.co.nz
- **Wellington:** InterIslander Ferry Arahura
- **Westland:** Weld St., westland@voyager.co.nz

For more detailed information, pick up a brochure called "Directory of the Visitor Information Network" at any New Zealand VIN office.

# DEPARTMENT OF CONSERVATION

With a head office in Wellington, P.O. Box 10-420, 04-471-0726, www.doc.govt.nz, New Zealand's DOC is an excellent source of information. The DOC has 14 conservancy offices and field centers located throughout the country. The organization's Maori name, Te Papa Atawhai, means "a treasure chest to care for."

Here is contact information for DOC offices located near activities and nature settings described in this book.

*North Island*

**Hauraki Gulf Maritime Park**
Parks Information Centre
Ferry Building, Quay St.
Auckland, 09-303-1530

**Northland Conservation Park**
P.O. Box 842
Whangarei, 09-438-0299

**Pirongia Forest Park**
Private Bag, 3072
Hamilton, 07-838-3363

**Pureora Forest Park Field Centre**
RD 7, Te Kuiti, 07-878-4773

**Te Urewera National Park**
Aniwaniwa Visitor Centre
Private Bag, Wairoa,
06-837-3803

**Tongariro National Park**
Whakapapa Visitor Centre
c/o Post Office
Mount Ruapehu, 07-892-3729

**Whanganui National Park**
Private Bag 3016
Whanganui, 06-345-2402

**Whirinaki Forest Park**
Te Ikawhenua Visitor Centre
P.O. Box 114, Murupara, 07-366-5641

*South Island*
**Abel Tasman National Park**
P.O. Box 97
Motueka, 03-528-9117,
or P.O. Box 53, Takaka, 03-525-8026

**Arthur's Pass National Park**
P.O. Box 8
Arthur's Pass, 03-318-9211

**Fiordland National Park**
**Visitor Centre**
P.O. Box 29

Te Anau, 03-249-7921
and Catlins Forest Park
20 Ryley St., Owaka, 03-415-8341

**Hanmer Forest Park**
Hurunui Visitor Centre
P.O. Box 6
Hanmer Springs, 03-3115-7128

**Marlborough Sounds**
P.O. Box 161,
Picton, 03-573-7477

**Mount Aspiring National Park**
Queenstown
P.O. Box 811, 03-442-7933

**Mount Cook National Park**
Visitor Centre, P.O. Box 5,
Mount Cook, 03-435-1819

**Paparoa National Park**
Visitor Centre, P.O. Box 1,
Punakaiki, 03-731-1895

**Stewart Island DOC**
P.O. Box 3
Stewart Island, 03-219-1130

**Westland National Park**
Franz Josef Glacier Visitor
Centre, P.O. Box 14
Franz Josef, 03-752-0796

# TOUR COMPANIES

Regional tour companies are described in detail—complete with contact information—in the eight regional chapters. Here are companies that cover routes throughout the country.

**New Zealand Nature Safaris,** 52 Holborn Dr., Stokes Valley 6008, 0800-697-232, fax 04-563-7324, nzns@globe.co.nz, www.nzsafaris.co.nz, offers small-group guided safaris and wilderness hikes throughout New Zealand. The safaris mix vehicle-based camping with overnight hiking trips to remote locations. Experienced knowledgeable guides are all New Zealanders—many have degrees in ecology, biology, or earth science. This eco-sensitive company donates NZ$10 to the N.Z. Wildlife Research Fund for every person booked.

**Flying Kiwi Wilderness Expeditions**, Koromiko, RD 3, Blenheim, New Zealand, 03-573-8126, fax 03-573-8128, flying.kiwi@xtra.co.nz, combines camping, hiking, and bicycling with experiences like bungy jumping and sky diving. Expeditions visit some of New Zealand's most gorgeous landscapes.

Other nature-oriented tour operators include **Down Under Connections**, based in Atlanta, Georgia, 800/937-7878 or 404/255-1922, fax 404-255-1066. **The Adventure Center**, 1311-NZ 63rd St., Emeryville, CA 94608, 800/227-8747 or 510/654-1879, nz@adventure-center.com, organizes Great Walks, sea kayaking, bicycle tours, natural history tours, and other adventures in New Zealand. **New Zealand Walkabout** specializes in nature, hiking, and the outdoors; contact Pacific Exploration Company, Box 3042-G, Santa Barbara, CA 93130, 805/569-0722, fax 805/569-0722. **New Zealand Travelers**, Inc, P.O. Box 605, Dept. V, Shelburne, VT 05482, 800/362-2718 or 802/985-8865, fax 802/985-8865, features walking tours for "travelers—not tourists."

For regional tour operators, consult the tour operators listed in each chapter. For high-adrenaline adventures, the New Zealand Way brand has been awarded to the following Queenstown companies for their high standards of excellence and environmental responsibility.

- J. Hackett Bungy, The Station, Shotover and Camp Sts., 03-442-7100, bungyjump@ajhackett.co.nz
- The Helicopter Line, The Station, Shotover and Camp Sts., 03-442-3034, hlinfo@helicopter.co.nz
- Pipeline Bungy, 27 Shotover St., 03-442-5455, bungy@pipeline.co.nz

- Raging Thunder Adventures, Shotover and Camp Sts., 03-442-7318, raftinfo@raft.co.nz
- Skydive Tandem, 03-021-325-961, paqltd@voyager
- Shotover Jet, The Station, Shotover and Camp Sts., 03-442-8570

# EMBASSIES AND CONSULATES

In the United States, New Zealand has an embassy at 37 Observatory Circle NW, Washington, D.C., 20008, 202/328-4848, fax 202/667-5227, and consulates in other major cities. In Canada, consult the New Zealand High Commission, Suite 727, Metropolitan House, 99 Bank St., Ottawa, Ontario K1P 6G3, 613/238-5991, fax 613/238-5707. In the United Kingdom, the high commission is located at New Zealand House, The Haymarket, London SW1Y 4TQ, 0171-973-0366, fax 0171-973-0370. In Germany, the New Zealand embassy is at Bundeskanzlerplatz 2-10, Bonn 53113; in Italy at Via Zara 28, Rome 00198; in the Netherlands at Carnegielaan 10, 2517 KH, The Hague.

In Auckland, the United States consulate is located at the General Building, Shortland and O'Connell Sts., 09-303-2724. In Wellington, the U.S. embassy is at 29 Fitzherbert Terrace, Thorndon, 04-472-2068. Foreign consulates for many countries are also in Christchurch; call the U.S. office at 03-379-004.

# RECOMMENDED READING

### Nonfiction

*Classic New Zealand Adventures* (Compass Star Publications Ltd., 1997), written by a quartet of New Zealand outdoorsmen, describes more than 200 adventures.

*New Zealand: A Century of Images* (Te Papa Press, 1998) was written and edited by Paul Thompson, curator of Wellington's excellent Te Papa museum.

About half the world's population inhabits the countries of the Pacific Rim; a dozen or so of these countries account for half the world's economic growth. In *Pacific Rising: the Emergence of a New World Culture* (Prentice Hall Press, 1991), author Simon Winchester looks at the role New Zealand and other countries play while he freeze-frames this moving economic picture.

*Nomads of the Wind: A Natural History of Polynesia,* by Peter Crawford (BBC Books, 1993), traces the origins of Polynesian people (including the Maoris), their voyages of discovery, and their special relationship with the sea and the land.

*The Maoris of New Zealand* by Graham Wiremu (Rourke Publications, 1989) describes the history, culture, and daily life of the Maori people, amid their changing world.

*Fly for Less: The Ultimate Guide to Bargain Airfares* by Gary E. Schmidt is a well-researched aid to getting good value for airfare to New Zealand and elsewhere. *The Toll-Free Traveler,* compiled by Don and Betty Martin, provides useful toll-free numbers in a slim paperback guide. American travelers will find it useful in planning a trip to New Zealand or anywhere else.

*Pocket Guide to New Zealand Wines and Vintages* by Michael Cooper (Hodder & Stoughton, Ltd., 1990) discusses New Zealand's wine regions and various styles. Contact the South Pacific Traveller's Booksource for the *New Zealand Bed & Breakfast Book.* In the United States, phone 800/234-4552 or e-mail sptbooks@nvi.nvi.net. Ask for information about the voucher program, a free brochure, and a listing of hard-to-find New Zealand travel books and maps.

Regional references include *Wild Dunedin* by Neville Peat and Brian Patrick (University of Otago Press, 1995), *The Catlins* by Neville Peat (University of Otago Press, 1998), and *The Port Hills: A Guide to the Walking Tracks on the Port Hills* by Mark Pickering (1994; contact P.O. Box 4510, Christchurch). Pickering (with co-author Rodney Smith) has also written *101 Great Tramps in New Zealand, Walk Away! A Guide to Walking Places in Canterbury; The Southern Journey,* which follows South Island historical routes from Farewell Spit to Milford Sound; *Wild Walks,* with separate books on North Island and South Island describing 60 short walks in each; and *Stepping Back: Historic Walks in the South Island.*

## Fiction

Most New Zealand authors create an evocative sense of place; a few novels have been made into films. You can obtain a reading list from the New Zealand Book Council/Te Kaunihera Pukapuka o Aotearoa,

P.O. Box 11-377, Wellington, 04-499-1569, fax 04-499-1424. You can order an array of New Zealand books, including hard-to-find volumes, from New Zealand: Books Abroad, P.O. Box 17-244, Wellington 6005, 04-475-4040; they ship anywhere.

Although New Zealand-born Katherine Mansfield lived for a time in England, some of her best writing is set in her native land. Look for *The Urewera Notebook* and *The Short Stories of Katherine Mansfield*, often covered in literature classes. Alan Duff's novel *Once Were Warriors* has been made into a film and will also become a musical. Keri Hulme, who lives on South Island's west coast in tiny Okarito, won the Booker Prize in 1985 for her novel *The Bone People*. Philip Temple's *Beak of the Moon* concerns keas, New Zealand's alpine parrots, and humans who intrude on wilderness habitats. Janet Frame's *An Angel at My Table*, the autobiography of a young woman recovering from mental illness, was later made into a film by New Zealander Jane Campion. Maurice Shadbolt is known for *The Season of the Jew*, among other works. Author Witi Ihimaeroa examines relationships between Maoris and pakehas. Margaret Mahy has written more than 100 books for children, and Tessa Duder writes for young adults.

# INDEX

# *Guidebooks that* really *guide*

## City•Smart™ Guidebooks
Pick one for your favorite city: *Albuquerque, Anchorage, Austin, Calgary, Charlotte, Chicago, Cincinnati, Cleveland, Denver, Indianapolis, Kansas City, Memphis, Milwaukee, Minneapolis/St. Paul, Nashville, Pittsburgh, Portland, Richmond, Salt Lake City, San Antonio, San Francisco, St. Louis, Tampa/St. Petersburg, Tucson.*
US $12.95 to 15.95

## Retirement & Relocation Guidebooks
*The World's Top Retirement Havens, Live Well in Honduras, Live Well in Ireland, Live Well in Mexico.*
US $15.95 to $16.95

## Travel•Smart® Guidebooks
Trip planners with select recommendations to *Alaska, American Southwest, Arizona, Carolinas, Colorado, Deep South, Eastern Canada, Florida, Florida Gulf Coast, Hawaii, Illinois/Indiana, Kentucky/Tennessee, Maryland/Delaware, Michigan, Minnesota/Wisconsin, Montana/Wyoming/Idaho, New England, New Mexico, New York State, Northern California, Ohio, Pacific Northwest, Pennsylvania/New Jersey, South Florida and the Keys, Southern California, Texas, Utah, Virginias, Western Canada.* US $14.95 to $17.95

## Rick Steves' Guides
See *Europe Through the Back Door* and take along guides to *France, Belgium & the Netherlands; Germany, Austria & Switzerland; Great Britain & Ireland; Italy; Scandinavia; Spain & Portugal; London; Paris;* or *Best of Europe.* US $12.95 to $21.95

## Adventures in Nature
Plan your next adventure in *Alaska, Belize, Caribbean, Costa Rica, Guatemala, Hawaii, Honduras, Mexico.*
US $17.95 to $18.95

## Into the Heart of Jerusalem
A traveler's guide to visits, celebrations, and sojourns.
US $17.95

## The People's Guide to Mexico
This is so much more than a guidebook—it's a trip to Mexico in and of itself, complete with the flavor of the country and its sights, sounds, and people. US $22.95

**JOHN MUIR PUBLICATIONS
A DIVISION OF AVALON TRAVEL PUBLISHING
5855 Beaudry Street, Emeryville, CA 94608**

*Please check our web site at www.travelmatters.com for current prices and editions, or see your local bookseller.*

# Cater to Your Interests on Your Next Vacation

**The 100 Best Small Art Towns in America 3rd edition**
Discover Creative Communities, Fresh Air, and Affordable Living
U.S. $16.95

**Healing Centers & Retreats**
Healthy Getaways for Every Body and Budget
U.S. $16.95

**Cross-Country Ski Vacations, 2nd edition**
A Guide to the Best Resorts, Lodges, and Groomed Trails in North America
U.S. $15.95

**Gene Kilgore's Ranch Vacations, 5th edition**
The Complete Guide to Guest and Resort, Fly-Fishing, and Cross-Country Skiing Ranches
U.S. $22.95

**Yoga Vacations**
A Guide to International Yoga Retreats
U.S. $16.95

**Watch It Made in the U.S.A., 2nd edition**
A Visitor's Guide to the Companies That Make Your Favorite Products
U.S. $17.95

**The Way of the Traveler**
Making Every Trip a Journey of Self-Discovery
U.S. $12.95

**Kidding Around®**
Guides for kids 6 to 10 years old about what to do, where to go, and how to have fun in *Atlanta, Austin, Boston, Chicago, Cleveland, Denver, Indianapolis, Kansas City, Miami, Milwaukee, Minneapolis/St. Paul, Nashville, Portland, San Francisco, Seattle, Washington D.C.*
U.S. $7.95

 **JOHN MUIR PUBLICATIONS**
**A DIVISION OF AVALON PUBLISHING**
**5855 Beaudry Street, Emeryville, CA 94608**

*Available at your favorite bookstore.*

# ABOUT THE AUTHOR

Sally McKinney, a native of Indiana, has written travel features for newspapers throughout the United States and Canada. Writing assignments have taken her all over the world. She is a member of the Society of American Travel Writers.